METAPHOR

METAPHOR

A Practical Introduction

ZOLTÁN KÖVECSES

Exercises written with
Szilvia Csábi,
Réka Hajdú,
Zsuzsanna Bokor,
& Orsolya Izsó

OXFORD
UNIVERSITY PRESS

2002

OXFORD

UNIVERSITY PRESS

Oxford   New York
Athens   Auckland   Bangkok   Bogotá   Buenos Aires   Cape Town
Chennai   Dar es Salaam   Delhi   Florence   Hong Kong   Istanbul   Karachi
Kolkata   Kuala Lumpur   Madrid   Melbourne   Mexico City   Mumbai   Nairobi
Paris   São Paulo   Shanghai   Singapore   Taipei   Tokyo   Toronto   Warsaw

and associated companies in
Berlin   Ibadan

Copyright © 2002 by Zoltán Kövecses

Published by Oxford University Press, Inc.
198 Madison Avenue, New York, New York 10016

Oxford is a registered trademark of Oxford University Press

Library of Congress Cataloging-in-Publication Data
Kövecses, Zoltán.
Metaphor : a practical introduction / Zoltán Kövecses ;
exercises written with Szilvia Csábi, Réka Hajdú, Zsuzsanna Bokor, and Orsolya Izsó
    p. cm.
Includes bibliographical references.
ISBN-13 978-0-19-514510-6; 978-0-19-514511-3(pbk.)

ISBN 0-19-514510-0; ISBN 0-19-514511-9 (pbk.)
1. Metaphor.   I. Title.
PN228.M4 K68 2001
808—dc21   2001036570

9 8 7

Printed in the United States of America
on acid-free paper

To

GEORGE

&

MARK

Preface:
The Study of
Metaphor

For most of us, metaphor is a figure of speech in which one thing is compared to another by saying that one is the other, as in *He is a lion*. Or, as the *Encyclopaedia Britannica* puts it: "*metaphor* [is a] figure of speech that implies comparison between two unlike entities, as distinguished from *simile*, an explicit comparison signalled by the words 'like' or 'as.'" [emphases in the original]. For example, we would consider the word *lion* to be a metaphor in the sentence "Achilles was a *lion* in the fight." We would probably also say that the word is used metaphorically in order to achieve some artistic and rhetorical effect, since we speak and write metaphorically to communicate eloquently, to impress others with "beautiful," esthetically pleasing words, or to express some deep emotion. Perhaps we would also add that what makes the metaphorical identification of Achilles with a *lion* possible is that *Achilles* and *lions* have something in common, namely, their bravery and strength.

Indeed, this is a widely shared view—the most common conception of metaphor, both in scholarly circles and in the popular mind (which is not to say that this is the *only* view of metaphor). This traditional concept can be briefly characterized by pointing out five of its most commonly accepted features. First, metaphor is a property of words; it is a linguistic phenomenon. The metaphorical use of *lion* is a characteristic of a linguistic expression (that of the word *lion*). Second, metaphor is used for some artistic and rhetorical purpose, such as when Shakespeare writes "all the world's a *stage*." Third, metaphor is based on a resemblance between the two entities that are compared and identified. Achilles must share some features with lions in order for us to be able to use the word *lion* as a metaphor for Achilles. Fourth, metaphor is a conscious and deliberate use of words, and you must have a special talent to be able to do it and do it well. Only great poets or eloquent speakers, such as, say, Shakespeare and Churchill, can be its masters. For instance, Aristotle makes the following statement to this effect: "The greatest thing by far is to have command of metaphor. This alone cannot be imparted by another; it is the mark of genius." Fifth, it is also commonly held that metaphor is a figure of speech that we can do without; we use it for special effects, and it is not an inevitable part of everyday human communication, let alone everyday human thought and reasoning.

A new view of metaphor that challenged all these aspects of the powerful traditional theory in a coherent and systematic way was first developed by George Lakoff and Mark Johnson in 1980 in their seminal study: *Metaphors We Live By*. Their conception has become known as the "cognitive linguistic view of metaphor." Lakoff and Johnson challenged the deeply entrenched view of metaphor by claiming that (1) metaphor is a property of concepts, and not of words; (2) the function of metaphor is to better understand certain concepts, and not just some artistic or esthetic purpose; (3) metaphor is often *not* based on similarity; (4) metaphor is used effortlessly in everyday life by ordinary people, not just by special talented people; and (5) metaphor, far from being a superfluous though pleasing linguistic ornament, is an inevitable process of human thought and reasoning.

Lakoff and Johnson showed convincingly that metaphor is pervasive both in thought and everyday language. Their insight has been taken up by recent dictionary preparers as well. For instance, *Cobuild's Metaphor Dictionary* has examples of metaphors, such as the following (metaphorical expressions in the example sentences or phrases are italicized):

(1) He was an *animal* on Saturday afternoon and is a disgrace to British football.
(2) There is no painless way to get inflation down. We now have an excellent *foundation on which to build*.
(3) Politicians are being blamed for the *ills* of society.
(4) The *machinery* of democracy could be *created* quickly but its spirit was just as important.
(5) Government grants have enabled a number of the top names in British sport *to build* a successful career.
(6) . . . a local *branch* of this organization.
(7) Few of them have the qualifications . . . *to put an ailing* company *back on its feet*.
(8) The Service will continue *to stagger from* crisis *to* crisis.
(9) Her career was *in ruins*.
(10) How could any man ever understand the *workings* of a woman's mind?
(11) Scientists *have taken a big step* in understanding Alzheimer's disease.
(12) They selectively *pruned* the workforce.
(13) . . . *cultivating* business relationships that can lead to major accounts.
(14) The coffee was perfect and by the time I was halfway through my first cup my brain *was ticking over much more briskly*.
(15) Let's hope he can *keep* the team *on the road to* success.
(16) Everyone says what a happy, *sunny* girl she was.

(17) It's going to be a *bitch* to replace him.

(18) The province is quite close to *sliding into* civil war.

(19) They remembered her as she'd been *in the flower* of their friendship.

(20) Vincent met his father's *icy* stare evenly.

(21) With its economy *in ruins*, it can't afford to involve itself in military action.

(22) ... French sex *kitten* Brigitte Bardot.

Some of these examples would be considered by most people to be obvious cases of metaphor, while some of them would perhaps be considered less obvious. Nevertheless, it can be claimed that most of the metaphorical linguistic expressions above are not literary and that most of them are not intended to exhibit some kind of rhetorical flourish. Indeed, most of them are so mundane that a very commonly heard charge can be leveled at them—namely, that they are simply "dead" metaphors—metaphors that may have been alive and vigorous at some point but have become so conventional and commonplace with constant use that by now they have lost their vigor and have ceased to be metaphors at all (such as 6 and 13).

The "dead metaphor" account misses an important point; namely, that what is deeply entrenched, hardly noticed, and thus effortlessly used is most active in our thought. The metaphors above may be highly conventional and effortlessly used, but this does not mean that they have lost their vigor in thought and that they are dead. On the contrary, they are "alive" in the most important sense—they govern our thought—they are "metaphors we live by." One example of this involves our comprehension of the mind as a machine. In the list above, two sentences reflect this way of thinking about the mind:

(10) How could any man ever understand the *workings* of a woman's mind?

(14) The coffee was perfect and by the time I was halfway through my first cup my brain *was ticking over much more briskly*.

We think of the mind as a machine. Both lay people and scientists employ this way of understanding the mind. The scientists of today use the most sophisticated machine available as their model—the computer. Lakoff and Johnson call this way of understanding the mind THE MIND IS A MACHINE metaphor. In their view, metaphor is not simply a matter of words or linguistic expressions but of concepts, of thinking of one thing in terms of another. In the examples, two very different linguistic expressions capture aspects of the same concept, the mind, through another concept, machines. In the cognitive linguistic view as developed by Lakoff and Johnson, metaphor is conceptual in nature. In this view, metaphor ceases to be the sole device of creative literary imagination; it becomes a valuable cognitive tool without which neither poets nor you and I as ordinary people could live.

This discussion is not intended to suggest that the ideas mentioned above in what we call the cognitive linguistic view of metaphor did not exist before

1980. Obviously, many of them did. Key components of the cognitive theory were proposed by a diverse range of scholars in the past two thousand years. For example, the idea of the conceptual nature of metaphor was discussed by a number of philosophers, including Locke and Kant, several centuries ago. What is new, then, in the cognitive linguistic view of metaphor? Overall, what is new is that it is a comprehensive, generalized, and empirically tested theory.

First, its comprehensiveness derives from the fact that it discusses a large number of issues connected with metaphor. These include the systematicity of metaphor; the relationship between metaphor and other tropes; the universality and culture-specificness of metaphor; the application of metaphor theory to a range of different kinds of discourse such as literature; the acquisition of metaphor; the teaching of metaphor in foreign language teaching; the nonlinguistic realization of metaphor in a variety of areas such as advertisements; and many others. It is not claimed that these issues have not been dealt with at all in other approaches; instead, the claim is that not all of them have been dealt with within the same theory.

Second, the generalized nature of the theory derives from the fact that it attempts to connect what we know about conceptual metaphor with what we know about the working of language, the working of the human conceptual system, and the working of culture. The cognitive linguistic view of metaphor can provide new insights into how certain linguistic phenomena work, such as polysemy and the development of meaning. It can also shed new light on how metaphorical meaning emerges. It challenges the traditional view that metaphorical language and thought is arbitrary and unmotivated. And offers the new view that both metaphorical language and thought arise from the basic bodily (sensorimotor) experience of human beings. As it turns out, this notion of "embodiment" very clearly sets off the cognitive linguistic view from the traditional ones.

Third, it is an empirically tested theory in that researchers have used a variety of experiments to test the validity of the major claims of the theory. These experiments have shown that the cognitive view of metaphor is a psychologically viable one, that is, it has psychological reality. Further experiments have shown that, because of its psychological reality, it can be seen as a key instrument not only in producing new words and expressions but also in organizing human thought, and that it may also have useful practical applications, for example, in foreign language teaching. I will try to deal with most of these topics in this book, although as can be expected from a book of this sort, I will only be able to offer a glimpse of them.

Up until most recently, metaphor has been primarily studied by philosophers, rhetoricians, literary critics, psychologists, and linguists, such as Aristotle, Hume, Locke, Vico, Herder, Cassirer, Buhler, I. A. Richards, Whorf, Goodman, Max Black, to mention just a few names from the thousands of people who have done work on metaphor over the past two thousand years. Today, an increasing number of cognitive scientists, including cognitive linguists, engage in the research on metaphor. The reason is that metaphor plays a role in human thought, understanding, and reasoning and, beyond that, in the creation of our social, cultural, and psychological reality. Trying to understand metaphor, then, means attempting to understand a vital part of who we are and what kind of world we live in.

Lakoff and Johnson initiated this new study of metaphor over twenty years ago. In fact, it was their work that has defined in part cognitive linguistics itself as we know it today. Many scholars from a variety of disciplines have since contributed to this work over the years and have produced new and important results in the study of metaphor. What has exactly happened in the past two decades in the cognitive linguistic study of metaphor? This is what this book is about.

FURTHER READING

If you want to read up on the background to the study of metaphor, in general, including some of the scholars mentioned above, the best available collection of essays is Andrew Ortony (ed.), *Metaphor and Thought* (1993), second edition. What makes this volume especially important reading is that it contains several essays that represent rival views to the cognitive linguistic one. This is also the time to begin to read George Lakoff and Mark Johnson's *Metaphors We Live By*, the work that "started it all." An excellent survey of the view of metaphor developed by Lakoff and Johnson and others is Ray Gibbs (1994). This work also discusses a great deal of psychological evidence supporting the cognitive linguistic view of metaphor. Jäkel (1999) provides a useful survey of the most important predecessors of the cognitive linguistic view. If you are interested in the history of the study of metaphor, you should look at Mark Johnson's (1981) *Philosophical Perspectives on Metaphor*. The most recent representative collection of papers in the cognitive spirit is the volume edited by Gibbs and Steen (1999). The metaphor dictionary referred to above is *Cobuild English Guides, 7: Metaphor* (1995).

Acknowledgments

I dedicate this book to George Lakoff and Mark Johnson, without whose work this book could not have been written.

I am grateful to Donald Freeman, Ray Gibbs, and Mark Turner for their extensive comments and suggestions on the entire manuscript. Their help meant a lot more for me than just taking scholarly advice.

I want to thank Günter Radden and Michael White for providing many detailed comments on early forms of the manuscript.

Szilvia Csábi, Zsuzsanna Bokor, Réka Hajdú, and Orsolya Izsó have prepared the bulk of the exercises and helped me in various other ways in working on this book. Their generous help is much appreciated. I am also thankful to my students who participated in my courses on metaphor over the years and gave me valuable feedback on several issues in the book. They include Zsuzsanna Bokor, Szilvia Csábi, Judit Ferenczy, Márta Hack, Réka Hajdú, Orsolya Izsó, Katalin Jobbágy, Ágnes Király, Nikolett Köves, Orsolya Sági, and Judit Szirmai. I thank Katalin Jobbágy for creating the drawing in chapter 17.

But, as always, the most beautiful metaphors came from Lacó and Ádi.

Budapest   Z. K.
October, 2000

Contents

METAPHOR

1

What Is
Metaphor?

Consider the way native speakers of English often talk about life—either their own lives or those of others:

> People might say that they try to give their children an education so they will get a good start in life. If their children act out, they hope that they are just going through a stage and that they will get over it. Parents hope that their children won't be burdened with financial worries or ill health and, if they face such difficulties, that they will be able to overcome them. Parents hope that their children will have a long life span and that they will go far in life. But they also know that their children, as all mortals, will reach the end of the road. (based on Winter, 1995, p. 235)

This way of speaking about life would be regarded by most speakers of English as normal and natural for everyday purposes. The use of phrases such as *to get a good start, to go through a stage, to get over something, to be burdened, to overcome something, a long life span, to go far in life, to reach the end of the road*, and so on would not count as using particularly picturesque or literary language. Below is a list of additional phrases that speakers of English use to talk about the concept of life:

> He's *without direction* in life.
> I'm *where I want to be* in life.
> I'm *at a crossroads* in my life.
> She'll *go places* in life.
> He's never *let* anyone *get in his way.*
> She's *gone through* a lot in life.

Given all these examples, we can see that a large part of the way we speak about life in English derives from the way we speak about journeys. In light of such examples, it seems that speakers of English make extensive use of the

3

domain of journey to think about the highly abstract and elusive concept of life. The question is: Why do they draw so heavily on the domain of journey in their effort to comprehend life? Cognitive linguists suggest that they do so because thinking about the abstract concept of life is facilitated by the more concrete concept of journey.

1. Conceptual Metaphor

In the cognitive linguistic view, metaphor is defined as understanding one conceptual domain in terms of another conceptual domain. (The issue of precisely what is meant by "understanding" will be discussed in section 3.) Examples of this include when we talk and think about life in terms of journeys, about arguments in terms of war, about love also in terms of journeys, about theories in terms of buildings, about ideas in terms of food, about social organizations in terms of plants, and many others. A convenient shorthand way of capturing this view of metaphor is the following: CONCEPTUAL DOMAIN (A) IS CONCEPTUAL DOMAIN (B), which is what is called a **conceptual metaphor**. A conceptual metaphor consists of two conceptual domains, in which one domain is understood in terms of another. A conceptual domain is any coherent organization of experience. Thus, for example, we have coherently organized knowledge about journeys that we rely on in understanding life. We will discuss the nature of this knowledge below.

We thus need to distinguish conceptual metaphor from **metaphorical linguistic expressions**. The latter are words or other linguistic expressions that come from the language or terminology of the more concrete conceptual domain (i.e., domain B). Thus, all the expressions above that have to do with life and that come from the domain of journey are linguistic metaphorical expressions, whereas the corresponding conceptual metaphor that they make manifest is LIFE IS A JOURNEY. The use of small capital letters indicates that the particular wording does not occur in language as such, but it underlies conceptually all the metaphorical expressions listed underneath it.

The two domains that participate in conceptual metaphor have special names. The conceptual domain from which we draw metaphorical expressions to understand another conceptual domain is called **source domain**, while the conceptual domain that is understood this way is the **target domain**. Thus, life, arguments, love, theory, ideas, social organizations, and others are target domains, while journeys, war, buildings, food, plants, and others are source domains. The target domain is the domain that we try to understand through the use of the source domain.

2. Some Examples of Conceptual Metaphor

To see that we do indeed talk about these target domains by making use of such source domains as war, journey, food, let us consider some classic examples of each from Lakoff and Johnson's *Metaphors We Live By*. Following the conventions of cognitive linguistics, I will use small capitals for the statement of conceptual metaphors and italics for metaphorical linguistic expressions.

AN ARGUMENT IS WAR
Your claims are *indefensible*.
He *attacked every weak point* in my argument.
His criticisms were *right on target*.
I *demolished* his argument.
I've never *won* an argument with him.
You disagree? Okay, *shoot!*
If you use that *strategy*, he'll *wipe* you *out*.
He *shot down* all of my arguments.

LOVE IS A JOURNEY
Look *how far* we've *come*.
We're *at a crossroads*.
We'll just have to *go our separate ways*.
We can't *turn back* now.
I don't think this relationship is *going anywhere*.
Where are we?
We're *stuck*.
It's been a *long, bumpy road*.
This relationship is a *dead-end street*.
We're just *spinning our wheels*.
Our marriage is *on the rocks*.
We've *gotten off the track*.
This relationship is *foundering*.

THEORIES ARE BUILDINGS
Is that the *foundation* for your theory?
The theory needs more *support*.
We need *to construct* a *strong* argument for that.
We need *to buttress* the theory with *solid* arguments.
The theory will *stand or fall* on the *strength* of that argument.
So far we have *put together* only the *framework* of the theory.

IDEAS ARE FOOD
All this paper has in it are *raw* facts, *half-baked* ideas, and *warmed-over* theories.
There are too many facts here for me *to digest* them all.
I just can't *swallow* that claim.
Let me *stew* over that for a while.
That's *food* for thought.
She *devoured* the book.
Let's let that idea *simmer on the back burner* for a while.

This is just a small sample of all the possible linguistic expressions that speakers of English commonly and conventionally employ to talk about the target domains above. We can state the nature of the relationship between the conceptual metaphors and the metaphorical linguistic expressions in the following way: the linguistic expressions (i.e., ways of talking) make explicit, or are manifestations of, the conceptual metaphors (i.e., ways of thinking). To put the same thing differently, it is the metaphorical linguistic expressions that reveal the existence of the conceptual metaphors. The terminology of a source domain that is utilized in the metaphorical process is one kind of evidence for the existence of conceptual metaphor. But it is not the only kind, and we will survey other kinds of evidence in later chapters.

An important generalization that emerges from these conceptual metaphors is that conceptual metaphors typically employ a more abstract concept as target and a more concrete or physical concept as their source. Argument, love, idea, social organization are all more abstract concepts than war, journey, food, and plant. This generalization makes intuitive sense. If we want to better understand a concept, we are better off using another concept that is more concrete, physical, or tangible than the former for this purpose. Our experiences with the physical world serve as a natural and logical foundation for the comprehension of more abstract domains. This explains why in most cases of everyday metaphors the source and target domains are not reversible. For example, we do not talk about ideas as food or journey as love. This is called the principle of **unidirectionality**; that is, the metaphorical process typically goes from the more concrete to the more abstract but not the other way around.

3. Conceptual Metaphor as a Set of Mappings

So far we have used the word "to understand" to characterize the relationship between two concepts (A and B) in the metaphorical process. But what does it mean exactly that A is understood in terms of B? The answer is that there is a set of systematic **correspondences** between the source and the target in the sense that constituent conceptual elements of B correspond to constituent elements of A. Technically, these conceptual correspondences are often referred to as **mappings**.

Let us look at some cases where elements of the source domain are mapped onto elements of the target domain. Let's take the LOVE IS A JOURNEY conceptual metaphor first. When we use the sentence *We aren't going anywhere*, the expression *go somewhere* indicates traveling to a destination, in this particular sentence, a journey which has no clear destination. The word *we* obviously refers to the travelers involved. This sentence then gives us three constituent elements of journeys: the travelers, the travel or the journey as such, and the destination. However, when we hear this sentence in the appropriate context, we will interpret it to be about love, and we will know that the speaker of the sentence has in mind not real travelers but lovers, not a physical journey but the events in a love relationship, and not a physical destination at the end of the journey but the goal(s) of the love relationship. The sentence

The relationship is foundering suggests that somehow relationships are conceptually equated with the vehicles used in journeys. The sentence *It's been a bumpy road* is not about the physical obstacles on the way but about the difficulties that the lovers experience in their relationship. Furthermore, talking about love, the speaker of *We've made a lot of headway* will mean that a great deal of progress has been made in the relationship, and not that the travelers traveled far. And the sentence *We're at a crossroads* will mean that choices have to be made in the relationship, and not that a traveler has to decide which way to go at a fork in the road.

Given these interpretations, we can lay out a set of correspondences, or mappings between constituent elements of the source and those of the target. (In giving the correspondences, or mappings, we reverse the target-source order of the conceptual metaphors to yield source-target. We adopt this convention to emphasize the point that understanding typically goes from the more concrete to the more abstract concept.)

Source: JOURNEY		*Target*: LOVE
the travelers	⇒	the lovers
the vehicle	⇒	the love relationship itself
the journey	⇒	events in the relationship
the distance covered	⇒	the progress made
the obstacles encountered	⇒	the difficulties experienced
decisions about which way to go	⇒	choices about what to do
the destination of the journey	⇒	the goal(s) of the relationship

This is the systematic set of correspondences, or mappings, that characterize the LOVE IS A JOURNEY conceptual metaphor. Constituent elements of conceptual domain A are in systematic correspondence with constituent elements of conceptual domain B. From this discussion it might seem that the elements in the target domain have been there all along and that people came up with this metaphor because there were preexisting similarities between the elements in the two domains. This is not so. The domain of love did not have these elements *before it was structured* by the domain of journey. It was the application of the journey domain to the love domain that provided the concept of love with this particular structure or set of elements. In a way, it was the concept of journey that "created" the concept of love. To see that this is so, try to do a thought experiment. Try to imagine the goal, choice, difficulty, progress, etc. aspects of love without making use of the journey domain. Can you think of the goal of a love relationship without at the same time thinking of trying to reach a destination at the end of a journey? Can you think of the progress made in a love relationship without at the same time imagining the distance covered in a journey? Can you think of the choices made in a love relationship without thinking of choosing a direction in a journey? The difficulty of doing this shows that the target of love is not structured independently of and prior to the domain of journey. Another piece of evidence for the view that the target of love is not structured independently of any source domains is the following. In talking about the elements that structure a target domain, it is often difficult to name the elements without recourse to the language of the source. In the present example, we talk about the *goals* associated with love, but this is just a slightly "disguised" way of talking about destinations given in the source; the word *goal* has an additional literal or physical use—not just a metaphorical one. In the same way, the word *progress* also has a literal or physical meaning and it comes from a word meaning "step, go." These examples show that many elements of target concepts come from source domains and are not preexisting.

We can now consider another example of how correspondences, or mappings, make up a conceptual metaphor.

SOCIAL ORGANIZATIONS ARE PLANTS
He works for the local *branch* of the bank.
Our company is *growing*.
They had to *prune* the workforce.
The organization was *rooted* in the old church.
There is now a *flourishing* black market in software there.
His business *blossomed* when the railways put his establishment within
    reach of the big city.
Employers *reaped* enormous benefits from cheap foreign labour.

This seems to be characterized by the following set of mappings:

Source: PLANT		*Target:* SOCIAL ORGANIZATION
(a) the whole plant	⇒	the entire organization
(b) a part of the plant	⇒	a part of the organization
(c) growth of the plant	⇒	development of the organization
(d) removing a part of the plant	⇒	reducing the organization
(e) the root of the plant	⇒	the origin of the organization
(f) the flowering	⇒	the best stage, the most successful stage
(g) the fruits or crops	⇒	the beneficial consequences

Notice that in this case as well, constituent elements of plants correspond systematically to constituent elements of social organizations, such as companies, and the words that are used about plants are employed systematically in connection with organizations. This correspondence can be seen in all of the mappings, except mapping (a), which is merely assumed by the sentence: "He works for the local *branch* of the bank." The mappings (indicated by the letters used above) and the matching expressions that make them manifest in the PLANTS metaphor are listed below:

(b) *branch*
(c) *is growing*
(d) *prune*
(e) *root*

(f) *blossom, flower*
(g) *fruits*

In light of the discussion so far, we can ask: What does it mean then to know a metaphor? It means to know the systematic mappings between a source and a target. It is not suggested that this happens in a conscious manner. This knowledge is largely unconscious, and it is only for the purposes of analysis that we bring the mappings into awareness. However, when we know a conceptual metaphor, we use the linguistic expressions that reflect it in such a way that we do not violate the mappings that are conventionally fixed for the linguistic community. In other words, not any element of B can be mapped onto any element of A. The linguistic expressions used metaphorically must conform to established mappings, or correspondences, between the source and the target.

4. The Importance of Metaphor

But how important is metaphor in our lives and how important is it to study? One of the best (but not quite serious) illustrations of the seriousness and importance of metaphor can be found in the myth of Oedipus. As part of the myth, Oedipus arrives in Thebes where he finds that a monster, called the Sphinx, is guarding the road to the city. She poses riddles to everyone on their way to Thebes and devours them if they are unable to solve the riddles. So far, everyone has been devoured when Oedipus arrives. The Sphinx asks him the riddle: Which is the animal that has four feet in the morning, two at midday, and three in the evening? Without hesitation Oedipus answers: Man, who in infancy crawls on all fours, who walks upright in maturity, and in his old age supports himself with a stick. The Sphinx is defeated and kills herself. Oedipus thus becomes the king of Thebes. How was Oedipus able to solve the riddle? At least a part of this must have been his knowledge of conceptual metaphor. There appear to be two metaphors operative in figuring out the riddle. The first is the metaphor THE LIFE OF HUMAN BEINGS IS A DAY. Oedipus must have been helped by the correspondences that obtain between the target concept of life and the source domain of day. Morning corresponds to infancy, midday to mature adulthood, and evening to old age. Since he knew these mappings, he offered the correct solution. Another, and maybe less important, metaphor that may have played a part is HUMAN LIFE IS A JOURNEY. This metaphor is evoked by the frequent mention and thus the important role of feet in the riddle. Feet evoke the concept of journey that may provide a clue to the successful solution of the riddle through the HUMAN LIFE IS A JOURNEY metaphor. This reading is reinforced by the fact that much of the myth is a tale of Oedipus's life in the form of a journey.

All in all, Oedipus's life, at least on this occasion, is saved in part by his knowledge of metaphor. Can there be a more important reason and better motivation to find out about metaphor?

5. Some Questions about Metaphor

Given this characterization of metaphor in cognitive linguistics, several important questions arise. The answers to these questions will make up much of the rest of this book. They include the following.

(1) *Common source and target domains.* If we want to get a good idea of the range of conceptual metaphors in English, we have to ask three specific questions: (a) What are the most common abstract targets in English? That is, given the many abstract domains, do all of them require an equal amount of metaphorical understanding? (b) What are the most common source concepts? That is, given the large number of potential source domains from the physical world, do all of them participate in metaphorical understanding to the same degree? and (c) Which sources are used to understand which targets? That is, given the most common targets and sources, is it the case that any source can be used to comprehend any target? These issues will be discussed in chapter 2.

(2) *Kinds of metaphor.* Are all conceptual metaphors like the ones we have dealt with so far? It will be shown that there are distinct kinds within the larger category of conceptual metaphor and that it is possible to classify metaphors in a variety of ways. The characterization of the distinct classes will enable us to see the subtle differences in the nature, function, and power of metaphor. This will be the topic of chapter 3.

(3) *Metaphor in literature.* The language of literature is often metaphorical. What can the view of metaphor as presented here contribute to the study of literature? Indeed, what is the relationship between everyday metaphor and metaphor used in literature? This issue will be discussed in chapter 4.

(4) *Nonlinguistic realizations of conceptual metaphors.* It was mentioned above that we use primarily linguistic evidence for the existence of conceptual metaphors. But there are other kinds of available evidence as well. Conceptual metaphors manifest themselves, or are realized, in ways other than linguistic. What then are the most common ways in which conceptual metaphors are realized in a culture? I will try to provide an answer in chapter 5.

(5) *The basis of metaphor.* It was pointed out that there is a potentially vast range of target and an equally huge range of source domains. If any source domain could be paired with any target domain, we would have completely arbitrary conceptual metaphors. However, this does not seem to be the case. Only some connections or pairings between sources and targets are acceptable. This indicates that there are certain limitations on what can become conceptual metaphors. What are the limitations that possibly motivate metaphorical links between A and B? I will take up this issue in chapter 6.

(6) *Partial mappings.* It was claimed that conceptual metaphors can be characterized by the formula A IS B. This would assume that an entire target domain would be understood in terms of an entire

source domain. This obviously cannot be the case because it would mean that one conceptual domain would be exactly the same as another. I will show that mappings can be, and are, only partial. Only a part of B is mapped onto a part of A. We need to ask which parts of the source are mapped onto which parts in the target. The issue is addressed in chapter 7.

(7) *Metaphorical entailments.* We have seen above that conceptual metaphor consists of a set of mappings between a source and a target. Given the rich knowledge we have about concrete source domains, how much and what knowledge is carried over from source B to target A? In other words, to what extent do we make use of this rich knowledge about sources beyond the basic constituent elements as discussed in the mappings above? Why isn't everything carried over from B to A? What determines what is not carried over? An explanation will be offered in chapter 8.

(8) *The scope of metaphor.* Most of the specific source domains appear to characterize not just one target concept but several. For instance, the concept of war applies not only to arguments but also to love, the concept of building not only to theories but also to societies, the concept of fire not only to love but also to anger, etc. What is the scope of metaphorical source domains and what determines it? We will deal with the issue in chapter 9.

(9) *Metaphor systems.* Some conceptual metaphors appear to cluster together to form larger subsystems of metaphor. Do we have any idea what some of these larger subsystems are? What might the overarching metaphorical system of English look like? I will describe systems of metaphor in chapter 10.

(10) *Another figure: metonymy.* Metaphor is closely related to several other "tropes"; most important, to metonymy. What are the similarities between them and how do they differ from each other? I will try to characterize the relationship between metaphor and metonymy in chapter 11.

(11) *The universality of conceptual metaphors.* Some conceptual metaphors appear to be at least near-universal. What can possibly determine the universality of these metaphors? The issue is raised and answered in chapter 12.

(12) *Cultural variation in metaphor.* Other metaphors tend to be culture-specific. Indeed, what kind of variation is there in metaphor? In addition to varying cross-culturally, do they also vary subculturally, individually, geographically? I will offer some tentative answers to these questions in chapter 13.

(13) *Idioms and metaphor.* One aspect of language where metaphor figures prominently is idioms. Idioms are often metaphorical. How can we characterize the relationship between idioms and metaphor on the basis of the cognitive linguistic view? I will address the issue in chapter 14.

(14) *Metaphor in the study of language.* But metaphor is important not only in idioms but also in many other areas of the study of language. What can linguistics gain from the cognitive approach to metaphor? I will discuss some examples of the usefulness of

the cognitive view of metaphor in the study of language in chapter 15.

(15) *Blending and metaphor.* The cognitive view of metaphor is not a closed system of ideas. There are some recent developments that add to, enhance, and complement this system. One of the most significant of these is the theory of "network models." This new development will be the topic of chapter 16.

These are some of the issues that we have to focus on if we wish to understand the metaphorical process in some of its complexity. I will return to these issues in subsequent chapters of this book.

SUMMARY

We have made a distinction between **conceptual metaphors** and **metaphorical linguistic expressions**. In conceptual metaphors, one domain of experience is used to understand another domain of experience. The metaphorical linguistic expressions make manifest particular conceptual metaphors. The conceptual domain that we try to understand is called the **target domain** and the conceptual domain that we use for this purpose is the **source domain**.

Understanding one domain in terms of another involves a set of fixed **correspondences** (technically called **mappings**) between a source and a target domain. This set of mappings obtains between basic constituent elements of the source domain and basic constituent elements of the target. To know a conceptual metaphor is to know the set of mappings that applies to a given source-target pairing. It is these mappings that provide much of the meaning of the metaphorical linguistic expressions (or linguistic metaphors) that make a particular conceptual metaphor manifest.

There are several issues that arise in connection with this view of metaphor. The answers to these issues will be discussed in subsequent chapters of the book.

FURTHER READING

Lakoff and Johnson (1980) introduce the notion of conceptual metaphor. Their book contains many of the conceptual metaphors discussed in the chapter, as well as more linguistic examples for these metaphors. Lakoff (1993) is a survey of a more sophisticated later version of the cognitive linguistic view. The idea that conceptual metaphor is constituted by a set of mappings between a source and a target domain is discussed primarily on the basis of the same paper by Lakoff. The LIFE IS A JOURNEY metaphor is discussed by Lakoff (1994) and Winter (1995). Helpful comments on correspondences, or mappings, can be found in Lakoff and Kövecses (1987).

Gerard Steen (1999) offers an "identification procedure" for metaphorical expressions. Several authors deal with the issue of metaphor identification and the research of metaphor in general in a volume edited by Cameron and Low (1999).

Criticisms of the early forms of the cognitive view of metaphor can be found in Holland (1982), Ortony (1988), and Wierzbicka (1986).

EXERCISES

1. Match the corresponding constituent elements of the source (indicated by numbers) and the target domains (indicated by letters) in the LOVE IS WAR metaphor. In other words, what are the mappings?

   1. the battles in the war

   2. the belligerents in the war

   3. the damage in the war to the belligerents

   4. the strategies for the war actions

   5. the victory of a belligerent

   6. to surrender to a belligerent

   (a) the damage in love to the lovers

   (b) to allow the partner to take control

   (c) the dominance of a partner

   (d) the events of the love relationship

   (e) the lovers in the love relationship

   (f) the plans for the love relationship

2. Which metaphor, i.e., which source domain and which target domain, can you recognize in the linguistic expressions *I'll take my chances*; *The odds are against me*; *I've got an ace up my sleeve*; *He's holding all the aces*; *It's a toss-up*?

3. What linguistic expressions can you collect as examples of the metaphor TIME IS MONEY?

4. What mappings characterize the THEORIES ARE BUILDINGS conceptual metaphor? With the help of the examples given in the chapter, lay out the set of correspondences, or mappings, between elements of the source and those of the target domains.

2

Common
Source and
Target Domains

I t was shown in the previous chapter that conceptual metaphors consist of a source domain and a target domain, as well as a set of mappings between them. It was also noted that the source domains are typically more concrete or physical and more clearly delineated concepts than the targets, which tend to be fairly abstract and less delineated ones. What, then, are the most commonly used source and target domains? In other words, which clearly delineated physical concepts are used most commonly in understanding which less clearly delineated abstract concepts?

I will make use of two kinds of evidence in examining this issue. One kind of evidence is provided by various metaphor dictionaries and lists of conceptual metaphors, such as the *Master Metaphor List*. I have also looked at several metaphor dictionaries to find out which sources and targets occur most frequently. These dictionaries include the *Cobuild Metaphor Dictionary*, the metaphor section of *Rodale's Phrase Finder*, the *Metaphors Dictionary*, the *Dictionary of Everyday English Metaphors*, and *Roget's Thesaurus* to mention the best-known ones. I tried to determine which sources are employed most commonly to understand which common targets. I did not do a systematic study, but I feel that what I found is consistent across the metaphor dictionaries that were consulted. The other source of evidence comes from the research of scholars working within the cognitive linguistic tradition. I have surveyed most of the available literature on conceptual metaphor in order to see which sources and which targets stand out quantitatively in this body of research. Again, I feel that the findings based on this research are consistent with the findings based on the survey of metaphor dictionaries: roughly the same conceptual domains stand out as the most common sources and targets in both.

Another issue that I will pay some attention to is that of the directionality of conceptual metaphors; that is, the question of the reversibility of source and target domains. This issue was already mentioned in the previous chapter. In this chapter, however, we will look at a much greater number of examples that will allow us to be more confident in one of the basic claims of the cognitive linguistic view of metaphor; namely, that in most cases source and target domains are not reversible.

1. Common Source Domains

In studying the most common source domains, I found that the most systematic comprehensive survey is provided by the *Cobuild Metaphor Dictionary*. I have supplemented the list of sources offered by this metaphor dictionary with some additional ones from my survey of metaphor research. Below, I will briefly mention the most frequent sources.

1.1. The Human Body

The human body is an ideal source domain, since, for us, it is clearly delineated and (we believe) we know it well. This does not mean that we make use of *all* aspects of this domain in metaphorically understanding abstract targets. The aspects that are especially utilized in metaphorical comprehension involve various parts of the body, including the head, face, legs, hands, back, heart, bones, shoulders, and others. Some examples follow:

the *heart* of the problem
to shoulder a responsibility
the *head* of the department

Actually, one of my students, Réka Hajdú, did a comprehensive study of a recent American collection of metaphorical idioms titled *Figurative Idioms* by George Nagy. She counted all the body-based metaphorical idioms in the dictionary and found that out of 12,000 idioms, well over two thousand have to do with the human body. This remarkable finding shows that a large portion of metaphorical meaning derives from our experience of our own body. The "embodiment" of meaning is perhaps *the* central idea of the cognitive linguistic view of metaphor and indeed of the cognitive linguistic view of meaning. As can be expected, the human body plays a key role in the emergence of metaphorical meaning not only in English and other "Western" languages and cultures, but also scholars, such as Bernd Heine and others, have abundantly demonstrated its central importance in human conceptualization in languages and cultures around the world. I will return to the discussion of embodiment in several later chapters.

1.2. Health and Illness

Health and illness are, of course, aspects of the human body. Both the general properties of health and illness and particular illnesses frequently constitute metaphorical source domains. Some examples include:

a *healthy* society
a *sick* mind
She *hurt* my feelings.

1.3. Animals

The domain of animals is an extremely productive source domain. Human beings are especially frequently understood in terms of (assumed) properties of animals. Thus, we talk about someone being a *brute*, a *tiger*, a *dog*, a *sly fox*, a *bitch*, a *cow*, a *snake*, and so on. But the metaphorical use of animal terms is not limited to human beings, as indicated by the example "It will be a *bitch* to pull this boat out of the water." In this instance, the term *bitch* denotes any difficult situation. The body parts of animals are also commonly used in the metaphorical conceptualization of abstract domains. This way of understanding nonphysical domains is also very common in languages of the world, as Heine and his colleagues show.

1.4. Plants

People cultivate plants for a variety of purposes: for eating, for pleasure, for making things, and so on. In our metaphorical use, we distinguish various parts of plants; we are aware of the many actions we perform in relation to plants; and we recognize the many different stages of growth that plants go through. Here are some examples:

a *budding* beauty
He *cultivated* his friendship with her.
the *fruit* of her labor
Exports *flourished* last year.

1.5. Buildings and Construction

Human beings build houses and other structures for shelter, work, storage, and so on. Both the static object of a house and its parts and the act of building it serve as common metaphorical source domains. Some examples follow:

a *towering* genius
He's *in ruins* financially.
She *constructed* a coherent argument.

1.6. Machines and Tools

People use machines and tools to work, play, fight, and for pleasure. Again, both the machines and tools and the activities related to them show up as metaphorical expressions, as illustrated by the examples below:

the *machine* of democracy
conceptual *tools*
She *produces* a book every year.

1.7. Games and Sport

People play and they invent elaborate activities to entertain themselves. Games and sport are characterized by certain properties that are commonly utilized for metaphorical purposes. For example, many games have rules and this property occurs in examples such as "He *plays by the rules*" and "We want an *even playing field*." Additional examples from the domain of games and sport include:

> *to toy* with the idea
> He tried to *checkmate* her.
> He's a *heavyweight* politician.

1.8. Money and Economic Transactions (business)

From very early on, people living in human society have engaged in economic transactions of various kinds. These transactions often involve the use of money and commodities in general. The commercial event involves a number of entities and actions: a commodity, money, handing over the commodity, and handing over the money. Our understanding of various abstract things is based on this scenario or parts of it. Below are some examples:

> *Spend* your time wisely.
> I tried *to save* some energy.
> She *invested a lot* in the relationship.

1.9. Cooking and Food

Cooking food as an activity has been with us ever since the beginnings of humanity. Cooking involves a complex process of several elements: an agent, recipe, ingredients, actions, a product, just to mention the most important ones. The activity with its parts and the product serve as a deeply entrenched source domain. Here are some examples:

> What's your *recipe* for success?
> That's a *watered-down* idea.
> He *cooked up* a story that nobody believed.

1.10. Heat and Cold

Heat and cold are extremely basic human experiences. We feel warm and cold as a result of the temperature of the air that surrounds us. We often use the heat domain metaphorically to talk about our attitude to people and things.

Here are a few examples to illustrate:

in the *heat* of passion
a *cold* reception
an *icy* stare
a *warm* welcome

As the example with the word *icy* shows, the properties of warm and cold sometimes appear as weather conditions.

The domain of fire is related to that of heat. In addition to using fire to keep ourselves warm, we also use fire to cook, to destroy things, etc. This source domain is especially common in the metaphorical conceptualization of passions and desires, such as rage, love, hate, and some others. For example, a person can be described as "*burning* with love" or "*smoldering* with anger." But the source domain of fire enables us to observe an interesting aspect of many conceptual metaphors. Often, in the case of conceptual metaphors, a typical source domain can also be further conceptualized by another source; that is, source domains can become target domains. Thus, the domain of fire itself, a typical source for many conceptual metaphors, can also be understood metaphorically in terms of other domains. As an example, consider the FIRE IS A HUNGRY ANIMAL metaphor, which produces linguistic metaphors such as "The fire *devoured* everything" and "The fire was already *licking* at the first row of houses." The same process producing "metaphor chains" can be noticed in the body metaphor discussed above; that is, the human body can also function as a target domain, as when we say "I feel a little *rusty* today." This "chain-producing" aspect of metaphor has not been explored in the cognitive linguistic approach, and its mechanism is unaccounted for.

1.11. Light and Darkness

Light and darkness are also basic human experiences. The properties of light and darkness often appear as weather conditions when we speak and think metaphorically. Let us see some examples:

a *dark* mood
She *brightened* up.
a *cloud* of suspicion
There was a *cloud* over their friendship.
I do not have the *foggiest* idea.
She was in a *haze* of confusion.

1.12. Forces

There are various kinds of forces: gravitational, magnetic, electric, mechanical. We see these forces as operating on and affecting us in many ways. The forces take many shapes in the physical world: waves, wind, storm, fire, and agents pushing, pulling, driving, sending another thing. These forces effect various changes in the thing acted on. There are as many different effects as there are different forces. The metaphorical conceptualization of several abstract domains in terms of forces is reflected in the examples below:

> She *swept me off my feet.*
> You're *driving* me nuts.
> Don't *push* me!
> I was *overwhelmed.*

1.13. Movement and Direction

Movement—either self-propelled or otherwise—is yet another basic experience. Movement can involve a change of location or it can be stationary (as in the case of shaking, for instance). When it involves a change of location, it is associated with direction: forward and backward, up and down. Changes of various kinds are conceptualized metaphorically as movement that involves a change of location. This is indicated by the examples:

> He *went* crazy.
> She solved the problem *step by step.*
> Inflation is *soaring.*
> Our economy is *galloping ahead.*

Obviously, this is not a complete survey of domains that participate in conceptual metaphors as sources. Further sources include various basic entities, such as containers, substances, physical objects, and several others. I will come back to these in the next chapter. Common source domains also include the various properties of objects and substances, such as their shape, color, size, hardness, transparency, sharpness, weight, and many more. However, despite the representative nature of the list, we get a sense of the most common source domains and the kind of world that our most common metaphors depict. In this world, it seems, there are people, animals, and plants; the people live in houses, they have bodies, they eat, they get sick and get better; they move around and travel; they live in a physical environment with all kinds of objects and substances in it; the objects and substances have all kinds of properties; the physical environment affects the people; and the people make tools, work, and engage in various other transactions with other people. This is an extremely simplified world, but it is exactly the simplified nature of this world that enables us to make use of parts of it in creating more abstract ones.

2. Common Target Domains

In the same way as the source domains apply to several targets, the targets also have several sources. Target domains are abstract, diffuse, and lack clear delineation; as a result, they "cry out" for metaphorical conceptualization. I can only survey here the most common target domains and their most important sources.

2.1. Emotion

The domain of emotion is a par excellence target domain. Emotion concepts such as anger, fear, love, happiness, sadness, shame, pride, and so on are primarily understood by means of conceptual metaphors. The source domains of emotion concepts typically involve forces. Thus, we have examples like

> She was deeply *moved*.
> He was *bursting* with joy.
> He *unleashed* his anger.

Given that emotions are largely comprehended via force metaphors, it is not surprising that, etymologically, the word *emotion* derives from the Latin *e* meaning "out" and *movere* meaning "to move."

2.2. Desire

As regards metaphorical conceptualization, desire is similar to emotion. It is also comprehended as a force, not only as a physical one but also often as a physiological force like hunger or thirst. It is also often understood in terms of heat. Some examples include:

> The jacket I saw in the shopwindow *pulled* me into the store.
> She is *hungry for* knowledge.
> I am *starved for* affection.
> He's *burning* to go.

2.3. Morality

Moral categories such as good and bad, as well as honesty, courage, sincerity, honor, and their opposites, are largely understood by means of more concrete source concepts. Among these, economic transactions, forces, straightness, light and dark, and up-down orientation are especially important, as the examples below indicate:

> I'll *pay* you *back for* this.
> She *resisted* the temptation.
> He's a *straight* shooter.
> He's a *shady* character.
> That was a *lowly* thing to do.

2.4. Thought

How the human mind works is still little known. This situation makes it no surprise that people, both lay persons and experts, try to understand the mind by resorting to metaphors of various kinds. Rational thought is comprehended as work—the manipulation of objects in a workshop. Less active aspects of thought are understood in terms of perception, such as seeing. Some examples to demonstrate this follow:

> She's *grinding out* new ideas.
> He *hammered* the point home.
> He *searched for* the memory.
> I *see* your point.

2.5. Society / Nation

The concepts of society and nation are extremely complex, and this complexity calls for metaphorical understanding. Common ways of comprehending society and nation involve the source concepts of person and family.

> What do we *owe* society?
> *neighboring* countries
> a *friendly* nation
> the founding *fathers* of the country

Other aspects of society are viewed as machines or the human body:

> the *machinery* of democracy
> the *functioning* of society
> the *ills* of society

2.6. Politics

Politics has to do with the exercise of power. Political power is conceptualized as physical force. Politics has many additional aspects that are understood by means of a variety of further source domains, including games and sport, business, and war.

> They *forced* the opposition out of the House.
> The president *plays hardball*.
> There was a great deal of *haggling* over the issue.
> The *fight erupted* over abortion.

2.7. Economy

Economy is usually comprehended via metaphor. Its most commonly used source domains include building, plants, journey (movement, direction), as shown by the examples:

> Germany *built a strong* economy.
> the *growth* of the economy
> They *pruned* the budget.
> China's economy is *galloping ahead*.

2.8. Human Relationships

Human relationships include such concepts as friendship, love, and marriage. These and similar concepts are metaphorically viewed as plants, machines, and buildings, as shown by the examples:

Their friendship is *in full flower*.
It's a *budding* relationship.
They had *to work on* their relationship.
They *built a strong* marriage.

2.9. Communication

We conceive of human communication as involving a speaker and a hearer, a message consisting of some meaning encoded in linguistic expressions, and a transfer of this message from the speaker to the hearer along some channel. Metaphorically, we view the linguistic expressions, meanings, and the transfer of the message as containers, objects, and sending, respectively. Here are some examples to illustrate this:

You are *putting* too many ideas *into* a single sentence.
That's a *dense* paragraph.
She *gave* me a lot of information.

It should be pointed out here that this metaphor is not the only one for communication, but it represents the most common "folk theory" of what human communication involves. This metaphor will be dealt with in greater detail in chapter 6.

2.10. Time

Time is a notoriously difficult concept to understand. The major metaphor for the comprehension of time is one according to which time is an object that moves. Many common everyday expressions demonstrate this:

The time will *come* when . . .
Christmas is *coming up* soon.
Time *flies*.
in the *following* week . . .
Time *goes by* fast.

2.11. Life and Death

Life and death are concepts that are heavily metaphorical in nature. Their metaphorical conceptualization is pervasive in both everyday language and literary works. As we saw in the first chapter, life is understood as a journey to some destination. Moreover, it is metaphorically day, light, warmth, and others. Birth is conceived of as arrival, whereas death is viewed as departure, as well as night, darkness, and cold.

The baby will *arrive* soon.
Grandpa is *gone*.
His father *passed away*.

2.12. Religion

Key aspects of religion involve our view of God and our relationship to God. (Notice that to use a personal pronoun to replace the word God would already require metaphorical understanding: Should we refer to God as *it* or *him* or *she*?) God, similar to the concepts of society and nation, is conceptualized as a person: Father, Shepherd, King, etc. It follows from the metaphor that believers are viewed as God's children, sheep, subjects, etc. Other aspects of religious experience involve the conceptualization of such notions as eternity, life after/before death, and so on which are necessarily metaphorical, since we have no experience of them.

2.13. Events and Actions

Events and actions are superordinate concepts that comprise a variety of different kinds of events and actions. For example, reading, making a chair, doing a project in the lab, plowing, or whatever are kinds of actions. Aspects of events and actions are often comprehended as movement and force. These aspects include such notions as change, cause, purpose, means, and so on. Here are some examples that show this:

He *went* crazy.
She *turned* thirty last month.
You're *driving* me nuts.
The goal *sent* the crowd into a frenzy.
She has *reached* her goals in life.

As can be seen, these common target domains can be roughly classified as psychological and mental states and events (emotion, desire, morality, thought), social groups and processes (society, politics, economy, human relationships, communication), and personal experiences and events (time, life, death, religion). The superordinate concepts of events and actions are difficult to place in this scheme. Another difficulty is to see exactly how the simplified world, as depicted in the most common source domains, fits and "maps onto" the groups of common target domains described above. However, in chapter 10 on metaphor systems I will attempt to work out this "fit," at least in its most general outline.

The survey above also enables us to reinforce the conclusion that conceptual metaphors are mostly **unidirectional**. While we commonly talk about the *illness* of society, the *machinery* of political decision-making, and the *heat* of passion, we do not or much less commonly talk about the *society* of illness, the *political decision-making* of machinery, or the *passion* of heat. In some cases, however, the source and target can be reversed. Take the ANGER IS STORM metaphor, with examples such as "It was a *stormy* meeting" or "He *stormed* out of the room." But we can also have A STORM IS ANGER (AN ANGRY PERSON), as exemplified by expressions such as "*angry* waves" or "The storm was *raging* for hours." However, when source and target domains of conceptual metaphors are reversed, there typically occur certain stylistic shifts in the value of the linguistic metaphors. In the present example, the reversal of the usual source-target pairing results in expressions that are not everyday but literary or formal. Interestingly, linguistic metaphors that are isolated, not systematic, that is, ones that do not belong to a conceptual metaphor, seem to be more easily reversible. Take, for instance, the metaphorical statement "The surgeon is a *butcher*." Its reversed version is also acceptable: "The butcher is a *surgeon*." However, in this case there is a shift of meaning. While the statement of the surgeon being a butcher is considered very negative, the reverse statement of the butcher being a surgeon is considered as something positive. Reversibility is found commonly in isolated metaphors of the form *a* is *b* (where *a* and *b* are linguistic expressions, not conceptual domains) that are based on subcategorization, as in the present example the surgeon is classified as a butcher and the butcher as a surgeon.

SUMMARY

In this chapter, we have surveyed some of the most common source and target domains. These source domains include the HUMAN BODY, HEALTH AND ILLNESS, ANIMALS, MACHINES AND TOOLS, BUILDINGS AND CONSTRUCTION, PLANTS, GAMES AND SPORT, COOKING AND FOOD, ECONOMIC TRANSACTIONS, FORCES, LIGHT AND DARKNESS, HEAT AND COLD, and MOVEMENT AND DIRECTION.

The common targets include EMOTION, DESIRE, MORALITY, THOUGHT, SOCIETY, RELIGION, POLITICS, ECONOMY, HUMAN RELATIONSHIPS, COMMUNICATION, EVENTS AND ACTIONS, TIME, and LIFE AND DEATH. The target domains fall into such higher groups as psychological and mental states and events, social groups and processes, and personal experiences.

These findings provide overwhelming evidence for the view that conceptual metaphors are *unidirectional*: they go from concrete to abstract domains; the most common source domains are concrete, while the most common targets are abstract concepts. In this way, conceptual metaphors can serve the purpose of understanding intangible, and hence difficult-to-understand, concepts.

FURTHER READING

Metaphors We Live By by Lakoff and Johnson (1980) is the classic study of the contemporary view of metaphor in cognitive linguistics. It deals with several source and target domains. Gibbs (1994) discusses several of the source and target domains I have mentioned in this chapter and provides evidence for the ubiquity of metaphor in everyday thought. These are basic works that should be read by anyone interested in the cognitive linguistic view of metaphor.

Jäkel (1995) describes a large system of metaphors relating to the mind and thought, in which the mind is viewed as a workshop and thought as the manipulation of tools and objects. Jäkel (1993) tests the notion of the unidirectionality of metaphor and finds that in the majority of cases conceptual metaphors are not reversible. Johnson (1987), in contrast to Jäkel (1995), lays emphasis on a different metaphorical source domain in discussing the mind and human thought processes: understanding-as-seeing. Johnson (1992) is a discussion of morality as moral accounting. Kövecses (1986, 1988, 1990, 1991a, 1991b) are analyses of various emotion concepts. Kövecses (1994) discusses Alexis de Tocqueville's metaphors for society in general and American democracy in particular. Kövecses (2000a) explores the system of emotion metaphors, making use of Talmy's force dynamics. Lakoff (1987) contains, in case study one, a detailed examination of metaphors for sexual desire. Lakoff (1990, 1993) looks at metaphors for events and actions in general and finds that they are structured by movement and force as their source domains. Lakoff (1993, 1994) and Radden (1997) examine the concept of time as conceptualized in terms of moving objects. Lakoff (1992) contains a discussion of some of the most important metaphors for nation and politics. Lakoff (1996) explores in detail the American conception of morality and its relation to politics. This book also contains discussions of metaphors for God. Lakoff and Turner (1989) investigate metaphors for life and death, as well as time, in literary texts. Quinn (1987, 1991) offers intensive studies of the American view of marriage on the basis of interview materials. Radden (1995) describes idioms that have movement and direction as their source domain. Reddy (1979) is a study of the metaphors for communication and introduces some of the basic insights into the nature of metaphor in the cognitive linguistic view. Adamson et al. (1996) and Rohrer (1995) analyze the American political scene using the cognitive linguistic approach to metaphor. Sweetser (1990) contains a chapter in which she describes a system of metaphors for the mind and thought that she calls the Mind-as-Body metaphor. Talmy (1988) calls attention to the importance of "force dynamics" in the study of language and cognition; he treats the notion of force as a major source domain in the conceptualization of a variety of abstract concepts. Turner (1987) analyzes the system of kinship in English as a source domain in works of literature.

Metaphor lists and dictionaries:

Master Metaphor List
Cobuild Metaphor Dictionary
The Phrase Finder
Dictionary of Everyday English Metaphors
Metaphors Dictionary
Roget's Thesaurus

EXERCISES

1. Below you can read parts of a magazine article from *Time*, June 10, 1996. What are the source and target domains of the italicized metaphorical expressions in the following passage?

   "The Right Way to Peace?" (p. 28)
   Which way now? In this year of elections that could *redirect* history—in Israel, Russia, the US—the first has been decided. Israelis have picked a Prime Minister in conservative 46-year-old Likud leader Benjamin Netanyahu. And the change in policies that this country will now pursue will have consequences affecting half the globe. Sometimes statesmen *stumble blindly over an epochal crossroads they do not know is there.* Others are given the chance to *see the fork in the road ahead and decide deliberately which way to go.* Folly, wrote historian Barbara Tuchman, is when leaders knowingly *choose the wrong path.*

2. In the chapter, you read about God being conceptualized in several different ways. Look at the following quotes from hymns (religious songs) and decide which conceptualization is used.

   (a) Dearest children, God is near you,
   Watching o'er you day and night
   And delights to own and bless you
   If you strive to do what's right.

   (b) The Lord my pasture will prepare
   . . . feed me . . .
   And guard me with a watchful eye
   My noonday walks he will attend
   And all my silent midnight hours defend.

   (c) Beneath his watchful eye, His saints will securely dwell
   That hand which bears all nature up Shall guard his children well.
   Why should this anxious load Press down your wary mind
   Haste to your Heavenly Father's throne And sweet refreshment find.

3. The following quotation hides a different kind of religious conceptualization. How would you describe this? What metaphors do you recognize?

   Jesus, Savior pilot me Over life's tempestuous sea
   Unknown waves before me roll, Hiding rock and treach'rous shoal.
   Chart and compass came from thee: Jesus, Savior, pilot me.

4. In the chapter we described forces as one of the typical source domains. In the following metaphorical linguistic examples, identify the various kinds of forces and the abstract domains to which these forces apply.

   (a) I was *drawn* to him.
   (b) The film caused a *storm* of controversy.
   (c) After a *whirlwind* romance the couple announced their engagement in July and were married last month.
   (d) . . . the *hurricane* of grief and anger swept the nation.

3

Kinds of
Metaphor

In the first chapter, we saw that metaphor can be characterized with the formula *A IS B*, where the target domain (A) is comprehended through a source domain (B). This comprehension is based on a set of mappings that exist between elements of A and elements of B. To know a conceptual metaphor is to know this set of mappings. It was also pointed out that metaphor in the cognitive linguistic view means primarily conceptual metaphor, as opposed to linguistic metaphor. That is, we distinguish between a conceptual metaphor with the form *A IS B* and its metaphorical linguistic expressions. The metaphorical expressions that characterize *A IS B* formulas are regarded as the linguistic realizations or manifestations of underlying conceptual metaphors. It was noted, however, that conceptual metaphors can be realized in other than linguistic ways (such as myths)—a point to which we will return in chapter 5.

But the question arises whether all conceptual metaphors are like the ones we have characterized so far. In the present chapter, I will show that there are distinct kinds of **conceptual metaphor** and that it is possible to classify metaphors in a variety of ways. These include classifications according to the **conventionality, function, nature,** and **level of generality of metaphor.** (In chapter 9, I will further distinguish metaphors according to their complexity, classifying them as "simple" or "complex.") It is possible to classify metaphors in several other ways, but these are the ways that play an especially important role in the cognitive linguistic view.

1. The Conventionality of Metaphor

A major way in which metaphors can be classified is their degree of conventionality. In other words, we can ask how well worn or how deeply entrenched a metaphor is in everyday use by ordinary people for everyday purposes. This use of the notion of conventionality is different from the way this concept is usually used in linguistics, semiotics, and the philosophy of language. The typical application of the term in these fields is synonymous with that of the term "arbitrary," especially as this is used in explaining the nature of linguistic signs (where it is pointed out that "form" and "meaning" are related to each other in an arbitrary fashion). However, the term "conventional" is used here in the sense of well established and well entrenched. Thus, we can say that a metaphor is highly conventional or conventionalized (i.e., well established and deeply entrenched) in the usage of a linguistic community.

Since there are both conceptual metaphors and their corresponding linguistic expressions, the issue of conventionality concerns both conceptual metaphors and their linguistic manifestations. The metaphors, both conceptual and linguistic, we saw as examples in the previous chapters were all highly conventionalized, in that speakers of English use them naturally and effortlessly for their normal, everyday purposes when they talk about such concepts as argument, love, social organizations, life, and so on. Consider again the metaphors below:

ARGUMENT IS WAR: I *defended* my argument.
LOVE IS A JOURNEY: We'll just have to *go our separate ways.*
THEORIES ARE BUILDINGS: We have *to construct* a new theory.
IDEAS ARE FOOD: I can't *digest* all these facts.
SOCIAL ORGANIZATIONS ARE PLANTS: The company *is growing fast.*
LIFE IS A JOURNEY: He had a *head start* in life.

The metaphorical expressions given as illustrations of the conceptual metaphors above are highly conventionalized, that is, they are well worn or even cliched. Most speakers would not in fact even notice that they use metaphor when they use the expression *defend* in connection with arguments, *construct* in connection with theories, *go our separate* ways in connection with love, *grow* in connection with company, *digest* in connection with ideas, *head start* in connection with life. For native speakers of English these are some of the most ordinary and natural ways to talk about these subject matters.

Conventional conceptual metaphors, such as ARGUMENT IS WAR, LOVE IS A JOURNEY, IDEAS ARE FOOD, THEORIES ARE BUILDINGS, etc., are deeply entrenched ways of *thinking about* or *understanding* an abstract domain, while conventional metaphorical linguistic expressions are well worn, cliched ways of *talking about* abstract domains. Thus, both conceptual and linguistic metaphors can be more or less conventional. For example, a conventional way of thinking about theories is in terms of buildings and about life in terms of a journey. In addition, there are conventional ways of talking about the same domains. Thus, we use the verb *to construct* to talk about some aspects of theories and the noun *head start* to talk about some aspects of life. It is customary to refer to the conventional nature of linguistic expressions with the adjective *conventionalized* and thus talk about conventionalized (rather than conventionàl) metaphorical linguistic expressions.

Highly conventional metaphors are at one end of what we can call the *scale of conventionality*. At the opposite end of the scale, we find highly unconventional or novel metaphors. To illustrate, let us give an example of both:

LIFE IS A JOURNEY
(a) He had a *head start* in life.
(b) Two roads diverged in a wood, and I—
    I took the one less traveled by,
    And that has made all the difference.

Both of these examples are linguistic metaphors that manifest the same conceptual metaphor. The example in (b) comes from Robert Frost's poem "The Road Not Taken." Obviously, Frost uses the conventional LIFE IS A JOURNEY metaphor in unconventional ways. He employs linguistic expressions from the journey domain that have not been conventionalized for speakers of English; "two roads diverged" and "I took the one [road] less traveled by" are not worn out, cliched linguistic expressions to talk about life in English. As linguistic metaphors, they strike us as unconventional and novel, but the conceptual metaphor that they realize remains conventional. While it may be difficult for most of us to conceive of life in other than the JOURNEY conceptual metaphor, we probably couldn't find these linguistic expressions in a dictionary or hear them every day from ordinary speakers for everyday purposes of communication.

These examples of the LIFE IS A JOURNEY conceptual metaphor appear to support the widespread view that novel metaphorical expressions have their source in poetry or literature. But unconventionalized metaphorical expressions do not only come from the realm of arts, strictly conceived. There are many creative speakers who can produce novel linguistic metaphors based on conventional conceptual metaphors. Some well-known categories of these speakers in English include sports journalists, politicians, (church) ministers, certain speakers of Black English, authentic users of slang, graffiti writers, writers of song lyrics, and others.

To give a couple of examples of this, consider first the following cliché:

Stop the world. I want to get off.

Obviously, the author of this line had the conventional conceptual metaphor LIFE IS A JOURNEY in mind but used unconventionalized linguistic expressions that make it manifest.

Another conceptual metaphor for life is LIFE IS A SPORTING GAME. This is the metaphor that American politician Ross Perot used, when he commented in June 1992 on the nation's high medical costs with the following words: "We're buying a front row box seat, and we're not even getting to see a bad show from the bleachers." While he uses here a conventional conceptual metaphor for life, the linguistic expressions that he employs are unconventionalized.

While it is easy to find unconventionalized metaphorical linguistic expressions that realize conventional conceptual metaphors, it is less easy to find unconventional conceptual metaphors for a given target domain. Take the concept of love, as an example. Love is metaphorically conceptualized in many ways; in addition to LOVE IS A JOURNEY, we understand it in terms of FIRE (*burning* with love); PHYSICAL UNITY (We are *as one*); INSANITY (I'm *madly* in love); ECONOMIC EXCHANGE (She *invested a lot* in that relationship); PHYSI-CAL FORCES (She *attracts* me *irresistibly*); NATURAL FORCES (He was *swept off his feet*); ILLNESS (She *has it bad*); MAGIC (I'm *enchanted*); RAPTURE (He was *high on* love); WAR (She eventually *surrendered*); GAME (She's *playing hard to get*); and so on. These are all highly conventional ways of concep-tualizing love; they are age-old and deeply entrenched ways of thought con-cerning love in Anglo-American (and even more generally in Western) cul-ture. Do people think of love in terms of concepts other than these? Not really. Most people comprehend their love experiences and lead their love lives via such conventional conceptual metaphors. It seems that the understanding of love through these source domains provides a sufficiently comprehensive and coherent notion of the concept. However, when experiences fall outside the range of these conventional mechanisms or when people cannot make sense of them in a coherent way, they may and often do employ less conventional source domains. Lakoff and Johnson point out one such unconventional conceptual metaphor: LOVE IS A COLLABORATIVE WORK OF ART. While the conventional metaphors mentioned above focus largely on passive aspects of romantic love, the COLLABORATIVE WORK OF ART metaphor emphasizes the more action-oriented aspects of it. If love is a collaborative work of art, the two lovers should be able to work out their common goals, the premises of the work, the responsibilities that they do and do not share, the ratio of control and letting go in the creation, the costs and the benefits of the project, and so on. It is clear that the notion of love will be very different for those who "live by" this metaphor. The unconventionality of this conceptual meta-phor is shown by the fact that Lakoff and Johnson do not provide any meta-phorical linguistic expressions to demonstrate it. The reason for this, in all probability, is that there are no such conventionalized expressions.

The LOVE IS A COLLABORATIVE WORK OF ART metaphor is the product of two ordinary people attempting to make sense of their everyday love ex-periences. Artists, poets, and scientists also often do the same; they offer us new ways and possibilities in the form of new, unconventional conceptual metaphors to see the world around us. One example of this occurred when William P. Magee said at a United Nations NGO meeting in 1993: "Life is a mirror. If you smile, it smiles back at you; if you frown, it frowns back." LIFE IS A MIRROR is not a conventional conceptual metaphor; Magee used an in-ventive, unconventional metaphor.

2. The Cognitive Function of Metaphor

When we ask what the function of metaphor is for ordinary people in think-ing about and seeing the world, we're asking a question about the cognitive function of metaphor. Conceptual metaphors can also be classified according to the cognitive functions that they perform. On this basis, three general kinds of conceptual metaphor have been distinguished: structural, ontological, and orientational.

2.1. Structural Metaphors

So far in this book we have been concerned with what we call **structural metaphors**. In this kind of metaphor, the source domain provides a relatively rich knowledge structure for the target concept. In other words, the cognitive function of these metaphors is to enable speakers to understand target A by means of the structure of source B. As we saw in chapter 1, this understanding takes place by means of conceptual mappings between elements of A and elements of B.

For example, the concept of time is structured according to motion and space. Given the TIME IS MOTION metaphor, we understand time in the following way:

We understand time in terms of some basic elements: Physical objects, their locations, and their motion.

There is a background condition that applies to this way of understanding time: The present time is at the same location as a canonical observer.

Given the basic elements and the background condition, we get the following mappings:

Times are things.
The passing of time is motion.
Future times are in front of the observer; past times are behind the observer.
One thing is moving, the other is stationary; the stationary thing is the deictic center.

This set of mappings structures our notion of time in a clear way. The TIME IS MOTION conceptual metaphor exists in the form of two special cases in English: TIME PASSING IS MOTION OF AN OBJECT and TIME PASSING IS AN OBSERVER'S MOTION OVER A LANDSCAPE. The two versions can be seen in such examples as:

TIME PASSING IS MOTION OF AN OBJECT
The time will *come* when . . .
The time has long since *gone* when . . .
The time for action has *arrived*.
In the weeks *following* next Tuesday . . .
On the *preceding* day . . .
I'm looking *ahead* to Christmas.

Thanksgiving is *coming up* on us.
Time is *flying by*.

In this version of the TIME IS MOTION metaphor, the observer is fixed and times are objects moving with respect to the observer. Times are oriented with their fronts in their direction of motion. The other version of the TIME IS MO-TION metaphor is:

TIME PASSING IS AN OBSERVER'S MOTION OVER A LANDSCAPE
There's going to be trouble *along the road*.
His stay in Russia *extended* over many years.
He *passed* the time happily.
We're *coming up* on Christmas.
We're *getting close* to Christmas.

Whereas in the first version the observer is fixed, in this second version times are fixed locations and the observer is moving with respect to time.

The TIME IS MOTION metaphor (as specified in the mappings and the differences in the two versions) accounts for a large number of linguistic metaphors in English. The mappings not only explain why the particular expressions mean what they do, but they also provide a basic overall structure, hence understanding, for our notion of time. Without the metaphor it would be difficult to imagine what our concept of time would be. Most structural metaphors provide this kind of structuring and understanding for their target concepts.

2.2. Ontological Metaphors

Ontological metaphors provide much less cognitive structuring for target concepts than structural ones do. Their cognitive job seems to be to "merely" give an ontological status to general categories of abstract target concepts. What this simply means is that we conceive of our experiences in terms of objects, substances, and containers, in general, without specifying exactly what kind of object, substance, or container is meant. Since our knowledge about objects, substances, and containers is rather limited at this general level, we cannot use these highly general categories to understand much about target domains. This is, as has been seen, the job of structural metaphors, which provide an elaborate structure for abstract concepts.

But it is nevertheless a cognitively important job to assign a basic status in terms of objects, substances, etc. to many of our experiences. The kinds of experiences that require this the most are those that are not clearly delineated, vague, or abstract. For example, we do not really know what the mind is, but we conceive of it as an object (note the use of the word *what* in the first part of this sentence). This way we can attempt to understand more about it.

In general, ontological metaphors enable us to see more sharply delineated structure where there is very little or none.

Source Domains	*Target Domains*
PHYSICAL OBJECT	⇒ NONPHYSICAL OR ABSTRACT ENTITIES (e.g., the mind)
	EVENTS (e.g., going to the race), ACTIONS (e.g., giving someone a call)
SUBSTANCE	⇒ ACTIVITIES (e.g., a lot of running in the game)
CONTAINER	⇒ UNDELINEATED PHYSICAL OBJECTS (e.g., a clearing in the forest)
	⇒ PHYSICAL AND NONPHYSICAL SURFACES (e.g., land areas, the visual field)
	⇒ STATES (e.g., in love)

Given that undelineated experiences receive a more delineated status via ontological metaphors, speakers can use these metaphors for more specific jobs: (1) to refer to, to quantify, to identify aspects of the experience that has been made more delineated. For example, conceiving of fear as an object, we can conceptualize it as "our possession." Thus, we can linguistically refer to fear as *my fear* or *your fear*. Cases like this are the least noticeable types of conceptual metaphor. (2) Once a "nonthing" experience has received the status of a thing through an ontological metaphor, the experience so conceptualized can be structured further by means of structural metaphors. If we conceptualize the mind as an object, we can easily provide more structure for it by means of the "machine" metaphor for the mind (as in: "My mind is *rusty* this morning").

We can conceive of **personification** as a form of ontological metaphor. In personification, human qualities are given to nonhuman entities. Personification is very common in literature, but it also abounds in everyday discourse, as the examples below show:

His theory *explained* to me the behavior of chickens raised in factories.
Life has *cheated* me.
Inflation is *eating up* our profits.
Cancer finally *caught up* with him.
The computer *went dead* on me.

Theory, life, inflation, cancer, computer are not humans, but they are given qualities of human beings, such as explaining, cheating, eating, catching up, and dying. Personification makes use of one of the best source domains we have—ourselves. In personifying nonhumans as humans, we can begin to understand them a little better.

2.3. Orientational Metaphors

Orientational metaphors provide even less conceptual structure for target concepts than ontological ones. Their cognitive job, instead, is to make a set of target concepts coherent in our conceptual system. The name "orientational metaphor" derives from the fact that most metaphors that serve this function have to do with basic human spatial orientations, such as up-down, center-periphery, etc. It would perhaps be more appropriate to call this type of conceptual metaphor "coherence metaphor," which would be more in line with the cognitive function these metaphors perform.

By coherence, we simply mean that certain target concepts tend to be conceptualized in a uniform manner. For example, all the following concepts are characterized by an "upward" orientation, while their "opposites" receive a "downward" orientation.

> MORE IS UP; LESS IS DOWN: Speak *up*, please. Keep your voice *down*, please.
>
> HEALTHY IS UP; SICK IS DOWN: Lazarus *rose* from the dead. He *fell* ill.
>
> CONSCIOUS IS UP; UNCONSCIOUS IS DOWN: Wake *up*. He *sank* into a coma.
>
> CONTROL IS UP; LACK OF CONTROL IS DOWN: I'm *on top* of the situation. He is *under* my control.
>
> HAPPY IS UP; SAD IS DOWN: I'm feeling *up* today. He's really *low* these days.
>
> VIRTUE IS UP; LACK OF VIRTUE IS DOWN: She's an *upstanding* citizen. That was a *low-down* thing to do.
>
> RATIONAL IS UP; NONRATIONAL IS DOWN: The discussion *fell* to an emotional level. He couldn't *rise above* his emotions.

Upward orientation tends to go together with positive evaluation, while downward orientation with a negative one. But positive-negative evaluation is not limited to the spatial orientation up-down. It has been pointed out that various spatial image schemas are bipolar and bivalent. Thus, whole, center, link, balance, in, goal, front are mostly regarded as positive, while their opposites, not whole, periphery, no link, imbalance, out, no goal, and back as negative. Just to give one example, it is remarkable that in English the phrase *half the man* denotes someone who is not positively viewed, as in *He is half the man he used to be.* Obviously, the "whole" vs. "not whole" opposition is at work here.

3. The Nature of Metaphor

Metaphors may be based on both knowledge and image. Most of the metaphors we have discussed so far are based on our basic knowledge of concepts. In them, basic knowledge structures constituted by some basic elements are mapped from a source to a target. But there is another kind of conceptual metaphor that can be called **image-schema metaphor**, in which it is not conceptual elements of knowledge (like traveler, destination, obstacles, etc. in the case of JOURNEY) that get mapped from a source to a target, but conceptual elements of image-schemas. We began to see such conceptual metaphors in the previous section, when we looked at orientational metaphors. We will continue to examine such metaphors in the present one.

Let's take the following examples with the word *out*:

pass out
space out
zone out
tune out
veg out
conk out
rub out
snuff out
out of order
be out of something

As can be seen, the phrases above have to do with such events and states as losing consciousness, lack of attention, something breaking down, death, absence of something, etc. All of these indicate a negative state of affairs, as has been just explained in the previous section.

However, the more important point for the discussion of image-schema metaphors is that these metaphors map relatively little from source to target. As the name image-schema implies, metaphors of this kind have source domains that have skeletal image-schemas, such as the one associated with *out*. By contrast, structural metaphors are rich in knowledge structure and provide a relatively rich set of mappings between source and target. Image-schemas are not limited to spatial relations, such as "in-out." There are many other "schemas" that play a role in our metaphorical understanding of the world. These basic image-schemas derive from our interactions with the world: we explore physical objects by contact with them; we experience ourselves and other objects as containers with other objects in them or outside of them; we move around the world; we experience physical forces affecting us; and we also try to resist these forces, such as when we walk against the wind. Interactions such as these occur repeatedly in human experience. These basic physical experiences give rise to what are called image-schemas, and the image-schemas structure many of our abstract concepts metaphorically. Here are some examples:

Image-Schema	Metaphorical Extension
in-out	I'm *out* of money.
front-back	He's an *up-front* kind of guy.
up-down	I'm feeling *low*.
contact	*Hold on*, please. ("Wait")
motion	He just *went* crazy.
force	You're *driving* me insane.

An interesting property of image-schemas is that they can serve as the basis of other concepts. Thus, for instance, the motion schema underlies the concept of a journey. The motion schema has the parts, initial point, movement, and end point, to which correspond in journeys the point of departure, the travel, and the destination. In this way, most apparently nonimage-schematic concepts (such as journey) seem to have an image-schematic basis. The target domains of many structural metaphors can then be seen as image-schematically structured by their source (such as LIFE IS A JOURNEY).

But there are other kinds of image-based metaphors that are richer in imagistic detail. These conceptual metaphors do not employ image-schemas but rich *images*. We can call them *image metaphors*. They can be found in both poetry and other kinds of discourse. Let's look at some examples from slang:

(a) A. What 'you doin'? B. Watering the plants.
(b) He laid pipe.

Sentence (a) describes an act of urination, while (b) an act of copulation (or for some speakers, defecation or both) in English slang. Both sentences utilize image metaphors that map a detailed set of images from the source to the target. Let us analyze sentence (a) as a demonstration of this point. In the sentence, the person watering the plants is the person urinating, the water is the urine, the watering can is the penis, the intended goal of the action of watering is the ground where the urine is directed. Notice that there is no general structural metaphor involved in this mapping. The mapping is of the *one-shot* kind that is generated by two images that are brought into correspondence by the superimposition of one image onto the other. These are **one-shot image metaphors**.

4. Levels of Generality of Metaphor

Conceptual metaphors can be classified according to the level of generality at which they can be found. As we saw above, image-schemas are structures with very little detail filled in. For example, the "motion" schema has only initial location, movement along a path, and final location. This highly generic schema gets filled in with much more detail in the case of the concept of a journey: we may have a traveler, a point of departure, a means of travel (e.g., a car), a travel schedule, difficulties along the way, a destination, a guide, and so on. The journey schema is much more detailed than the "motion" schema. Another property of such generic-level schemas as "motion" is that they can be filled in not just one but in many ways. The motion schema can be realized not only as a journey but also as a walk, a run, a hike, mountain climbing, etc. These are specific-level instances of the generic motion schema. All of these would instantiate the schema in a different way, but they would have the same underlying generic-level structure of the motion schema.

Now conceptual metaphors can be generic-level or specific-level ones. The metaphors that we have seen so far were all specific-level ones: LIFE IS A JOURNEY, AN ARGUMENT IS WAR, IDEAS ARE FOOD, etc. Life, journey, argument, war, ideas, food are specific-level concepts. Schematic structures underlying them are filled in a detailed way, as we have seen in the case of a journey. In addition to these metaphors, there are generic-level ones. These include such metaphors as EVENTS ARE ACTIONS, GENERIC IS SPECIFIC, and what is known as THE GREAT CHAIN metaphor (we will discuss this last one in chapter 10). As can be seen, events, actions, generic, specific are all generic-level concepts. They are defined by only a small number of properties, which is to say that they are characterized by extremely skeletal structures. For example, in the case of events, an entity undergoes some change typically caused by some external force. There are many different kinds of events: dying, burning, loving, inflation, getting sick, freezing, the wind blowing, etc. These are all specific instances of the generic concept of event. Unlike the generic-level concept of event, the specific cases are filled in with specific detail. For example, in death there is an entity, typically a human, who gets old or gets sick, as a result of which he or she ceases to exist. Notice that the characterization of event does not mention any of these elements. However, the general structure of death shares the skeletal structure of generic event: in death, an entity undergoes some change as a result of some force (time-age or illness).

Generic-level metaphors are designed to perform special jobs—jobs that are different from those of specific-level metaphors that we have examined so far. The EVENTS ARE ACTIONS metaphor, for example, accounts for many cases of personification, as we will see in the next chapter. The GENERIC IS SPECIFIC metaphor helps us interpret proverbs and other cliched phrases. Proverbs often consist of specific-level concepts. Take the proverb "The early bird catches the worm." "Bird," "catch," and "worm" are specific-level concepts. The interpretation of the proverb is facilitated by the metaphor GENERIC IS SPECIFIC. It tells us to interpret the proverb at a generic level: the early bird is anyone who does something first, catching is obtaining something, and the worm is anything obtained before others. Thus, the generic meaning of the proverb is something like "If you do something first, you will get what you want before others." Given this generic-level interpretation, the proverb can apply to a wide range of cases that have this generic structure. One such case is when you go and stand in line early for a ticket to a popular Broadway show and you do get a ticket, while others who come late do not. This example shows how the GENERIC IS SPECIFIC metaphor can give us a generic-level interpretation of a specific-level proverb and then allows us to apply the generic interpretation to a specific case that has the appropriate underlying generic structure.

SUMMARY

Metaphors can be conceptual and linguistic. Conceptual metaphors involve two concepts and have the form A is B, where concept A is understood in terms of concept B. Linguistic metaphors, or metaphorical linguistic expressions, are linguistic manifestations of conceptual metaphors.

Metaphors can be classified in many ways. Four of these are especially relevant to the cognitive linguistic view of metaphor; classification according to the conventionality, function, nature, and level of generality of metaphor.

Both linguistic and conceptual metaphors may be highly *conventionalized* or they may be *unconventional, or novel*. We have seen that a highly conventional conceptual metaphor may receive expression by means of a highly unconventional metaphorical linguistic expression.

According to their cognitive function, conceptual metaphors can be of three kinds: structural, orientational, and ontological. **Structural metaphors** map the structure of the source domain onto the structure of the target and in this way allow speakers to understand one domain in terms of another. **Orientational metaphors** have primarily an evaluative function. They make large groups of metaphors coherent with each other. **Ontological metaphors** provide extremely fundamental but very crude understanding for target concepts. These fundamental but crude understandings often serve as the bases of structural metaphors. Conceptual metaphors may utilize not only (propositional) knowledge but also *images* of various kinds (including not only visual images). Images that have extremely general schematic structure are called **image-schemas**. Image-schemas of various sorts, such as the container or force schemas, structure many abstract concepts metaphorically. Images that are not based on recurrent experience with a generic structure but capture a specific experience are called **one-shot images**. These can also participate in metaphorical understanding.

Conceptual metaphors can also be **specific-level** and **generic-level**. Most conceptual metaphors are at the specific level, in that they employ concepts that are at a specific level of generality. Some conceptual metaphors are generic-level, such as EVENTS ARE ACTIONS and GENERIC IS SPECIFIC. Generic-level metaphors have special jobs designed for them in the working of our metaphorical conceptual system.

FURTHER READING

Lakoff and Johnson (1980) and Lakoff and Turner (1989) discuss the varying degrees of conventionality of metaphor. Conceptual metaphors of the structural, orientational, and ontological kinds were introduced by Lakoff and Johnson (1980). The role of images and image-schemas in metaphorical understanding is emphasized by Lakoff (1987) and Johnson (1987), as well as Talmy (1988) and Sweetser (1990). Lakoff and Turner (1989) draw the distinction between specific- and generic-level metaphors. Krzeszowski (1993) discusses the evaluative function of many image-schemas.

EXERCISES

   1. Which orientational metaphor pairs do these linguistic examples refer to?

     (a) an upstanding citizen; a low trick; a low-down thing
     (b) lofty position; to rise to the top; the bottom of social hierarchy

(c) high spirits; to be depressed; to be low

(d) in top shape; to fall ill; to drop dead.

2. Identify the conceptual metaphors underlying the following proverbs, graffitis, or quotations. Are the conceptual metaphors conventional ("C") or extensions ("E") of conventional metaphors?

(a) You cannot harness happiness.

(b) No herb will cure love.

(c) My life is an open book. All too often open at the wrong page. (Mae West)

(d) Go down the ladder when you marry a wife, go up when you choose a friend.

(e) A man without a wife is but half a man.

3. Read the poem by William Wordsworth. Determine what is personified in it.

Composed Upon Westminster Bridge
September 3, 1802
Earth was not anything to show more fair:
Dull would he be of soul who could pass by
A sight so touching in its majesty:
This City now doth, like a garment, wear
The beauty of the morning; silent, bare,
Ships, towers, domes, theatres, and temples lie
Open unto the fields, and to the sky;
All bright and glittering in the smokeless air.
Never did sun more beautifully steep
In his first splendour, valley, rock, or hill;
Ne'er saw I, never felt, a calm so deep!
The river glideth at his own sweet will:
Dear God! the very houses seem asleep;
And all that mighty heart is lying still!

4. Find unconventionalized linguistic examples in poetry for one of the following conventional conceptual metaphors PEOPLE ARE PLANTS, LIFE IS A PLAY, or DEATH IS DEPARTURE.

5. Listen to the song "Love Is Blindness" by U2 and identify the kinds of metaphors. Which are conventional? Which are unconventional?

4

Metaphor
in Literature

What is the relationship between the metaphors used in ordinary language and those used in literature, including poetry? Do literary metaphors constitute a distinct and independent category from ordinary metaphors? There is a widespread notion among lay people and scholars alike that the "real" source of metaphor is in literature and the arts. It is believed that it is the creative genius of the poet and the artist that creates the most authentic examples of metaphor. When we examine this notion from the point of view of cognitive linguistics, we will find that the idea is only partially true, and that everyday language and the everyday conceptual system contribute a great deal to the working of the artistic genius.

This is not to claim, however, that poets and writers never create new, original metaphors. They obviously do. And when they produce new metaphors, these often "jump out" from the text; they have a tendency to be noteworthy by virtue of their frequently anomalous character. Consider the following example from Gabriel García Márquez's novel *Love in the Time of Cholera*, as analyzed by Ray Gibbs:

> Once he tasted some chamomile tea and sent it back, saying only, "This
> stuff tastes of window." Both she and the servants were surprised
> because they had never heard of anyone who had drunk boiled window,
> but when they tried the tea in an effort to understand, they understood:
> it did taste of window. (1994, p. 261)

What is tea like that tastes like window? This is obviously an unconventional metaphor that was created by the author in order to offer a new and different perspective on an aspect of reality. Original, creative *literary metaphors* such as this are typically less clear but richer in meaning than either everyday metaphors or metaphors in science.

I. Ordinary and Poetic Language

But original, creative literary metaphors of the structural kind seem to be less frequent in literature than those metaphors that are based on our everyday, ordinary conceptual system. One of the startling discoveries of work on poetic language by cognitive linguists is the recognition that most poetic language is based on conventional, ordinary conceptual metaphors. As a first example to demonstrate this point, let us take the following poem by the nineteenth-century poet Christina Georgina Rossetti:

> Does the road wind up-hill all the way?
> Yes, to the very end.
> Will the day's journey take the whole long day?
> From morn to night, my friend.
>
> But is there for the night a resting place?
> A roof for when the slow, dark hours begin.
> May not the darkness hide it from my face?
> You cannot miss that inn.
>
> Shall I meet other wayfarers at night?
> Those who have gone before.
> Then must I knock or call when just in sight?
> They will not keep you standing at that door.
>
> Shall I find comfort, travel-sore and weak?
> Of labour you shall find the sum.
> Will there be beds for me and all who seek?
> Yea, beds for all who come.

Is this poem about a day's hard journey to an inn at the end of a road winding uphill? It is unlikely that anyone would interpret it this way. We can be fairly certain that it is concerned with issues of life and death. But what makes us so confident that the poem has this "deeper," underlying interpretation? Given the cognitive linguistic view of metaphor, we can suggest that our judgment is based on a conceptual metaphor that links life and death to a journey. The metaphor is by now well known to us: LIFE IS A JOURNEY and DEATH IS THE END OF THE JOURNEY. Although life and death are not mentioned at all in the poem, the journey metaphor for life and death guides us in making sense of the poem. This interpretation is reinforced by additional metaphors that are employed in the poem and that are conventional in our everyday conceptual system as well. The line "From morn to night, my friend" evokes the A LIFETIME IS A DAY metaphor; the words "for when the slow, dark hours begin" evoke the conventional metaphor LIFE IS LIGHT; DEATH IS DARK; the line "But is there for the night a resting place?" evokes the conventional metaphors DEATH IS NIGHT and DEATH IS REST; etc. These conventional metaphors that are part of our everyday conceptual system guide and direct us to the idea that the poem is not simply about a journey during the day that ends at night but about life and death. We feel that this is a natural interpretation because the metaphors that link the concept of journey to the concepts of life and death are so natural.

Now let us examine another poem, one by Emily Dickinson:

> I taste a liquor never brewed
> From tankards scooped in pearl.
> Not all the Frankfort berries
> Yield such an alcohol.
>
> Inebriate of air am I
> And debauchee of dew,
> Reeling through endless summer days
> From inns of molten blue.
>
> When landlords turn the drunken bee
> Out of the foxglove's door,
> When butterflies renounce their drams,
> I shall but drink the more,
>
> Till seraphs swing their snowy hats
> And saints to windows run
> To see the little tippler
> From the manzanilla come!

How do we know that this is a love poem? This is not a completely trivial question, since the word *love* does not occur in the poem at all. Again, part of the answer is that our interpretation of the poem is guided by certain metaphors that we are thoroughly familiar with. As we noted in the previous chapter, love is conceptualized metaphorically in many ways. These conventional metaphors include LOVE IS A NUTRIENT and LOVE IS A RAPTURE. Some everyday linguistic examples for them include "I'm *sustained* by love," "I'm *starved for* your affection," "I'm *drunk with* love," etc. There is some conceptual overlap between these two metaphors, in that alcohol that can produce rapture is also a nutrient. We can see the poem as a poetic example of these overlapping metaphors.

As a final illustration, let us take a look at the poem of a seventeenth-century American poet, Anne Bradstreet, entitled "To My Dear and Loving Husband."

> If ever two were one, then surely we.
> If man were loved by wife, then thee;
> If ever wife was happy in a man,
> Compare with me, ye women, if you can.
> I prize thy love more than whole mines of gold
> Or all the riches that the East doth hold.
> My love is such that rivers cannot quench,
> Nor ought but love from thee, give recompense.
> Thy love is such I can no way repay.

The heavens reward thee manifold, I pray.
Then while we live, in love let's so persevere
That when we live no more, we may live ever.

This poem also seems to be based on familiar, conventional metaphors of love: LOVE IS A UNITY (as in "She is my *better half*" and "We're *inseparable*"), LOVE IS AN ECONOMIC EXCHANGE (as in "I'm *putting more* into this than you are"), and LOVE IS A NUTRIENT: FOOD OR DRINK (as in "I'm *sustained* by love") or LOVE IS FIRE (as in "Betty was my old *flame*"), the last one depending on our interpretation of the word *quench* in the poem. Although the verb *quench* can be interpreted both as an example of NUTRIENT (FOOD/DRINK) and of FIRE, in this particular case the latter interpretation seems to be the one intended by the poet (assuming the influence of the Bible on the author's images). This is what the King James Version of the Bible says in the Song of Solomon (8: 6, 7):

> Set me as a seal upon thine heart, as a seal upon thine arm: / for love is strong as death; jealousy is cruel as the grave: / the coals thereof are coals of fire, which has the most vehement flame.

> Many waters cannot quench love, neither cannot floods drown it: / if a man would give all the substance of his house for love, it would utterly be contemned.

All of the conceptual metaphors mentioned above are made use of in the poem:

> If ever two were one, then surely we.—LOVE IS A UNITY
> Thy love is such I can no way repay.—LOVE IS AN ECONOMIC EXCHANGE
> My love is such that rivers cannot quench,—LOVE IS A NUTRIENT/ FIRE

In this section, we have dealt with only three examples, but there are many more similar cases. They point to the same general conclusion: that the metaphors used by poets are based on everyday conventional metaphors. Gibbs, following Lakoff and Turner, puts this in the following way:

> My claim is that much of our conceptualization of experience is metaphorical, which both motivates and constrains the way we think creatively. The idea that metaphor constrains creativity might seem contrary to the widely held belief that metaphor somehow liberates the mind to engage in divergent thinking. (1994, p. 7)

Ordinary metaphors, then, are not things that poets and writers leave behind when they do their "creative" work. On the contrary, there is accumulating evidence that suggests that "creative" people make heavy use of conventional, everyday metaphors, and that their creativity and originality actually derive from them. But now we are faced with a new question: How does this exactly happen? What is the more precise relationship, then, between ordinary and literary metaphors?

2. Poetic Reworking of Ordinary Metaphors

George Lakoff, Mark Turner, and Ray Gibbs have pointed out that poets regularly employ several devices to create novel unconventional language and "images" from the conventional materials of everyday language and thought. These include: **extending, elaboration, questioning,** and **combining.**

2.1. Extending

In **extending,** a conventional conceptual metaphor associated with certain conventionalized linguistic expressions is expressed by new linguistic means that is based on introducing a new conceptual element in the source domain. We saw an example of this by Robert Frost in the previous chapter:

> Two roads diverged in a wood, and I—
> I took the one less travelled by.
> And that has made all the difference.

The example employs the conventional metaphor LIFE IS A JOURNEY and expresses it in a novel way. What is novel here is the element that in the case of two roads leading to the same destination one road may be more or less traveled than the other. The same conventional metaphor is extended in Dante:

> In the middle of life's road
> I found myself in a dark wood.

The novelty here derives from the unconventional element that life's road may pass through a dark wood. Dante extends the metaphor by adding this unconventional aspect to it. What we find in common in the two cases is that both poets take the LIFE IS A JOURNEY conventional metaphor and describe it by means of unconventionalized language that is conceptually based on an "unused" element of the source.

2.2. Elaboration

Elaboration is different from extension, in that it elaborates on an existing element of the source in an unusual way. Instead of adding a new element to the source domain, it captures an already existing one in a new, unconventional way. A good example of this is provided by Adrienne Rich's "The Phenomenology of Anger."

> Fantasies of murder: not enough:
> to kill is to cut off from pain.
> but the killer goes on hurting
>
> Not enough. When I dream of meeting
> the enemy, this is my dream:

> white acetylene
> ripples from my body
> effortlessly released
> perfectly trained
> on the true enemy
>
> raking his body down to the thread
> of existence
> burning away his lie
> leaving him in a new
> world; a changed
> man.

When we understand this poem, we activate in our mind one of the most conventional metaphors for anger: ANGER IS A HOT FLUID IN A CONTAINER. This perfectly ordinary metaphor is seen in such everyday linguistic examples as "*boiling* with anger," "*making one's blood boil*," "*simmer down*," "*blowing your stack*," and many others. In Rich's poem, the hot fluid gets elaborated as acetylene and the passive event of explosion is replaced by directing the dangerous substance of acetylene at the target of anger. When Rich modifies the hot fluid and turns it into a dangerous substance, she performs the (unconscious) act of elaborating on an everyday metaphor. A large part of the intuitive appeal of the poem derives from our (possibly unconscious) recognition of this familiar and completely mundane metaphorical view of anger.

2.3. Questioning

In the poetic device of **questioning**, poets can call into question the very appropriateness of our common everyday metaphors. To see an example of this, consider the following lines:

> Suns can set and return again,
> but when our brief light goes out,
> there's one perpetual night to be slept through.
>   (Catullus 5)

Here Catullus points out that at death some of our most common metaphors for life and death, A LIFETIME IS A DAY and DEATH IS NIGHT, cease to be appropriate. They become inappropriate because death is "one perpetual night to be slept through" which means that metaphorical death-as-night does not turn into day again: once we die, we do not live again. In other words, while the metaphors of A LIFETIME IS A DAY and DEATH IS NIGHT are preserved, their validity or appropriateness is called into question. A consequence of the metaphorical source domains (that day becomes night and night becomes day) does not apply to the target domains (life becomes death, but death does not become life again). Catullus observes that the metaphors are only partially appropriate.

Another example of demonstrating the mechanism of questioning can be found in Margaret Freeman's article, which stated that "much of Dickinson's poetry is structured by the extent to which she rejected the dominant metaphor of her religious environment, that of LIFE IS A JOURNEY THROUGH TIME, and replaced it with a metaphor more in accordance with the latest scientific discoveries of her day, that of LIFE IS A VOYAGE IN SPACE" (1995, 643). Thus, the cognitive mechanism of questioning the validity of accepted metaphors may be part of the "creed" of an artist.

2.4. Combining

Combining is perhaps the most powerful mechanism to go beyond our everyday conceptual system (but still using the materials of everyday conventional thought). Let's take the following lines from one of Shakespeare's sonnets:

> In me thou seest the twilight of such day
> As after sunset fadeth in the west;
> Which by and by black night doth take away,
> Death's second self that seals up all in rest.

These lines combine at least five everyday conceptual metaphors: LIGHT IS A SUBSTANCE, EVENTS ARE ACTIONS, LIFE IS A PRECIOUS POSSESSION, A LIFETIME IS A DAY, and LIFE IS LIGHT. The process of combining can activate, and thus be based on, several everyday metaphors at the same time. Let's take the clause "black night doth take away [the twilight]." In this single clause, we find the following metaphors combined.

> black: LIFETIME IS A DAY, LIFE IS LIGHT, DEATH IS NIGHT
> night: DEATH IS NIGHT, LIFE IS LIGHT
> take away: LIFE IS A PRECIOUS POSSESSION, EVENTS ARE ACTIONS

3. Personification

We briefly introduced **personification** in the last chapter and saw that it occurs in everyday conventional language. Personification is a metaphorical device that is also used commonly in literature. This aspect of poetic language has been studied extensively from a cognitive linguistic view by George Lakoff and Mark Turner. One of the abstract concepts that is frequently personified in literature is time. We find time personified in several ways:

> TIME IS A THIEF
> How soon hath Time, the subtle thief of youth,
> Stolen on his wing my three and twentieth years!
> (Milton, Sonnet 7)

> TIME IS A REAPER
> Love's not Time's fool, though rosy lips and cheeks
> Within his bending sickle's compass come.
> (Shakespeare, Sonnet 116)

TIME IS A DEVOURER
Time, the devourer of everything
    (Ovid, Metamorphoses 15)

TIME IS A DESTROYER
Does it really exist, Time, the destroyer?
When will it crush the fortress on the peaceful
height?
    (Rainer Maria Rilke, *Sonnets to Orpheus*, 2)

TIME IS AN EVALUATOR
Time! the Corrector where our judgments err.
    (Byron, Childe Harold's Pilgrimage)

Time is a great legalizer, even in the field of morals.
    (Mencken)

TIME IS A PURSUER
But at my back I always hear
Time's winged chariot hurrying near.
    (Marvell, "To His Coy Mistress")

Personification permits us to use knowledge about ourselves to comprehend other aspects of the world, such as time, death, natural forces, inanimate objects, etc. One important question that arises in connection with personification is why we use the kinds of persons that we do for a target. Specifically, why do we use the source domains above (representing different kinds of persons) to understand time? Lakoff and Turner suggest that the answer has to do with the EVENTS ARE ACTIONS generic-level metaphor. Given this metaphor, we comprehend external events as actions. This entails an important consequence; namely, that we view events as produced by an active, willful agent. That is, since actions have such an agent, we will view events in the same way. The result will be the personification of events, such as time and death. Time is an external event that occurs independently from human beings, and thus, it can be seen as an agent, like a thief, reaper, pursuer, and so on. But why these particular agents? This is in part because we have certain metaphors for the concepts that time affects: life, people, etc. For example, given that LIFE IS A PRECIOUS POSSESSION, time can be conceptualized as a THIEF that steals that precious possession and given that PEOPLE ARE PLANTS, time can be conceptualized as a reaper that can kill people. More generally, we understand time nonmetaphorically as a CHANGER, an entity that can affect people and things, especially in adverse ways. This knowledge about time explains many of the personifications we use for time. Many other abstract concepts, such as death, can be analyzed in similar ways.

4. Image Metaphors

Poetry abounds in *image-based metaphors* that are rich in imagistic detail. As we saw in the previous chapter, these conceptual metaphors do not employ image-schemas but rich images. Consider the following example from poetry:

My wife . . . whose waist is an hourglass.

Here we have two detailed images: one for the body of a woman and one for an hourglass. The images are based on the shape of the two "objects." According to the metaphor, we take the image of the detailed shape of the hourglass and map it onto the detailed shape of the woman's body. What is especially noteworthy is that the words themselves in the metaphor do not say anything about which part of the hourglass should be mapped onto which part of the woman's body. Yet we know exactly which part maps onto which on the basis of the common shape. This is what makes image metaphors conceptual as well, rather than simply linguistic.

5. "Megametaphors"

Some metaphors, conventional or novel, may run through entire literary texts without necessarily "surfacing." What one sometimes finds at the surface level of a literary text are specific **micrometaphors**, but "underlying" these metaphors is a **megametaphor** that makes these surface micrometaphors coherent. Megametaphors, or **extended metaphors** (not to be confused with the device of extension above), have been studied by Paul Werth, who offers an excerpt from Dylan Thomas's work *Under Milk Wood* for illustration of this idea:

> It is spring, moonless night in the small town, starless and bible-black, the cobblestreets silent and the hunched, courter's-and-rabbits' wood limping invisible down to the sloeblack, slow, black, crowblack, fishingboat-bobbing sea. The houses are blind as moles (though moles see fine tonight in the snouting velvet dingles) or blind as Captain Cat there in the muffled middle by the pump and the town clock, the shops in mourning, and the Welfare Hall in widow's weeds. And all the people of the lulled and dumbfound town are sleeping now. (quoted in Werth, 1994, p. 84)

In the passage, inanimate things are characterized in terms of human properties: "the wood is hunched," "the wood is limping invisible down to the sea," "the houses are blind," "the middle of the town is muffled," "the shops are in mourning." The process of personification is at work here, in which some properties of a town are understood in terms of the properties of human beings. We could propose a number of specific, surface metaphors to account for the particular linguistic examples. For instance, we could say that darkness is viewed as blindness, silence as being muffled, roundness as being hunched, abstract movement as limping, and being unguarded as being lulled. But this would not explain why all the human properties that are mapped onto the aspects of the town are specific disabilities, such as blindness, being muffled, being hunched, limping, etc. According to Werth, there is a mega-metaphor, or extended metaphor, here: SLEEP IS DISABILITY. This metaphor provides a certain "undercurrent" to the micrometaphors that appear on the surface of the text. The connection between SLEEP IS PHYSICAL DISABILITY and the concept of town is provided by the metonymy THE TOWN STANDS FOR ITS INHABITANTS (or more generally, THE PLACE STANDS FOR THE PEOPLE IN THAT PLACE). The megametaphor becomes especially interesting if we consider that the concept of sleep often functions as a source domain for the concept of death. Since death is viewed as sleep and sleep is understood as a disability, death will also be seen as a disability: the utmost human disability in which we are blind, deaf, dumb, immobile, etc. The identification of sleep with death is pre-figured already in the passage above, where the author frequently mentions black-ness, darkness, and even mourning. In later passages of the work Dylan Thomas makes this connection explicit. For example: "Only you can see, in the blinded bedrooms . . . the yellowing, dickybirdwatching pictures of the dead." (p. 3.) Thus, the town is conceived as dead through a complex interaction of specific metaphors, metonymy, and an extended metaphor that runs through the text.

A further remarkable aspect of extended metaphors has to do with literary criticism. Donald Freeman has analyzed the text of Shakespeare's *Macbeth* with the machinery of cognitive linguistics. He found two extended metaphors that account for most of the language, characters, settings, events, and plot of this play: the PATH (MOTION) and the CONTAINER (IN-OUT) schemas. He found that Macbeth's career is largely characterized by paths and containers. For example, Macbeth says: "I am in blood / Stepped in so far that, should I wade no more, / Returning were as tedious as go o'er" (3.4.136–138). The path of Macbeth's career requires him to return, but he cannot anymore. Now what is interesting in connection with the critical work of this play is that the critics invariably use the same language and conceptualization of the work that the work itself uses. In other words, literary critics employ path and container metaphors to assess *Macbeth*. For instance, the path schema is clear in most literary critics' work, including W. Richardson's description: ". . . he [Macbeth] rushes headlong on his bane" and more recently, in Robert Watson's formulation: "Macbeth finds himself on a linear course into winter. . . ." Don Freeman concludes that these facts demonstrate a "unity of the language of and about *Macbeth*, as well as the unity of opinion about that unity, . . ." (1995, p. 707) which all arise from the source domains that the path and container schemas provide. It seems that the notion of extended metaphor offers new ways of understanding not only the text of the literary work but also the language and thought of the critics.

SUMMARY

Do literary metaphors constitute a special set among metaphors? Sometimes they do, but most of the time poets and writers use the same conceptual metaphors that ordinary people do. Nevertheless, we feel that literary metaphors are somehow special. This is because ordinary conceptual metaphors are regularly transformed by poets and writers in a number of ways: by (1) **extending**, (2) **elaboration**, (3) **questioning**, and (4) **combining**.

Personification is another common device used in literary texts. We showed why the abstract concept of time is personified the way it is. We explained this with the help of the generic-level metaphor EVENTS ARE ACTIONS.

Literary texts also abound in *image-based metaphors*. These are one-shot images that require the mapping of several elements of one image onto another. Although people are not explicitly instructed about which element of one image maps onto which element of another, they can perform the mappings successfully in the process of interpreting literary texts. Some metaphors extend through entire literary texts or large portions of them. These are called **extended metaphors** or **megametaphors**. They may not explicitly "surface" in the texts at all but tend to appear in the form of what we call **micrometaphors**.

FURTHER READING

The foundational work for the analysis of the relationship between everyday and poetic metaphor is George Lakoff and Mark Turner (1989). Lakoff and Turner write in detail about the devices that poets use to turn ordinary metaphors into poetic ones, as well as about image metaphors and personification. Turner (1991) describes the place and role of cognitive linguistics in the study of English in general. Ray Gibbs (1994) continues in the direction set by Lakoff and Turner, extending the analysis to fiction, formulating the key insights in a clear way, and offering psycholinguistic evidence for the claims made by cognitive linguists. Ray Jackendoff and David Aaron's (1991) review article provides a critical assessment of the Lakoff-Turner view.

Paul Werth (1994) analyzes megametaphors in fiction, while Donald Freeman (1995) looks at them in Shakespeare's Macbeth. Margaret Freeman (1995, 2000) writes about Emily Dickinson's poetry using the machinery of cognitive linguistics and she outlines a theory of "cognitive poetics." Antonio Barcelona (1995) demonstrates the usefulness of the approach in an analysis of love metaphors in Shakespeare's Romeo and Juliet. Gerard Steen (1994) provides a wide-ranging study of how people understand metaphors in literary texts. Andrew Goatley (1997) offers a panoramic view of the study of metaphor in literature. Elena Semino (1997) is another useful source for studying metaphoric language in literature.

EXERCISES

1. What are the conventional metaphors here, and what device is used to make them unconventional? Give the resulting unconventional metaphor.

   Drink me only with thine eyes
   And I will pledge with mine
   Or leave a kiss but in the *cup*
   And I'll not look for *wine*
   The *thirst* that from the soul doeth rise
   Doth ask a *drink divine*

But might I of Jove's *nectar sup*
I would not change for thine.
            (Ben Jonson, "Song to Celia")

2. In "The Fall of the House of Usher," Edgar Allan Poe uses a ballad,
   "The Haunted Palace," to illustrate the story and characterize the
   Usher family. In the ballad, the central image is that of a palace
   which corresponds to the human body. Try to work out the metaphors, together with the mappings, that are present in the poem.

   I. In the greenest of our valleys,
        By good angels tenanted,
        Once a fair and stately palace—
        Snow-white palace—reared its head.
        In the monarch Thought's dominion—
        It stood there!
        Never seraph spread a pinion
        Over fabric half so fair.

   II. Banners yellow, glorious, golden,
        On its roof did float and flow;
        (This—all this—was in the olden
        Time long ago)
        And every gentle air that dallied,
        In that sweet day,
        Along the ramparts plumed and pallid,
        A winged odor went away.

   III. Wanderers in that happy valley
        Through two luminous windows saw
        Spirits moving musically
        To a lute's well-tuned law,
        Round about a throne, where sitting
        (Porphyrogene!)
        In state his glory well befitting,
        The sovereign of the realm was seen.

   IV. And all with pearl and ruby glowing
        Was the fair palace door,
        Through which came flowing, flowing, flowing,
        And sparking evermore,
        A troop of Echoes whose sole duty
        Was but to sing,
        In voices of surpassing beauty,
        The wit and wisdom of their king.

   V. But evil things, in robes of sorrow,
        Assailed the monarch's high estate;
        (ah, let us mourn, for never morrow
        Shall dawn upon him, desolate!)
        And, round about his home, the glory
        That blushed and bloomed
        Is but a dim-remembered story
        Of the old time entombed.

VI. And travellers now within that valley,
Through the red-litten windows, see
Vast forms that move fantastically
To a discordant melody;
While, like a rapid ghastly river,
Through the pale door,
A hideous throng rush out forever,
And laugh—but smile no more.

3. You have already seen how conceptual metaphors work in the case
of myths: Oedipus's life was saved because he possibly made use of
certain conceptual metaphors when answering the riddle of the
Sphinx.
    Read Henry James's short story "The Beast in the Jungle." In this
story, tension arises from the fact that the main characters, May
Bartram and John Marcher become involved in a puzzle similar to
the riddle of the sphinx in the Oedipus-myth. Which conceptual
metaphor should Marcher have known in order to make sense of and
solve the riddle that the sphinx-like female character poses to him?

4. Which common everyday metaphor(s) do the following slogans
found in advertisements call into question? Look for other advertisements (in newspapers, among TV ads) which make use of the same
metaphors.

   (a) "Living without boundaries"—Ralph Lauren's Safari;
   (b) "Your world should know no boundaries"—Merrill Lynch;
   (c) "It's not trespassing when you cross your own boundaries"—
       Johnny Walker Scotch;
   (d) "I don't know where I end and you begin"—Calvin Klein's
       perfume Eternity
          (from John Leo's article "Decadence, the corporate way"; *US
          News & World Report*, August 28 / Sept. 4, 1995).

5. Read the following quote from Martin Luther King Jr.'s "I have a
dream" speech:

   It is obvious today that America has defaulted on [the Constitution
   and the Declaration of Independence] insofar as her citizens of color
   are concerned. Instead of honoring this sacred obligation, America
   has given the Negro people *a bad check; a check which has come
   back marked "insufficient funds."* We refuse to believe that *the Bank
   of Justice is bankrupt.* We refuse to believe that there are *insufficient
   funds* in the great vaults of opportunity of this nation. So we have
   come to *cash this check—a check* that will give us upon demand the
   riches of freedom and the security of justice.

   (a) What corresponds to the concepts of *check, funds,* and *to cash* in
       the target?
   (b) What are the source and target domains? Give the conceptual
       metaphor.
   (c) What mappings can you find between the source and the target?
   (d) In what ways is this an example of an unconventional conceptual
       metaphor?

5

Nonlinguistic Realizations of Conceptual Metaphors

As has been emphasized so far, metaphors are conceptual in nature. It was shown, furthermore, that conceptual metaphors have linguistic manifestations. We have called these manifestations metaphorical linguistic expressions. But if metaphors are primarily conceptual, then they must manifest themselves in other than linguistic ways. That is, if the conceptual system that governs how we experience the world, how we think, and how we act is partly metaphorical, then the (conceptual) metaphors must be realized not only in language but also in many other areas of human experience. These manifestations are called the **realization of conceptual metaphors**.

In the present chapter, I will offer some examples of cases where conceptual metaphors manifest themselves or are realized—mainly in nonlinguistic ways. The list of cases I will present is no doubt incomplete, but the reader may look for other ways in which conceptual metaphors are realized. Many of the cases briefly described below come from George Lakoff's work.

1. Movies and Acting

Films may be structured in their entirety in terms of conceptual metaphors. One metaphor that is particularly well suited for this is, of course, the LIFE IS A JOURNEY metaphor. Several movies depict a person's life as a journey of some kind.

In addition, individual images in a movie may be based on one or several conceptual metaphors. In the Walt Disney version of the movie *Pocahontas*, for example, one scene shows how Pocahontas and Captain John Smith fall in love with each other. The images through which this is conveyed include Pocahontas and John Smith cascading down a waterfall. This image is a realization of the conceptual metaphor FALLING IN LOVE IS PHYSICAL FALLING. In another Walt Disney production, *The Hunchback of Notre Dame*, the cruel judge of Paris feels an uncontrollable sexual desire for the beautiful gypsy girl Esmeralda. In this scene, the entire room and the palace where the scene takes place is covered in flames. The metaphor that is given visual expression here is SEXUAL DESIRE IS FIRE. But metaphorical realization does not only occur in Walt Disney productions. It is part and parcel of making classic movies as well. In the film *Phaedra,* the same SEXUAL DESIRE IS FIRE metaphor is realized, when Phaedra (played by Melina Mercouri) and Alexis (played by the young Anthony Perkins) begin to make love in front of an intense fire in the fireplace. Obviously, the intense fire corresponds to the intense sexual desire of the lovers.

A major conceptual metaphor for difficulty is DIFFICULTIES ARE BURDENS. Sometimes people do "act out" this metaphor, when they walk in such a way that suggests carrying a heavy load on one's shoulders. In these cases, physical symptoms can be seen as "enactments" of conceptual metaphors. A large part of learning the profession of acting involves the learning of how to act out certain conceptual metaphors.

2. Cartoons, Drawings, Sculptures, and Buildings

Cartoons are another rich source for the nonlinguistic realization of metaphors. In them, conceptual metaphors are often depicted in a "literal" way. An angry man may be drawn in such a way that smoke is coming out of his ears. This is based on the ANGER IS A HOT FLUID IN A CONTAINER metaphor. Furthermore, given the same metaphor, in a cartoon an angry person may literally explode or burst open.

Children often draw pictures that visually embody conceptual metaphors. A common metaphor (more precisely, personification) that is made use of by children is INANIMATE OBJECTS ARE PEOPLE. In a picture drawn by a five-year-old boy, for example, a house is personified. In this way, the house assumes many of the properties of human beings and is therefore structured conceptually in terms of this metaphor.

In sculptures as well, conceptual metaphors are often "enacted." For example, the sculpture of two people in love can be such that they are bound together or are inside each other or very close to each other, making real the metaphors LOVE IS A BOND, LOVE IS A UNITY, and LOVE IS CLOSENESS, respectively. Another metaphor that seems to underlie many sculptures is SIGNIFICANT IS BIG. This is especially clear in the case of what is known in art history as the "social realist" style, in which people are usually represented as oversized heroes, suggesting their presumed importance.

The same metaphor can be found in architecture, for example, in the pyramids of Egypt, which were meant to show the significance of the ruler buried in it. The structure of buildings may also make manifest certain metaphors. Church architecture is a good example. Christian churches are built in such a way that they point toward the sky, the assumed place where God lives, which seems to be based on the metaphor GOD IS UP. Thus, Christian churches metaphorically represent the connection between God and his believers who worship Him in the church.

3. Advertisements

A major manifestation of conceptual metaphors are advertisements. Part of the selling power of an advertisement depends on how well-chosen the conceptual metaphor is that the picture and/or the words used in the advertisement attempt to evoke in people. An appropriately selected metaphor may work wonders in promoting the sale of an item. For example, washing powders are frequently presented as good friends; this is based on the metaphor ITEMS TO SELL ARE PEOPLE, which is a kind of personification. A WASHING POWDER IS A FRIEND metaphor evokes in people the same attitudes and feelings that they have in connection with their good friends. Sexuality is also often relied on in advertisements. Cars are often shown as one's lovers, and the people in the ads or commercials behave toward them as if they really were; they hug them, they kiss them, they whisper to them, etc.

4. Symbols

Symbols in general and cultural symbols in particular may be based on well-entrenched metaphors in a culture. For instance, a common symbol of life is fire. This symbol is a manifestation of the metaphor LIFE IS FIRE that also appears in mundane linguistic expressions such as *to snuff out* somebody's life. To understand a symbol means in part to be able to see the conceptual metaphors that the symbol can evoke or was created to evoke. Consider, for example, the Statue of Liberty in New York City, as analyzed by Kövecses. The statue was created to evoke the idea that liberty was achieved in the United States (together with its "accompaniments"—knowledge and justice). This is displayed in the statue by means of several metaphors—metaphors for free action, history, and knowledge. Since ACTION IS SELF-PROPELLED MOVEMENT, free action will be UNINHIBITED SELF-PROPELLED MOVEMENT. This arises from the fact that the statue steps forward as broken shackles lie at her feet. Second, a common view of history is that it is a change from a period of ignorance and oppression to a period of knowledge and freedom. This is based on the metaphor that HISTORICAL CHANGE IS MOVEMENT FROM A STATE OF IGNORANCE TO A STATE OF KNOWLEDGE. What evokes this metaphor is the fact that the statue steps forward with a torch enlightening the world. Finally, we have the metaphor KNOWING IS SEEING. Given these metaphors, the statue may be regarded as an embodiment of the metaphorical source domains: UNINHIBITED MOVEMENT, MOVEMENT FROM DARK TO LIGHT, and SEEING.

But today the statue simply evokes in most Americans the image of a benevolent and wealthy country (America) that readily helps and accepts people who are in need (the poor immigrants). How can this interpretation be given to it? The reason in part is that Americans (but also others) have the metaphor A STATE OR A COUNTRY IS A PERSON, plus some conventional knowledge about women. The statue represents a woman, who is beckoning to the immigrants arriving, and who is a "mighty" but gentle woman, who readily welcomes her children to her home. The poem engraved on the plaque at the entrance to the statue suggests this interpretation:

> Not like the brazen giant of Greek fame,
> With conquering limbs astride from land to land;
> Here at our sea-washed, sunset gates shall stand
> A mighty woman with a torch, whose flame
> Is the imprisoned lightning, and her name
> Mother of Exiles. From her beacon-hand
> Glows world-wide welcome; her mild eyes command
> The air-bridged harbor that twin cities frame.
> "Keep ancient lands, your storied pomp!" cries she
> With silent lips. "Give me your tired, your poor,
> Your huddled masses yearning to breathe free,
> The wretched refuse of your teeming shore.
> Send these, the homeless, tempest-tost to me,
> I lift my lamp beside the golden door!"

5. Myths

Conceptual metaphors may be realized in myths in a variety of ways. One of these is when a metaphor functions as a key element in a myth. We have seen examples of this in the myth of Oedipus, in which the metaphors A LIFETIME IS A DAY and LIFE IS A JOURNEY serve as important elements in saving Oedipus's life from the Sphinx.

Another way in which metaphors participate in myths involves the "characters" of myths themselves. For example, it has been suggested by Pamela Morgan that Poseidon, the Greek god of the sea (and some other forceful things, like earthquakes, horses, and bulls), is really the god of uncontrollable external events in general. This is based on the observation that there exists a very general metaphor according to which UNCONTROLLABLE EXTERNAL EVENTS ARE LARGE, MOVING OBJECTS. Large, moving physical objects that exert a huge force on people include the sea. Poseidon can thus be seen as the god of uncontrollable external events in general, and not just god of the sea (or some other specific forceful entity).

6. Dream Interpretation

In Genesis Pharaoh has a dream: He is standing on the river bank when seven fat cows come out of the river, followed by seven lean cows that eat the seven fat ones and still remain lean. Then Pharaoh dreams again: This time he sees seven "full and good" ears of corn growing and then seven withered ears growing after them. The withered ears devour the good ears. Pharaoh calls on Joseph to interpret the two dreams. Joseph interprets the two as one dream. The seven fat cows and full ears are good years, and the seven lean cows and withered ears are famine years that follow the good years. This interpretation turned out to be the correct one. How was Joseph able to interpret the dream? How did he know that it was about years and time? The reason is that he was aware of a metaphor that has been with us ever since biblical times: TIMES ARE MOVING OBJECTS. We saw this metaphor in the previous chapter. A special case of moving objects is a river. Indeed, rivers are commonly employed to understand time metaphorically. Another conceptual metaphor that's needed for a fuller interpretation is ACHIEVING A PURPOSE IS EATING. This explains why we have cows and ears of corn in the dream. These were typical foods eaten at the time. Finally, Joseph relied on the metaphor RESOURCES ARE FOOD. By combining these conceptual metaphors, Joseph could arrive at the correct interpretation.

What this example shows is that much of the interpretation of dreams depends on everyday conceptual metaphors. In other words, dreams realize particular combinations of metaphors.

7. Interpretation of History

Metaphors also play some role in modern myths. We often use these myths to make sense of historical events. For example, Szilvia Csábi argues that much of the early history of America (the settlement by the English) was conceptualized in terms of some of the key events in the Bible, such as the movement of the Jewish people from Egypt to the Promised Land. This way of thinking about the settlement of America by the English Puritans was characteristic of not only the ordinary people who actually participated in the early settlement but also by those who later commented on this and thus tried to come up with a coherent account of it (one example being the later American commentator, Margaret Fuller). This account is couched in metaphor, and in the cognitive linguistic view we can refer to it as the metaphor: THE SETTLEMENT OF NORTH AMERICA BY THE ENGLISH SETTLERS IS THE MOVEMENT OF THE JEWS FROM EGYPT TO THE PROMISED LAND.

But the actual makers or agents of history can also consciously pattern their actions on a particular source domain. This is what happened in the Mormons' case, who, again, used the biblical account of the Jews' flight from Egypt into Israel as their source domain in a conscious way. They modeled their flight west to what is now the Salt Lake City area on the Jews' flight to Israel. The Mormons referred to their new home as Zion, and they were influenced in their choice of homeland by the fact of a river (that they called Jordan), leading from a freshwater lake (Utah Lake = Sea of Galilee) to a saltwater dead sea (Great Salt Lake = Dead Sea). Brigham Young, the leader of the Mormons, is supposed to have sat up in his sickbed, when the caravan reached a point where he could see the valley, and said "This is the place."

As a final illustration, consider the work of Alexis de Tocqueville, the nineteenth-century French social thinker, who attempted an interpretation of American democracy in the early decades of the nineteenth century. His book, *Democracy in America*, is still one of the most often referred to works on the subject. According to Kövecses, Tocqueville analyzes American democracy metaphorically as a highly defective person, whose defects have to be made up for and counterbalanced by external forces such as the legal system. This view of democracy depends crucially on the acceptance of the conceptual metaphor A STATE IS A PERSON. Tocqueville's argument is couched in terms of this metaphor throughout his work.

8. Politics and Foreign Policy

Politics in general is rife with conceptual metaphors. In American politics, for example, political thought (and discourse) is largely structured by the following metaphors: POLITICS IS WAR; POLITICS IS BUSINESS; SOCIETY IS A FAMILY; SOCIETY IS A PERSON; and THE PRESIDENTIAL ELECTION IS A RACE. To take just one example, given the POLITICS IS WAR metaphor, American society can be seen as composed of armies that correspond to political groups; the leaders of the armies correspond to political leaders; the weapons used by the army are the ideas and policies of the political groups; the objective of the war is some political goal, and so on. These metaphors are widely disseminated in the media and by the politicians themselves. Most important, they impose a particular order or pattern on political activities. They not only make sense of these activities but also structure them in imperceptible ways.

If a nation is conceived of as a person, then it is possible to think of neighboring countries as "neighbors," who can be friendly or hostile, strong or weak, and healthy or sick. Strength corresponds here to military strength and health to economic wealth. This metaphor has certain implications for foreign politics. A country can be identified as strong and another as weak. Since strength is associated with men and weakness with women, a militarily strong nation can be seen as "raping" a weak one when it attacks the weak nation. The case in point is the Gulf War of 1990, when Iraq attacked and occupied Kuwait. The attack was interpreted as the "rape" of Kuwait. This interpretation provided moral justification for the United States to go to war against Iraq. Iraq was seen as a villain, Kuwait as a victim, and the United States as a hero that rescues an innocent victim. At the very least, casting the events in terms of a "fairy tale scenario" helped the U.S. president to get support for an important decision; because of choosing the right metaphor, he managed to get his decision to go to war accepted by the American people.

9. Morality

Discourse about morality often involves two foundational conceptual metaphors: (1) MORALITY IS STRENGTH and (2) MORALITY IS NURTURANCE. These metaphors can be laid out in greater detail as follows:

(1) BEING GOOD IS BEING UPRIGHT
    BEING BAD IS BEING LOW
    DOING EVIL IS FALLING
    EVIL IS A FORCE
    MORALITY IS STRENGTH

According to this metaphorical system of morality, evil can act on an "upright" person, who can either "fall" (become bad) or remain upright (remain good). The evil can be either an external or an internal force. External evil may be a dangerous situation that causes fear. Internal evil may be, for example, the seven deadly sins. In either case, a moral person would apply a counterforce in an effort to overcome the force of evil and would be successful in overcoming it. Thus, in this view, moral "strength" is based on the notion of physical strength.

(2) THE COMMUNITY IS A FAMILY
    MORAL AGENTS ARE NURTURING PARENTS
    PEOPLE NEEDING HELP ARE CHILDREN NEEDING NURTURANCE
    MORAL ACTION IS NURTURANCE

In this metaphor, morality appears to be more of an "other-directed" issue than a "self-directed" issue. In the "strength" metaphor there is only a single moral agent, whereas in the nurturance version there are two agents—people who need help and people who have a responsibility to provide that help. It is not the case that the two metaphors exclude each other in the actual practice of morality in everyday life. They are used together on most occasions, but different people may give different priorities to them. For some people, morality is primarily defined in terms of the MORALITY IS STRENGTH metaphor, whereas for others it is defined mostly in terms of MORALITY IS NURTURANCE.

Interestingly, the different priorities given to the two metaphors may account for two conceptions of politics—conservatism and liberalism. If one considers the MORALITY IS STRENGTH metaphor as more important, this person is likely to be attracted to conservative ideals and ideas in politics. On the other hand, if someone considers the "nurturance" metaphor more important as regards morality, this person is more likely to be a liberal concerning political issues. How is this possible? The link between one's moral and political views is provided by a metaphor of nation we have already mentioned above: A NATION OR SOCIETY IS A FAMILY. Society is conventionally viewed as a family with the state as a parent and citizens as children. The two views of morality that were briefly outlined above imply different conceptions of a family. In the "moral strength" metaphor, the family consists of independent and self-reliant individuals and morality is taught and learned primarily through discipline (to resist evil). In the "nurturance" metaphor, the family consists of people who have a moral obligation to help each other to begin with. In this family, morality is taught and learned less through discipline than through nurturance. Now the priorities given to the two metaphors will have implications for one's political views because the two conceptions of family and morality will influence one's view of the nation as a family. The metaphor-based notion of morality will have different consequences for one's political views. Morality and politics will fuse into *moral politics*.

10. Social Institutions

Certain social institutions may also be based on conceptual metaphors. Consider the use of "grades" in school. In the United States, the letter grades "A," "B," "C," "D," and "E" or "F" are used, but these are merely disguised forms of numbers, either going from 1 to a higher number such as 5 or from 5 to 1. This common practice exists in many countries throughout the world. The metaphor that seems to underlie the social institution of "grading" is QUALITY IS QUANTITY. According to this metaphor, matters of quality, such as knowledge, skills, understanding, sensitivity, are comprehended through units of quantity such as numbers. In some cultures, the quantification of qualitative things has reached huge proportions. For example, in the United States, achievements in sport are primarily interpreted through quantification of some kind. This is especially common in baseball, where statistics of all kinds are used to "measure" achievements.

11. Social Practices

Some metaphors can create certain social practices. One of these is the SEEING IS TOUCHING metaphor. This is the metaphor at work when we say things like "He couldn't *take his eyes off* of her." The same metaphor generates the social practices of "avoiding eye contact" with someone we do not know and "undressing someone with one's eyes." The prohibition against this is also based on SEEING IS TOUCHING. Both of these cases make a conceptual metaphor "real" in everyday social practice.

12. Literature

Literature is perhaps the most obvious area in which conceptual metaphors can be found. As we saw in the previous chapter, literature commonly makes use of unconventional(ized) metaphorical expressions that are based on conventional conceptual metaphors. In this sense, the creativity of literature is constrained by our everyday metaphorical conceptual system.

But all the examples we discussed in chapter 4 were linguistically realized metaphors. However, literature also contains metaphors that are realized nonlinguistically. The most interesting cases of the nonlinguistic realization of conceptual metaphors in literature are those where an entire literary genre is based on a given metaphor. One of the subgenres of literature is biography. In biography it is common to conceptualize one's life in terms of a story.

What makes this a nonlinguistic metaphor is that it is the entire plot that is cast as if it were a story. This practice is based on the LIFE IS A STORY conceptual metaphor. When the telling of one's life is presented as if it were a story, it gains its structure from the metaphor LIFE IS A STORY. Furthermore, fairy and folktales frequently employ this metaphor to present the lives of the characters participating in them. In short, the most common way of giving the history of one's life is in terms of the LIFE IS A STORY metaphor.

Another subgenre within fiction seems to be structured by what we called the LIFE IS A JOURNEY metaphor. One example of this is *The Pilgrim's Progress*. The two metaphors can also combine to yield a mixture of the two subgenres. When this is the case, the story of one's life is based on the historical account of a journey. In all these cases, it is the actions and events of one's life that are structured by a conceptual metaphor. Thus, it is the plot itself that manifests a certain conceptual metaphor, as this becomes especially clear when a novel or short story is turned into a film.

SUMMARY

In addition to conceptual metaphors being expressed linguistically, they can also be realized in many other ways. These nonlinguistic ways include movies and acting, cartoons, drawings, sculptures, buildings, advertisements, myths, dream interpretation, the interpretation of history, cultural symbols, politics and foreign policy, morality, "moral politics," social institutions, social practices, the nonlinguistic structure of certain literary genres, and many others that have not been discussed here. One such case is where metaphors are realized in gestures. There is a growing body of research into metaphorical aspects of gestures.

In light of these cases, we can conclude that conceptual metaphor pervades much of our social, artistic, psychological, intellectual, and cultural lives. Metaphor is present not only in the way we speak but also in much of our nonlinguistic reality. This insight makes the cognitive linguistic view of metaphor especially valuable to nonlinguists as well. At the same time, sensitivity to metaphor in language may help us discover conceptual metaphors in many nonlinguistic areas of human experience.

FURTHER READING

A listing, together with a brief discussion, of the realization of conceptual metaphors in nonlinguistic areas is given in Lakoff (1993) and Gibbs (1994). D. Schön (1979) is an early analysis that shows how metaphors can be real. A highly relevant work in the same spirit is Shore (1996), in which he shows some of the major organizing metaphors of American culture. P. Morgan's work is discussed in Lakoff (1993). Csábi (1997) analyzes the metaphors that structure the early American Puritan experience. Kövecses (1994) looks at the ways Tocqueville's understanding of American democracy is influenced by certain conceptual metaphors. Kövecses (1995a) employs the machinery of cognitive linguistics to "decode" the Statue of Liberty. Lakoff (1992) presents a metaphor analysis of the Gulf War. Adamson et al. (1996) examine the metaphors underlying much of American politics. American foreign policy is described in terms of metaphors by Chilton and Lakoff (1995). Lakoff (1996) shows how the notions and practice of morality and politics are intertwined and how both are structured by metaphor. Forceville (1996) and Ungerer (2000) study how metaphors are made use of in advertisements. Their work shows that the study of "pictorial metaphors" is very complex, raises several important theoretical questions, and thus deserves more attention by cognitive linguists. McNeill (1992) and Cienki (1998) have studied metaphorical gestures. Wilcox (2000) describes conceptual metaphors in American Sign Language.

EXERCISES

1. In this chapter you have encountered a symbol of the United States, the Statue of Liberty, in which several conceptual metaphors are realized. What other symbols of the United States and other countries can you think of in which a conceptual metaphor is realized?

2. Compare the following sentences:

   (i) Who seems to have run more?
   Harry ran and ran and ran.
   John ran.
   (ii) Who is taller; Harry or John?
   Harry is very very very tall.
   John is very tall.
   (iii) Who is bigger?
   Harry is bi-i-i-i-ig!
   John is big.

      (a) How do repetition and lengthening of words alter meaning?
      (b) Can you find a conceptual metaphor for sentences like the above?

3. As we saw in this chapter (in the section "Interpretation of History") there are several metaphors to describe a nation or the settlement of a country; for instance, the early settlement of America is often seen as the movement of the Jews from Egypt to Israel. However, nineteenth- and twentieth-century immigrants came to be described in different terms as the following statements demonstrate:

   (i) America has "lost control" of its borders but remains deeply divided over how to curb the inexorable *flood* of illegal immigration.
   (ii) The United States is receiving the largest *wave* of immigration in its history.
   (iii) This *influx* strains our facilities for assimilation.
   (iv) But America is poorly equipped with the *rising tide* of people seeking to come to the United States.
   (v) Here was another Asiatic *reservoir* of over 300 million souls threatening *to deluge* the coast.

      (a) How is the immigration process viewed in these sentences, i.e., what is the conceptual metaphor?
      (b) Is this a positive or a negative view? Why?

6

The Basis of
Metaphor

Our conceptual system contains thousands of concrete and thousands of abstract concepts. We noted, furthermore, that in the cognitive linguistic view metaphors are sets of mappings between a more concrete or physical source domain and a more abstract target domain. This situation raises the issue whether *any* concrete concept can serve as a source domain for *any* target concept. In other words, can we make use of any concrete concept in the process of understanding any abstract one?

The same issue arises in the most widely shared traditional view of metaphor, except that here the question is not why one concept rather than another is selected as a metaphorical source domain, but why one linguistic expression rather than another is chosen to speak metaphorically about something. The answer in this view is that there is a *similarity* between the two entities denoted by the two linguistic expressions, and hence, between the meanings of the two expressions. Thus, the constraint that limits the excessive production of metaphor is that there must be a similarity between the two entities compared. If the two entities are not similar in some respect, we cannot metaphorically use one to talk about the other.

The issue of whether there are constraints on the production of metaphors is closely related to another one: the issue of the predictability of metaphors. Can we predict what the metaphors are in a particular language and across languages? The notion of "predictability" characterizes formal theories of language (e.g., generative grammar) that (try to) model themselves on the "exact" sciences such as physics. In this view, which metaphors we have should be predictable, and if our theory can't predict them, the theory can be claimed to be unscientific.

Cognitive linguistics does not accept this view of what a theory should be capable of doing. In the description of metaphor in particular and of language in general, it breaks away from the notion of predictability and replaces this notion with *motivation*. As we will see at the end of the chapter and especially in chapter 12, the issue of which metaphors we have is not a matter of prediction but that of motivation; metaphors cannot be predicted, but they can be motivated.

1. The Similarity Constraint in the Traditional View

As we saw above, in the traditional view similarity is the basis of metaphor, and it also constrains the selection of particular linguistic expressions to talk about something else. A fairly typical example of this would be the expression "the *roses* on her cheeks." The example displays some typical features of the most widely held *traditional view of metaphor*:

(1) Metaphor is decorative or fancy speech. We use the word *roses* to talk about somebody's cheeks because we wish to create some special effect in the listener or reader (such as creating a pleasing image). We do not use the word *roses* as part of the process of conceptualizing and understanding one thing in terms of another.

(2) Metaphor is a linguistic, and not a conceptual, phenomenon. Whatever the intended effect or purpose is, in metaphor we simply use one word or expression instead of another word or expression, rather than one conceptual domain to comprehend another.

(3) The basis for using the word *roses* to talk about somebody's cheeks is the similarity between the color of some roses (pink or red) and that of the color of a person's cheeks (also pink or some light red). This similarity makes it possible for speakers to use the word *rose* instead of, say, the phrase *the pink skin on her cheeks* for some special effect. The similarity between some roses and some kinds of skin exists in reality before anyone uses *roses* to talk about somebody's cheeks.

(4) It is this preexisting kind of similarity between two things that constrains the possible metaphors speakers can employ for skins of some color. Given the color of this kind of skin on the cheeks, the rose is a good choice for a metaphor in a way in which many other things would not be; thus, for example, we could not talk metaphorically appropriately about the pinkish color on a person's cheeks by using the word *sky*, as in "the *sky* on her cheeks." The sky as we normally think of it (we take it to be blue) simply bears no resemblance to healthy pinkish skin on the cheeks. It is in this sense that in the traditional view certain preexisting similarities can determine or limit which linguistic expressions, rather than others, can be used to describe the world.

There is no doubt that this account of what linguistic expression can be used metaphorically in place of others applies to many cases. Preexisting similarity explains the selection of many metaphorical expressions in both conventional and unconventional language use. Nevertheless, there are many additional cases where the account fails. We have seen many examples so far where it would be impossible to account for the use of a metaphorical expression with the notion of preexisting similarity. What could possibly be the preexisting similarity between, say, "*digesting* food" and "*digesting* ideas," or between "We're *not going anywhere*," taken literally and "This relationship is *not going anywhere*," taken metaphorically. Similarly, what possible preexisting similarity exists between the concept of a journey and that of love?

For this reason, the cognitive linguistic view finds it important to provide an account of the selection of metaphorical source concepts (and their corresponding metaphorical linguistic expressions) that can also explain those cases where no obvious preexisting similarity between two entities can be found. This is the task to which we now turn.

2. The Grounding of Metaphors in the Cognitive Linguistic View

Can anything be a source domain for a particular target? If similarity cannot be taken to be a completely general account of the basis of metaphor, then what can? Or, to put the same question differently, what limits the selection of particular source domains for particular targets? For example, there is a large number of source domains for the target concept of love (roughly between twenty and thirty), but it is still a limited number. Not anything can function as a source concept for love. Quite simply, then, the question is why we have the sources that we do.

The cognitive linguistic view maintains that—in addition to objective, preexisting similarity—conceptual metaphors are based on a variety of human experience, including correlations in experience, various kinds of nonobjective similarity, biological and cultural roots shared by the two concepts, and possibly others. All of these may provide sufficient motivation for the selection of source B_1 over B_2 or B_3 for the comprehension of target A. Given such motivation, it makes sense to speakers of a language to use B_1, rather than, say, B_2 or B_3, to comprehend A. They consequently feel that the conceptual metaphors that they use are somehow natural.

Let us now see the major ways in which conceptual metaphors are grounded in experience, either perceptual, biological, or cultural. This kind of groundedness for conceptual metaphors is often referred to as the **experiential basis** or *motivation* of a metaphor.

2.1. Correlations in Experience

Some metaphors are grounded in correlations in our experience. It is important to see that correlations are not similarities. If event E_1 is accompanied by event E_2 (either all the time or just habitually), E_1 and E_2 will not be similar events; they will be events that are correlated in experience. For example, if the event of adding more fluid to a container is accompanied by the event of the level of the fluid rising, we will not say that the two events (adding more to a fluid and the level rising) are similar to each other. Rather, we will say that the occurrence of one event is correlated to the occurrence of another. This is exactly the kind of correlation that accounts for the conceptual metaphor MORE IS UP.

This metaphor operates with two concepts: quantity and verticality. Quantity consists of a scale that has MORE and LESS, while verticality consists of one that has UP and DOWN. We can ask two questions: Why is quantity understood in terms of verticality? And why is MORE understood as UP, while LESS as DOWN? The answer to the former is that there is in our everyday experience a correlation between quantity or amount and verticality. When issues of quantity arise, issues of verticality commonly arise. Simply, we understand changes in quantity in terms of changes in verticality. But why is MORE paired with UP and LESS with DOWN? This is because the more specific correlation is that when the quantity or amount of a substance increases (MORE), the level of the substance rises (UP) and when the quantity of the substance decreases (LESS), the level of the substance goes down (DOWN). There are hundreds of recurrent correlated experiences that motivate for us the conceptualization of MORE and LESS as UP and DOWN. We will see this metaphor as grounded in our recurrent everyday experiences. For the same reason, we will take the linguistic expressions that manifest this conceptual metaphor as well motivated. It will make sense for us to talk about the prices "going *up*," unemployment figures being "*high*," and turning the volume of the radio "*down*."

Next, consider the metaphor PURPOSES ARE DESTINATIONS, as it appears in such expressions as "*reaching one's goals*," "working *toward* a solution," or "the end being *in sight*." This metaphor is also grounded in correlations in human experience. If we want to do something, we often have to go to a particular place to do that thing. For example, if we want to drink beer, we either have to go to the store to buy beer or to a bar to have one there. That is, achieving a goal often requires going to a destination. In this sense, the concept of purpose or goal is correlated in our experience with the concept of going to a destination. This recurrent experience (of achieving goals by going to destinations) provides a strong experiential basis for the PURPOSES ARE DESTINATIONS metaphor.

Not all conceptual metaphors are grounded in correlated experience in such a direct way as MORE IS UP or PURPOSES ARE DESTINATIONS. In some cases, the experiential basis of a metaphor is less direct. Consider, for example, the LIFE IS A JOURNEY metaphor. It would be unreasonable to claim that there is any clear correlation in experience between life and journeys. But then how is this metaphor grounded? We can suggest that LIFE IS A JOURNEY is a special case of the more general metaphor PURPOSES ARE DESTINATIONS. We typically have certain goals in life (but this does not, of course, mean that *all* episodes in our life are purposeful). In other words, a life with a goal or a purposeful life is a special case of having purposes in general. Similarly, a journey, which is an attempt to reach a predetermined destination, is special case of reaching destinations in general. The class of events that we call "reaching destinations" is much broader than, and thus includes more, than just journeys. Given these observations, we can take the specific LIFE IS A JOURNEY metaphor to be a special case of the more general PURPOSES ARE DESTINATIONS metaphor. It then follows that the experiential basis that applies to the general case will also apply to the specific one. Thus, if a generic-level metaphor is grounded in correlated experience (as in the case of PURPOSES ARE DESTINATIONS), we do not need independent experiential basis for each specific-level metaphor that belongs to the generic-level one (as in the case of A (PURPOSEFUL) LIFE IS A JOURNEY). In sum, some metaphors are grounded in experience in less direct ways.

Some other metaphors have their experiential bases in the functioning of the human body. One of these is the metaphor ANGER IS HEAT. The heat metaphor for anger gains expression in language in many ways. Since the heat may be either the heat of a hot fluid or that of fire, metaphorical expressions that are instances of the ANGER IS HEAT metaphor can describe both. Thus, in English we have such words and phrases for anger as "*boil* with anger," "make one's *blood boil*," "be *stewing*," "be *seething*," "be *burned up*," "breathe *fire*," "*inflammatory* remarks," and so on. The ANGER IS HEAT metaphor is grounded in the experience that the angry person feels "hot." This is indicated by such expressions as "*hot*head," "be *hot* and bothered," "in the *heat* of the argument," and others. The experience of anger is, for us, correlated with the experience of body heat. This correlation of our emotional experience with our bodily experience serves as the basis of the metaphor ANGER IS HEAT in both of its versions: ANGER IS A HOT FLUID and ANGER IS FIRE.

Other emotional experiences may be associated with coldness rather than heat. This provides, for example, the experiential basis for the widespread conceptualization of fear in English as being cold. This can be seen in expressions such as "The thought *chilled* him," "He *had cold feet* to go inside," and "*Shivers* ran down her spine." Here again, emotional experience is felt to be associated with assumed or real changes in body temperature. The result is that speakers of English find both the expressions and the conceptual metaphor FEAR IS COLD natural and experientially motivated.

2.2. Perceived Structural Similarity

In the cases discussed in the previous section, two events are correlated and occur regularly and repeatedly in human experience. It is these correlations in experience that form the experiential basis of some conceptual metaphors. However, such correlations in experience should not be regarded as preexisting similarities between the two events. Thus, more of quantity and the level of a substance rising, achieving life goals and reaching destinations, and being angry and an increase in body heat are correlated events in our experiences, but this does not make them similar—at least not in the sense of objective, preexisting similarity.

However, there is a similarity of another kind that applies to some other conceptual metaphors and can thus form their experiential bases. These are cases that can be said to be based on some nonobjective similarity as perceived

by speakers of English. One example of this case is the conceptual metaphor
LIFE IS A GAMBLING GAME, as exemplified by the following expressions:

LIFE IS A GAMBLING GAME
I'll *take my chances*.
The *odds are against me*.
It's a *toss-up*.
If you *play your cards right*, you can do it.
Where is he when the *chips are down?*
He's *bluffing*.
Those are *high stakes*.
He *won big*.

These expressions depict human life as a gambling game. People perceive
certain similarities between life and gambling games, but these are not objective and preexisting similarities between them. The similarities arise as a result of metaphorically conceiving of life as a gambling game. We view our
actions in life as gambles and the consequences of those actions as either
winning or losing. Actions in life and their consequences are not inherently
gamblelike. In life, an action simply has some consequences, but we can conceive of the relationship between the action and its consequences in terms of
a gambling situation, in which a gamble (corresponding to an action in life)
results in winning or losing (corresponding to the consequence of the action).
We see a similarity between the relationship of gambles and winning or losing and life's actions and their consequences. When we see a similarity between the structure of one domain and that of another, we have cases where
there is a perceived structural similarity in the conceptual metaphor. Perceiving
life in terms of a gambling game is the process of understanding LIFE IS A
GAMBLING GAME. Whatever similarities arise from this perception will be
called *perceived structural similarities*. Similarities of this kind provide an important source of motivation for some conceptual metaphors.

The suggestion that some metaphors are characterized by *perceived similarities* has an interesting implication. It implies that some metaphors are not
based on similarity but generate similarities, as the analysis above shows.

2.3. Perceived Structural Similarity Induced by Basic Metaphors

In some other cases, the perception of structural similarity may be induced
by what was called ontological metaphors. It was observed that ontological
metaphors are extremely basic ones, in that they give object, substance, or
container "shape," or status, to entities and events that are not physical objects, substances, or containers. If two concepts (one abstract, the other concrete) share this basic shape or status, this can induce the perception of certain structural similarities between the two.

As an example, consider now the conceptual metaphor that was introduced
in chapter 1: IDEAS ARE FOOD. What helps or enables us to perceive struc-

tural similarities between the abstract concept of idea and that of food? First, let us see some of the perceived structural similarities between the two concepts. We cook food and we can *stew over* ideas; we swallow food and we can *swallow* a claim or insult; we chew food and we can *chew over* some suggestion; we digest food and we can or cannot *digest* an idea; we get nourishment from eating food and we are *nourished* by ideas. These similarities can be laid out as perceived structural similarities between the concepts of food and ideas.

Food
(a) we cook it
(b) we swallow it or refuse to eat it
(c) we chew it
(d) the body digests it
(e) digested food provides nourishment

Ideas
(a) we think about them
(b) we accept them or reject them
(c) we consider them
(d) the mind understands them
(e) understanding provides mental well-being

We can also represent these perceived structural similarities in the form of mappings:

(a) cooking   ⇒ thinking
(b) swallowing   ⇒ accepting
(c) chewing   ⇒ considering
(d) digesting   ⇒ understanding
(e) nourishment ⇒ mental well-being

These mappings can also be laid out as conceptual metaphors that provide the submappings of the IDEAS ARE FOOD metaphor:

(a) THINKING IS COOKING ("Let me *stew over* this.")
(b) ACCEPTING IS SWALLOWING ("I can't *swallow* that claim.")
(c) CONSIDERING IS CHEWING ("Let me *chew over* the proposal.")
(d) UNDERSTANDING IS DIGESTING ("I can't *digest* all these ideas.")
(e) MENTAL WELL-BEING IS PHYSICAL NOURISHMENT ("He *thrives on* stuff like this.")

But what facilitates the perception of these similarities for us? The perceived structural similarities are in all probability induced by some basic ideas we have about the mind:

The mind is a container.
Ideas are entities.
We receive ideas from outside of the mind and ideas go into the mind.

This view can be given as a set of interrelated ontological metaphors that characterize our conceptions of the mind and human communication:

THE MIND IS A CONTAINER
IDEAS ARE OBJECTS
COMMUNICATION IS SENDING IDEAS FROM ONE MIND-CONTAINER TO
   ANOTHER

This set of metaphors is known as the "conduit" metaphor. (It is called the "conduit" metaphor because ideas are assumed to travel along a conduit, as shown by sentences such as "His message *came across*.") These ontological metaphors for the mind arise from certain nonmetaphorical assumptions we make about the human body:

The body is a container.
Food consists of objects or substances.
We receive food from outside the body and it goes into the body.

Given these nonmetaphorical assumptions about the body and the ontological metaphors that map this understanding onto the mind, it makes sense for us that we talk and think about ideas and the mind in ways that reflect our structured knowledge about food and the body. This is how ontological metaphors may facilitate the perception of structural similarities between otherwise conceptually distant domains.

2.4. Source as the Root of the Target

In some other cases of conceptual metaphor, experiential basis is provided by a situation in which the source was the origin, or the "root," of the target. This kind of experiential basis comes in two versions: biological and cultural roots.

The source may be a *biological root* of the target and thus lead to the formation of a conceptual metaphor. Consider some metaphors for love and affection: LOVE IS A BOND (There's a *strong bond between* them), LOVE IS A UNITY (She is my *better half*), AFFECTION IS CLOSENESS (He's *close* to his grandmother). It is likely that these target domains have "selected" their source domains because the sources represent properties of such biologically determined states and events as the early mother-child relationship, sexuality, and birth. The notion of love seems to be based on such image-schematic properties as link, unity, and closeness which give rise to the source domains of BOND, UNITY, and CLOSENESS.

The root for the target may also be a *cultural root*. Take, for example, the ARGUMENT IS WAR metaphor. Why is the notion of war such a good (i.e., natural) source domain for the target concept of argument? The reason probably is that the verbal institution of arguments has evolved historically from the physical domain of fighting. Thus, the historical origin of the concept of argument (i.e., war or fighting) became a natural source domain for the target that has evolved from that origin (i.e., argument). The same root seems to apply to the metaphor SPORT IS WAR, as in "My team did not use the right *strategy*," "the two *battling* teams," "to go to a training *camp*," and many others. Many prototypical sports, such as soccer, rugby, American football, wrestling, boxing, evolved from war and fighting, and here again, the target domain took its historical origin as its source domain.

In addition to journeys and gambling games, a frequently used source domain for life is the concept of play; hence, the metaphor LIFE IS A PLAY, as in Shakespeare's famous lines "All the world is a stage, / And all the men and women merely players. / They have their exits and their entrances; / And one man in his time plays many parts" (*As You Like It* 2.7). The institution of the theater obviously evolved from everyday life. Life has thus acquired the concept of a theater play as its source domain.

As a matter of fact, from a contemporary perspective all these metaphors may be either based on correlations in experience (e.g., LOVE IS CLOSENESS) or on perceived structural similarity (e.g., SPORT IS WAR). What justifies the setting up of a separate category of metaphorical motivation in these cases is that the emergence of the metaphors is clearly based either on human biological evolution or on cultural history.

In sum, we have seen several types of basis for metaphor: literal, preexisting similarity, correlations in experience, perceived structural similarity (in two versions), and source as the root or origin of the target (in two versions). Joe Grady suggests a useful typology of metaphorical basis, or motivation, and distinguishes among three types of motivation for metaphor. In his system, there are thus correlation metaphors, resemblance metaphors, and GENERIC-IS-SPECIFIC metaphors. These cases correspond to the ones that have been identified in this chapter in the following way:

(1) correlation metaphors = correlations in experience, such as PUR-
POSES ARE DESTINATIONS (plus source as the origin of the target:
biological root)
(2) resemblance metaphors = perceived similarity (e.g., Achilles is a
lion)
(3) GENERIC-IS-SPECIFIC metaphors = perceived structural similarity,
such as LIFE IS A GAMBLING GAME (plus source as the origin of the
target: cultural root)

It might be possible that there exist other kinds of motivation for conceptual metaphors. Although it will take a long time for cognitive linguists to work out a comprehensive and more or less "final" list of the kinds of metaphorical basis, these motivations will surely be among them.

2.5. Motivation versus Prediction

In this chapter, we have seen a large number of conceptual metaphors whose metaphorical motivation or basis comes from a variety of factors, such as seeing correlation in experience, perceiving a similarity, the source being the root of the target, etc. These cases point to an important conclusion in the study of conceptual metaphors; namely, that we have the particular source-to-target mappings we do because we have "good" and human reasons to select certain sources for the conceptualization of certain targets over some other sources. Out of a large number of potential sources, we "choose" the ones that "make intuitive sense"—that is, the ones that emerge from human experience—either cognitive, physiological, cultural, biological, or whatever.

This conclusion is even more remarkable from the point of view of cross-linguistic comparison; experiential bases motivate the metaphors in particular languages, but they do not predict them. That is, a given language may not have a particular metaphor, though all human beings may have certain physiological experiences, such as body heat associated with anger. What can be predicted, however, is that no language will have source domains that contradict certain universal sensorimotor experiences in which targets are embedded. We will return to this issue in chapters 12 and 13.

SUMMARY

On what basis do we select the source domains for particular targets? In the traditional view, the selection of sources assumes an *objective, literal,* and *preexisting similarity* between the source and the target.

By contrast, the cognitive linguistic view maintains that the selection of source domains depends on human factors that reflect nonobjective, nonliteral, and nonpreexisting similarities between a source and a target domain. These are called the **experiential bases** *or motivation* of conceptual metaphors. Some of the common kinds of such similarities include: (1) *correlations in experience,* (2) *perceived structural similarity,* (3) *perceived structural similarity induced by basic metaphors,* (4) *source being the root of the target.* In this last case, the source may be either the biological or the cultural root of the target.

Conceptual metaphors have *motivation* (i.e., are motivated), not **prediction** (i.e., cannot be predicted). The source domains for a particular target cannot be predicted within a given language. The source-to-target mappings are merely motivated by the factors mentioned above. The same applies to cross-linguistic comparisons. We cannot expect the exact same metaphors to occur in all languages, but we cannot expect metaphors that contradict universal human experience either.

FURTHER READING

The traditional theory of metaphor, in its several versions, is discussed from a cognitive linguistic point of view by Lakoff and Turner (1989). Lakoff (1993) summarizes the main fallacies of several of the rival views on metaphor. Lakoff and Johnson (1980) offer a criticism of the "comparison view" of metaphor and challenge the notion that metaphor is based on objective, literal, preexisting similarity. They also outline some of the kinds of nonobjective similarities, such as correlation in experience and perceived structural similarity, on which conceptual metaphors are based. Lakoff (1987), Johnson (1987), Lakoff and Kövecses (1987) emphasize the embodied nature, hence, the motivation of conceptual metaphor. Lakoff (1987) points out that in a given conceptual system there is motivation, but not prediction. Grady (1999) offers a useful typology of metaphorical motivation, together with spelling out the advantages of the typology for a cognitive linguistic theory of metaphor. Something like "perceived structural similarity" as a basis for some metaphors has been suggested by Gentner (1983) in her studies of analogy, Jackendoff (1990) in his "thematic relations" hypothesis, and Murphy (1996).

EXERCISES

1. How are the following metaphors grounded: LOVE IS FIRE and LOVE IS A JOURNEY?
2. What other special cases of the PURPOSES ARE DESTINATIONS general metaphor can you think of, besides LIFE IS A JOURNEY and LOVE IS A JOURNEY—the ones mentioned in the chapter?
3. In this chapter, you have read about the MORE IS UP and the LESS IS DOWN metaphors. Expand on what you have learned. How are the HEALTHY IS UP and the SICK IS DOWN metaphors grounded in correlations in our experience?
4. Dance is metaphorically viewed as sex, as demonstrated by the saying: "Dancing is the perpendicular expression of a horizontal desire." What kind of motivation is involved in the DANCE IS SEX metaphor?

The Partial
Nature of
Metaphorical
Mappings

It has been emphasized throughout that conceptual metaphors can be characterized by the formula A IS B, in which a target domain, A, is understood in terms of a source domain, B. But this formulation of what conceptual metaphors involve is not precise enough. In the case of structural metaphors this would mean that an entire target concept is understood in terms of an entire source concept. However, this cannot be the case because concept A cannot be the same as another concept B. In discussing this issue the idea of mappings is relevant. It's been pointed out that a conceptual metaphor of the structural kind is constituted by a set of mappings between a source and a target. However, the mappings between A and B are, and can be, only partial. Only a part of concept B is mapped onto target A and only a part of target A is involved in the mappings from B. We need to ask which part(s) of the source are mapped onto which part(s) in the target.

1. Metaphorical Highlighting

Metaphorical **highlighting** applies to the target domain, whereas what we will call "metaphorical utilization" applies to the source domain. Concepts in general (both source and target) are characterized by a number of different aspects. When a source domain is applied to a target, only some (but not all) aspects of the target are brought into focus. Let us take, for example, THE MIND IS A BRITTLE OBJECT metaphor:

THE MIND IS A BRITTLE OBJECT
Her ego is very *fragile*.
You have *to handle him with care* since his wife's death.
He *broke* under cross-examination.
She is easily *crushed*.

The experience *shattered* him.
I'm *going to pieces*.
His mind *snapped*.
He *cracked up*.

This metaphorical source domain focuses on a single aspect of the concept of the mind. As the examples indicate, the main focus is on the aspect that we can call "psychological strength"—or, in this case, the lack of it. When a metaphor focuses on one or some aspects of a target concept, we can say that it *highlights* that or those aspect(s).

Highlighting necessarily goes together with **hiding**. This means that when a concept has several aspects (which is normally the case) and the metaphor focuses on one (or maybe two or three) aspect(s), the other aspects of the concept will remain hidden, that is, out of focus. Highlighting and hiding presuppose each other.

To see how the processes of highlighting and hiding jointly operate, consider some metaphors for the concept of argument.

> AN ARGUMENT IS A CONTAINER: Your argument has *a lot of content*.
>   What is the *core* of his argument?
> AN ARGUMENT IS A JOURNEY: We will *proceed in a step-by-step* fashion.
>   We have *covered a lot of ground*.
> AN ARGUMENT IS WAR: He *won* the argument. I couldn't *defend* that
>   point.
> AN ARGUMENT IS A BUILDING: She *constructed a solid* argument. We
>   have got a *good foundation* for the argument.

These metaphors focus on, or highlight, a number of the aspects of the concept of argument. They address the issue of the content of an argument, the basicness of its claims or points, the progress made, who controls it, its construction, and its strength. Given the examples above, the following can be suggested:

> The CONTAINER metaphor highlights the content and basicness of an
>   argument.
> The JOURNEY metaphor focuses on progress and content.
> The WAR metaphor's main focus seems to be the issue of control over
>   the argument.
> The BUILDING metaphor captures the aspects of the construction of an
>   argument and its strength.

As can be seen, the metaphors highlight certain aspects of arguments and at the same time hide other aspects of it. For instance, when the CONTAINER metaphor highlights issues of content and basicness, it simultaneously hides such other aspects as progress, control, construction, and strength. And the sole concern of the WAR metaphor for arguments appears to be the issue or aspect of control. It does not seem to enable us to think and talk about such aspects of arguments as content, construction, basicness, and so on. We can conclude, then, that different metaphors highlight different aspects of the same target concept and at the same time hide its other aspects.

1.1. Metaphorical Utilization

Another property of metaphorical mappings is that speakers tend to utilize only some aspects of a source domain in understanding a target. Whereas in the previous section it was shown that the focus of a source on a target was partial, in the process to be discussed in the present section I will show that only a part of the source is utilized for this purpose. Let us call this latter process partial metaphorical **utilization**.

We can continue with the example of the ARGUMENT IS A BUILDING metaphor. Here are some more metaphorical expressions for this metaphor:

> We've got the *framework* for a *solid* argument.
> If you don't *support* your argument with *solid* facts, the whole thing will *collapse*.
> You should try *to buttress* your argument with more facts.
> With the *groundwork* you've got, you can *build a strong* argument.

These linguistic metaphors can be taken to be fairly representative of the ARGUMENT IS A BUILDING metaphor; they appear to be highly conventionalized and widely used. Which parts of the concept of building do they utilize in the metaphorical comprehension of arguments? It appears that, typically and most conventionally, they make use of the construction, structure, and strength of a building. The metaphorical expressions make reference to the construction of a building with such words as *construct* and *build*; to the general structure of the building with such words as *framework*; and to its strength with such words as *buttress, solid, strong*, and *support*.

Notice that many aspects of our concept of building are not utilized in the metaphorical comprehension of arguments. Buildings typically have rooms and corridors; they have a roof; they are equipped with chimneys; they can be found on streets or roads; there are people living or working in them; they often have other houses next to them; they have windows and doors; they are built in a particular architectural style; and so on. It seems that all this information remains unutilized when the ARGUMENT IS A BUILDING metaphor is applied.

Let us look at one more example that illustrates the same process. Take the LOVE IS A NUTRIENT metaphor with some typical examples such as the following:

> I'm *starved for* affection.
> He *thrives* on love.
> I was *given new strength* by her love.
> She is *sustained* by love.
> She's love-*starved*.

The source domain utilizes and activates some aspects of the concept of nutrient, while leaving most of the concept un- or underutilized. Thus, to the extent that the expressions above are representative, the source domain of nutrient utilizes such aspects of the concept as the desire for nourishment (*starved*), the positive effects of being well nourished (*sustain, new strength, thrive*), and the negative consequences of a lack of nutrients (*being starved*). Overall, then, the nutrient metaphor for love utilizes chiefly the "hunger/thirst" and the corresponding "desire/effect" aspect of the concept of nutrient.

However, many things in connection with nutrients are left out of this picture. For example, no reference is conventionally made to the idea that nutrients come into the body from outside; that we digest nutrients in order to process them; that eventually some of the nutrient goes out of the body; that we may have to go out and buy nutrients; that we store them in the refrigerator or the pantry; that nutrients may go bad and can make us sick; and many more.

In sum, in the same way as metaphorical highlighting of the target is partial, metaphorical utilization of the source is partial as well. Given a source domain, only certain aspects of it are conceptually utilized and activated in the comprehension of a target domain. Highlighting and hiding are not processes that we can regard as being undesirable or "bad." Instead, we will see below that they are inevitable, since one source domain would not be sufficient to comprehend a target.

It is important to see, however, that we talk about partial metaphorical utilization in the course of *conventional* thought and language use. When we think and speak *unconventionally*, we can extend our conventional patterns of thought and language into what we called the "unutilized parts of the source." This was the topic of a previous chapter (see chapter 4), but we can illustrate the process with an example offered by the LOVE IS A NUTRIENT metaphor.

> An unconventional extension of the metaphorically utilized parts of
> LOVE IS A NUTRIENT: "My love is such that *rivers cannot quench*."
> (Anne Bradstreet, "To My Dear And Loving Husband")

(As we saw in chapter 4, this linguistic example can be interpreted as also belonging to the LOVE IS FIRE metaphor. This possibility, however, does not affect the point here.) The example represents a case in which the conventionally utilized part of the source is extended into a new part or aspect of the source concept.

Another point to keep in mind in connection with the discussion is that although just one or a few aspects of a source and target concept are utilized and highlighted in conceptual metaphors, the processes of utilization and highlighting concerning those aspects work according to normal principles of mappings. In other words, elements from one domain are mapped onto elements of another. As an illustration, let us take the LOVE IS A NUTRIENT metaphor. As has been seen, this metaphor highlights the aspects of desire for love and the consequence of love, while it utilizes the hunger and nourishment aspects of the concept of nutrient. But this correspondence of the aspects of nutrient and love is achieved via detailed mappings, as shown below:

NUTRIENT		LOVE
the hungry person	⇒	the person who desires love
food	⇒	love
hunger	⇒	the desire for love
physical nourishment	⇒	psychological strength
the effects of nourishment	⇒	the consequences of love

Thus, when we talk about utilization and highlighting in connection with a source and a target, respectively, we talk about two sides of the same coin. The utilized and highlighted aspects of a source and a target are brought together in a conceptual metaphor through a detailed set of mappings between some of the elements in the source and target domains.

2. Why These Particular Elements?

So far we have seen that the mappings between source and target are only partial; some elements of the source and the target are involved, but others are not.

This raises the question: Why are just these elements involved and not the others? To take a specific example, let us return to the ARGUMENT IS A BUILDING metaphor or its more general version THEORIES ARE BUILDINGS. We noted above that certain aspects of buildings such as construction, structure, and strength are utilized (with their respective elements in the mappings), whereas others such as tenants or windows or corridors are not. Why should this be the case? Joe Grady suggests the following solution.

The ARGUMENT (THEORY) IS A BUILDING metaphor is a complex one that is composed of **primary metaphors**. In this **complex metaphor** there are two such primary metaphors: LOGICAL STRUCTURE IS PHYSICAL STRUCTURE and PERSISTING IS REMAINING ERECT. Primary metaphors are motivated independently of complex ones. Whereas the ARGUMENT (THEORY) IS A BUILDING metaphor would be difficult to motivate (buildings and arguments/theories are not correlated in experience and they cannot be said to be structurally similar either), the two primary metaphors that constitute it can be. The experiential basis of LOGICAL STRUCTURE IS PHYSICAL STRUCTURE is the correlation between physical structures (like that of a house) and the abstract principles that enable us to make, take apart, rearrange, or otherwise manipulate them. In the case of PERSISTING IS REMAINING ERECT, the experiential basis is the correlation we repeatedly experience between things that remain erect or upright when they are functional, viable, and working, but fall down when they are not functional, viable, and working. Primary metaphors also have their independent language; in the present case, the language of the two primary metaphors may be independent of the complex metaphor AN ARGUMENT (THEORY) IS A BUILDING. Thus, we can talk about a "*strong* proposal," not only about a "*strong* argument" (LOGICAL STRUCTURE IS PHYSICAL STRUCTURE), and about a recipe that "*stood* the test of time," and not only about a theory *"standing* or *falling"* (PERSISTING IS REMAINING ERECT).

The combination of these two primary metaphors gives us what we know as the ARGUMENT (THEORY) IS A BUILDING metaphor. The combined version VIABLE LOGICAL STRUCTURES ARE ERECT PHYSICAL STRUCTURES captures those aspects of arguments/theories that have to do with structure, construction, and strength (or in Grady's wording structure and persistence). Since the complex metaphor is built out of these particular primary ones, we get an elegant explanation for why just these mappings participate in the metaphor and not others; why *framework* ("physical structure") and *buttress* ("remaining erect") are mapped, but *windows, chimneys, tenants* are not.

3. Why Do We Have Several Source Concepts for a Single Target?

As we have seen above, speakers of English have several conceptual metaphors for the concept of argument; that is, they resort to several source domains in understanding a single target domain—argument. This is typical of target domains. We use not just one but a number of source concepts to comprehend them. The question inevitably arises: Why should this be the case? Why don't we simply have one conceptual metaphor for a given target? The answer is straightforward in light of what we have shown in the previous two sections in the chapter:

> Since concepts (both target and source) have several aspects to them, speakers need several source domains to understand these different aspects of target concepts.

For example, the various aspects of the concept of argument, such as content, progress, and strength, will be comprehended via such conceptual metaphors as AN ARGUMENT IS A CONTAINER, AN ARGUMENT IS A JOURNEY, and AN ARGUMENT IS A BUILDING. In many cases, metaphors such as these enable speakers to make sense of various target concepts.

But how does this actually happen? How do several metaphors jointly produce an understanding for a given target domain? To get an idea of this, I will discuss the concept of happiness in some detail, as it is jointly characterized by a number of conceptual metaphors. Below is a list of the metaphors that speakers of English most commonly use to talk about happiness as an emotion. (The word *happiness*, in many of these instances, is replaceable and is often replaced by the word *joy*.) In the discussion of each of these metaphors, I will point out the most important mappings between the source and the target of this emotion.

The first three conceptual metaphors all give happiness an "upward orientation." The upward orientation of these metaphors makes the concept of happiness coherent with a number of other concepts; through the UP metaphors, it gets a highly positive evaluation.

BEING HAPPY IS BEING OFF THE GROUND
She was *on cloud nine.*
I was just *soaring* with happiness.
I'm *six feet off the ground.*
After the exam, I was *walking on air* for days.

BEING HAPPY IS BEING IN HEAVEN
That was *heaven* on earth.
I've died and *gone to heaven.*
It was *paradise* on earth.
I was *in seventh heaven.*

HAPPY IS UP
We had to cheer him *up.*
They were in *high* spirits.
Lighten *up!*
She lit *up.*

I prefer to keep these three metaphors distinct, since they are characterized by distinct but obviously related source concepts: being off the ground, being in heaven, and the general concept UP. The obvious relationship among them is that they are all "upward oriented."

Since light, as opposed to dark, is valued positively, the LIGHT metaphor also highlights the positive evaluation of happiness (*light up, brighten up, shine*). Furthermore, as several examples indicate, the happy person is characterized by a great deal of energy; the light appears to derive from an internal heat energy (cf. *radiate, glow, shine*).

HAPPINESS IS LIGHT
He *radiates* joy.
There was a *glow* of happiness in her face.
When she heard the news, she *lit* up.
Nothing to worry about, *brighten* up.
She was *shining* with joy.
Her face was *bright* with happiness.

The main emphasis of the VITALITY metaphor is that the happy person is energetic, active; he or she is "full of life."

HAPPINESS IS VITALITY
He was *alive* with joy.
I'm feeling *spry.*
I felt *vivacious.*
That *put some life* into them.
She's *animated* with joy.
I *got a big charge* out of it.

The CONTAINER metaphor's major focus is on the intensity and control aspects of happiness. It depicts happiness as a highly intense emotional state that may lead to difficulties in controlling it. Intensity in this metaphor is indicated by the quantity of the fluid in the container (*fill*) and by the corresponding inability of the subject of happiness to keep the fluid inside the container (*can't contain, brim over, overflow, burst*).

> HAPPINESS IS A FLUID IN A CONTAINER
> The sight *filled* them with joy.
> I *brimmed over* with joy when I saw her.
> She couldn't *contain* her joy any longer.
> He *bubbled over* with joy when he got his presents.
> She *overflowed* with joy.
> I was *bursting* with happiness.

Given the examples below, it seems that the CAPTIVE ANIMAL metaphor captures two aspects of happiness: giving up the attempt to control the emotion (*give way to, break loose, can't hold back*) and the need to communicate one's feelings to another (*can't keep it to myself*).

> HAPPINESS IS A CAPTIVE ANIMAL
> I couldn't *keep* my happiness *to* myself.
> She *gave way to* her feelings of happiness.
> His feelings of joy *broke loose*.
> He couldn't *hold back* tears of joy.

To the extent that we can take the following examples to be symptomatic of happiness, they seem to indicate that happiness is a powerful and intense emotion that we regard as taking control of us. That is, the OPPONENT metaphor suggests that there is an attempt at controlling the emotion on the part of the subject of happiness, but this struggle for control typically results in losing control for the happy person.

> HAPPINESS IS AN OPPONENT
> She was *overcome* with joy.
> Happiness *took complete control over* him.
> He was *knocked out*!
> She was *seized* by joy.

A rapture, or a high, is associated with energetic behavior. Another aspect of rapture is the pleasure it imparts. This depicts happiness as a very pleasurable experience. However, the major aspect of happiness that the RAPTURE metaphor highlights is excessiveness and loss of control. If we are *drunk* with joy, we do not quite know what we are doing.

> HAPPINESS IS A RAPTURE
> It was a *delirious* feeling.
> I was *drunk* with joy.

The experience was *intoxicating*.
I'm *on a natural high*.
I'm *high on* life.

According to the metaphor below, a happy person gets what he or she needs from the outside world (as a pig gets its slop, as a horse gets its hay, etc.). Such a person feels comfort and being in harmony with the surrounding world.

A HAPPY PERSON IS AN ANIMAL (THAT LIVES WELL)
He was happy as a *pig in slop*.
She was *chirping like a cricket*.
He is as happy as *a clam*.
He was as happy as a *pig in shit*.
He is as happy as a *horse in hay*.
She was *crowing* with excitement.
He was *wallowing in* a sea of happiness.

This metaphor shares some examples with the next one. Here, as well, the aspects of pleasurability and comfort or harmony with the world are focused on.

HAPPINESS IS A PLEASURABLE PHYSICAL SENSATION
I was *purring* with delight.
She was *crowing* with excitement.
He was *wallowing* in a sea of happiness.
I was *tickled pink*.

The next metaphor also highlights the feature of control. Insanity is a complete lack of control. Thus, the INSANITY metaphor suggests an even greater lack of control than the RAPTURE metaphor.

HAPPINESS IS INSANITY
They were *crazy* with happiness.
She was *mad* with joy.
I was *beside* myself.

If we are carried away and swept off our feet, we have no control over what is happening to us. And not only do we not have control over it, we can't help it either. In other words, we are passive in relation to the event or state that we are involved in. We are not the agents but the victims or patients. It is this aspect of the concept that is highlighted by the NATURAL FORCE metaphor.

HAPPINESS IS A NATURAL FORCE
She was *overwhelmed* with joy.
We were *carried away* with happiness.
He was *swept off his feet*.
I was *bowled over*.
They were *transported*.

We can now lay out the mappings for each of the metaphors for happiness in Table 7.1.

The highlighted elements in the target domain converge on a certain stereotypical concept of HAPPINESS. Given these mappings, we can characterize a good portion of the everyday concept of HAPPINESS as follows:

> You are satisfied. (from AN ANIMAL THAT LIVES WELL)
> You feel energized. (from VITALITY)
> You experience your state as a pleasurable one. (from PLEASURABLE PHYSICAL SENSATION, RAPTURE)
> You feel that you are in harmony with the world. (from AN ANIMAL THAT LIVES WELL)
> You can't help what you feel; you are passive in relation to your feelings. (from NATURAL FORCE)
> The intensity of your experiences is high. (from A FLUID IN A CONTAINER)
> Beyond a certain limit, an increase in intensity implies a danger that you will become dysfunctional, that is, will lose control. (from A FLUID IN A CONTAINER, A CAPTIVE ANIMAL, AN OPPONENT, NATURAL FORCE)
> It is not entirely acceptable to give free expression to what you feel (i.e., to become dysfunctional). (from A FLUID IN A CONTAINER, A CAPTIVE ANIMAL, AN OPPONENT)
> You try to keep the emotion under control. (from A FLUID IN A CONTAINER)
> You nevertheless lose control. (from A CAPTIVE ANIMAL, AN OPPONENT, A NATURAL FORCE) As a result, there is a lack of control over behavior. (from INSANITY)

This description results from the metaphorical mappings in the conceptual metaphors we have seen and constitutes a large portion of the concept of HAPPINESS. This is what we mean by understanding a concept jointly by several metaphors. However, the characterization of the concept of HAPPINESS as given above is incomplete. Thus, it is not claimed that *all* of the concept is metaphorically structured. Certain further aspects of it are structured by other than metaphorical means, including metonymy and literal concepts (on metonymy, see chapter 11).

A more complete description of HAPPINESS would look like this:

Cause of Happiness
You want to achieve something.
You achieve it.
There is an immediate emotional response to this.

Existence of Happiness
You are satisfied.
You display a variety of expressive and behavioral responses including brightness of the eyes, smiling, laughing, jumping up and down, and, often, even crying.
You feel energized.

Table 7.1

	Mappings	
Metaphor	Aspects of Source	Aspects of Target
BEING HAPPY IS BEING OFF THE GROUND	the goodness of being "up"	the goodness of happiness
BEING HAPPY IS BEING IN HEAVEN		
HAPPY IS UP		
HAPPINESS IS LIGHT	the goodness of being "light"	the goodness of happiness
	the energy of light	the energy that accompanies happiness
HAPPINESS IS VITALITY	the energy of vitality	the energy that accompanies happiness
HAPPINESS IS A FLUID IN A CONTAINER	the quantity of the fluid	the intensity of happiness
	trying to keeping the fluid inside	trying to control happiness
	the inability to control a large quantity of the fluid	the inability to control intense happiness
HAPPINESS IS A CAPTIVE ANIMAL	the inability to hold the animal back	the inability to control happiness
HAPPINESS IS AN OPPONENT	the inability to withstand the attack of an opponent	the inability to control happiness
HAPPINESS IS A RAPTURE	the physical pleasure of rapture	the emotional pleasantness of happiness
	the lack of control in a state of rapture	the lack of control in happiness
A HAPPY PERSON IS AN ANIMAL (THAT LIVES WELL)	the satisfaction of the animal	the harmony felt by the happy person
HAPPINESS IS A PLEASURABLE PHYSICAL SENSATION	the pleasurable physical sensation	the harmony felt by the happy person
HAPPINESS IS INSANITY	the mental lack of control over insanity	the emotional lack of control over happiness
	the inability to resist the force	the inability to control happiness
HAPPINESS IS A NATURAL FORCE	the physical helplessness	the emotional passivity

You also experience physiological responses, including warmth, agitation, and excitement.

The context for the state you are in is often a social one involving celebrations.

You have a positive outlook on the world.

You feel a need to communicate your feelings to others.

The feeling may "spread" to others.

You experience your state as a pleasurable one.

You feel that you are in harmony with the world.

You can't help what you feel; you are passive in relation to your feelings.

The intensity of your experiences is high.

Beyond a certain limit, an increase in intensity implies a danger that you will become dysfunctional, that is, will lose control.

It is not entirely acceptable to give free expression to what you feel (i.e., to become dysfunctional).

Attempt at Control

Because it is not entirely acceptable to communicate and/or give free expression to what you feel, you try to keep the emotion under control: You attempt not to engage in the behavioral responses, and/or not to display the expressive reactions, and/or not to communicate what you feel.

Loss of Control

You nevertheless lose control. As a result, there is a lack of control over behavior.

Action

You engage in the behavioral responses, and/or display expressive reactions, and/or communicate what you feel. You may, in addition, exhibit wild, uncontrolled behavior (often in the form of dancing, singing, and energetic behavior with a lot of movement).

As can be seen, part of the content of the concept HAPPINESS is not metaphorical (but literal and metonymic). However, without the extensive metaphorical contribution to this content, the concept could not be adequately described.

SUMMARY

Metaphorical mappings from a source to a target are only partial. Only a part of the source domain is utilized in every conceptual metaphor. We have called this *partial metaphorical utilization*. This partial structure of the source *highlights*, that is, provides structure for only a part of the target concept. We have called this *metaphorical highlighting*. The part of the target that falls outside the highlighted region is said to be *hidden*.

Why do we need several source domains to understand a target fully? This is because each source can only structure certain aspects of a target; no source domain can structure, and thus provide full understanding for, all aspects of a target.

There are **primary** and **complex metaphors**. Primary metaphors combine to form complex ones. The primary metaphors determine which particular elements of the source are mapped onto the target.

The source domains jointly produce the structure and content of abstract concepts. As we saw in the case of happiness, happiness can be described in terms of features that are largely metaphorical. This is not to say, however, that all features of abstract concepts are metaphorical; some of the them are literal and metonymic.

FURTHER READING

Lakoff and Johnson (1980) introduce the notions of metaphorical highlighting and hiding, chiefly elaborating on the metaphorical structure of the concept of communication as conceptualized by the "conduit" metaphor. They also discuss briefly the notion of utilization—using the terms "used" and "unused" as parts of a source. In addition, they show which metaphors map onto which aspect(s) of the target domain of argument. Grady and his colleagues (1996) explain why certain things do and certain other things do not get mapped from the source to the target by recourse to primary metaphors that constitute complex ones. Lakoff and Kövecses (1987) demonstrate in detail how a large number of metaphorical source domains jointly "produce" the target concept of anger. Kövecses (1986, 1988, 1990) demonstrates this process for such emotion concepts as anger, fear, pride, love, respect, and the superordinate concept of emotion itself. Barcelona (1986) does the same for sadness. Kövecses (1991b) provides a similar description for the concept of happiness. Quinn (1991) challenges the idea that metaphors can constitute or "produce" cultural models. Gibbs (1994) and Kövecses (1999) respond to Quinn. Kövecses (1995b) also offers a response to Quinn's claims, using cross-cultural data. Gibbs (1994) also provides a summary of experimental results that confirm the psychological reality and metaphorical nature of our cognitive models for abstract concepts such as anger. Allbritton (1995) contains further experimental evidence concerning the metaphorical nature of such concepts.

EXERCISES

1. Among other conceptual metaphors, the ones given in Table 7.2 characterize the concept of LOVE. What aspects of the source and target domains are utilized and highlighted in each of these conceptual metaphors?

Table 7.2

Metaphor	Example	Highlighted and Utilized Aspects
LOVE IS A JOURNEY	It's been a *long bumpy road.* Look *how far we've come.*	
LOVE IS A NUTRIENT	I am *starved for* love.	
LOVE IS FIRE	He is *burning with* love.	
LOVE IS MAGIC	I am *under her spell.*	

Table 7.3

Linguistic Examples	Conceptual Metaphors
1. Waves of depression came over him.	SADNESS IS A NATURAL FORCE
2. He brought me down with his remarks.	
3. He is in a dark mood.	
4. I am filled with sorrow.	
5. That was a terrible blow.	
6. Time heals all sorrows.	
7. He was insane with grief.	
8. He drowned his sorrow in drink.	
9. His feelings of misery got out of hand.	
10. She was ruled by sorrow.	

2. The following are some linguistic examples that characterize the concept of SADNESS.

   (a) Try to analyze them: identify the conceptual metaphors that the examples in Table 7.3 are manifestations of (e.g., SADNESS IS A NATURAL FORCE).

   (b) Now, using Table 7.4, take some of the conceptual metaphors and describe which aspects of *sadness* are highlighted/hidden by them.

   (c) Based on the results of your analysis, can you see any connections with the analysis of the concept of HAPPINESS given in the chapter?

3. The following is an unconventional extension of the metaphorically utilized parts of the DEATH IS SLEEP metaphor. Which part or aspect of the source concept is this an extension of? What is Shakespeare's attitude to the metaphor?

   To sleep? Perchance to dream! Ay, there's the rub;
   For in that sleep of death what dreams may come?
                       (William Shakespeare, *Hamlet*)

Table 7.4

Conceptual Metaphors	Highlighted Aspects	Hidden Aspects
1. SADNESS IS A NATURAL FORCE	Passivity Lack of control	Cause Attempt at control Behavioral responses
2.		
3.		
4.		
5.		
6.		
7.		
8.		
9.		
10.		

8

Metaphorical

Entailments

So far we have seen that conceptual metaphors consist of a set of mappings between a source and a target. Certain aspects of the source and those of the target are brought into correspondence with each other in such a way that constituent elements of the source correspond to constituent elements of the target.

In addition, we have rich knowledge about the source and these constituent elements. This extensive knowledge reflects our detailed and everyday understanding of the world; we know a lot about buildings, nutrients, journeys, war, containers, and so on and their constituents. Given the extensive everyday knowledge we have about concrete source domains and their elements, how much and what knowledge is carried over from source B to target A, relative to certain aspects of B and A that are involved in the mappings? In other words, to what extent do we make use of the *rich knowledge* about sources and their constituent elements beyond the *structure* that is defined by the *relationships* among the basic constituent elements?

As we saw in the discussion of the various metaphors for argument and love in the previous chapter, certain aspects of a source domain are utilized in the understanding of the targets. The aspects of the source are constituted by a small number of elements, and it is these elements that participate in the mappings. We have a great deal of additional knowledge about these sources and their constituent elements. As we saw, this knowledge is not involved in the mappings between the basic constituents. In other words, we have the picture in Figure 8.1.

The question is the following: Is the additional rich knowledge about the (constituent or nonconstituent) elements of a source domain completely ignored, or is it made use of for the purposes of metaphorical comprehension?

We saw an answer to this question in chapter 7, where the distinction between primary and complex metaphors was discussed. In this chapter we will look at another proposal that attempts to answer the same question: the

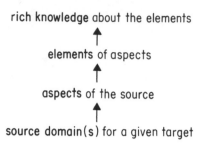

rich knowledge about the elements

↑

elements of aspects

↑

aspects of the source

↑

source domain(s) for a given target

Figure 8.1. The relationship among source domain, aspects of source, elements of aspects, and rich knowledge about elements.

"invariance hypothesis." However, before I discuss this, I need to clarify another theoretically important notion in the cognitive view of metaphor: that of "metaphorical entailments."

1. Metaphorical Entailments

When rich additional knowledge about a source is mapped onto a target, we will call it **metaphorical entailment** to distinguish it from most of the mappings we have seen so far. The examination of conceptual metaphors shows that many metaphors do map additional knowledge from the source onto the target. Metaphorical entailments are a common property of conceptual metaphors. Let me illustrate this with some examples.

We mentioned the metaphor AN ARGUMENT IS A JOURNEY in the previous chapter. We have the constituent element that the journey takes place along a path. The path corresponds to the progress of an argument. However, we also have some additional knowledge about journeys, namely, that we can stray from the path. That is, a nonconstituent element of the concept of JOURNEY in this metaphor is that we can "stray from the path" of our journey. This manifests itself in the metaphorical entailment that we can also "digress from" the line of an argument. In this case, we make use of an additional piece of knowledge about journeys to make sense of a possible feature of arguments.

Next, consider the metaphor POLITICS IS WAR that was referred to in chapter 2. It is not a constituent element of the domain of war that wars often "produce" war heroes; thus, the mapping "war heroes correspond to outstanding political leaders" is not a constituent mapping in the metaphor. Yet, this (nonconstituent) element of the concept of war may be utilized for the understanding of politics. This is exactly what happened recently in a particular conceptualization of American politics, as analyzed by Adamson et al. Rush Limbaugh, in his book *The Way Things Ought To Be*, makes use of the concept of WAR HEROES in his interpretation of the contemporary

American political scene, claiming that the conservatives have produced some war heroes or outstanding and devoted political leaders. (Incidentally, as it turns out, one of these is Rush Limbaugh himself.) In other words, Limbaugh activates the additional mapping that obtains between war heroes and outstanding political leaders in his particular conception of American politics. This activation yields a metaphorical entailment of the POLITICS IS WAR metaphor.

Metaphorical entailments can also structure entire conversations. One simple but clear example of this happened when the author met by accident a former phys ed teacher of his in a popular exercise center in Budapest. The following short conversation took place in Hungarian (a rough English translation is given):

TEACHER   You look like a healthy apple.

AUTHOR   I hope it's not rotten inside.

TEACHER   I hope, too, that it will last a long time.

Although this is a creative conversation, conversations like this are not at all infrequent in everyday life. In it, a completely conventional conceptual metaphor is introduced: PEOPLE ARE PLANTS (FRUITS). Given the mapping "an apple corresponds to a person," a property of the fruit—the piece of knowledge that an apple may be rotten inside although healthy-looking outside—is picked up by the second speaker and carried over. The first speaker, then, picks up another piece of knowledge concerning apples, when he expresses his hope that the apple will "last a long time." In this case, a conceptual metaphor is introduced into the conversation, and the participants carry on the conversation by picking out distinct pieces of knowledge associated with the source domain of this metaphor. In this sense, the activation of various metaphorical entailments of a conceptual metaphor can govern or structure a part or the whole of a conversation.

2. The Full Exploitation of Metaphorical Entailments

In the cases above, only one or just a few entailments of a metaphor have been exploited. In some other cases, however, the exploitation of a source's *metaphorical entailment potential* is almost complete. The present section will examine two such cases. In the first case, the metaphorical entailments of a source are carried over fully to a single target concept, while in the second case, the metaphorical entailments characterize a set of related target concepts.

2.1. Anger Is a Hot Fluid in a Container

Consider first a well-known metaphor for anger in English: ANGER IS A HOT FLUID IN A CONTAINER.

The constituent mappings of this metaphor are as follows:

the physical container	⇒	the angry person's body
the top of the container	⇒	the rational self of the angry person
the hot fluid inside the container	⇒	the anger
the degree of fluid heat	⇒	the intensity of anger
the cause of increase in fluid heat	⇒	the cause of anger

What we should do now is to see how much of the entailment potential of the source (HOT FLUID IN A CONTAINER) is carried over to the target of anger.

Let us begin by playing at being "naive" physicists, that is, ordinary people who do not know much about the science of physics. Even in this capacity, we know many things about the behavior of hot fluids in closed containers, which is to say that we possess a great amount of rich knowledge concerning this particular source. Among these are the following: We know that as the heat of the fluid increases, the level of the fluid in the container rises; we know that the heat produces steam; we know that the fluid and the steam exert pressure on the walls of the container; we know that beyond a certain limit the walls will burst as a result of too much pressure; we know that the fluid will come out of the container as a result of the explosion; we know that the pieces of the container will go flying all over the place; we know that this might be dangerous to people nearby, etc. This knowledge is completely coherent. Given our nonscientific or **folk understanding** of the behavior of hot fluids in closed containers, the pieces of knowledge in the description fit together in a structured way. This feature of the knowledge distinguishes it from the cases discussed above, where pieces of knowledge were more or less unsystematically selected and carried over to the target.

Now let us see what exactly is carried over to the concept of anger from the metaphorical entailment potential of the source. We can take linguistic usage to be evidence for the exploitation of this potential. In other words, if we find conventionalized linguistic expressions that indicate any of the above metaphorical entailments in talk about anger, we can assume that people often actually think in terms of this entailment potential. The metaphorical entailments below show that all the entailment potential given above is exploited by the ANGER IS A HOT FLUID IN A CONTAINER metaphor:

WHEN THE INTENSITY OF ANGER INCREASES, THE FLUID RISES
His pent-up anger *welled up* inside him.
She could feel her gorge *rising*.
We got a *rise* out of him.
My anger kept *building up* inside me.
Pretty soon I was in a *towering* rage.

INTENSE ANGER PRODUCES STEAM
She got all *steamed up*.
Billy's just *blowing off steam*.
I was *fuming*.

INTENSE ANGER PRODUCES PRESSURE ON THE CONTAINER
He was *bursting* with anger.
I could barely *contain* my rage.
I could barely *keep* it *in* anymore.

A variant of this involves:

THE ANGRY PERSON TRIES TO KEEP THE PRESSURE BACK
I *suppressed* my anger.
He *turned* his anger *inward*.
He managed to *keep* his anger *bottled up* inside him.

WHEN ANGER BECOMES TOO INTENSE, THE PERSON EXPLODES
When I told him, he just *exploded*.
She *blew up* at me.
We won't tolerate any of your *outbursts*.

This can be elaborated, using special cases:

Pistons: He *blew a gasket*.
Volcanoes: She *erupted*.
Electricity: I *blew a fuse*.
Explosives: She's *on a short fuse*.
Bombs: That really *set* me *off*.

WHEN AN ANGRY PERSON EXPLODES, PARTS OF HIM /HER
   GO UP IN THE AIR
I *blew my stack*.
I *blew my top*.
She *flipped her lid*.
He *hit the ceiling*.
I *went through the roof*.

WHEN AN ANGRY PERSON EXPLODES, WHAT WAS INSIDE
   HIM COMES OUT
His anger finally *came out*.
Smoke was pouring out of his ears.

This can be elaborated by using a special case:

ANIMALS GIVING BIRTH
She *was having kittens*.
My mother will *have a cow* when I tell her.

In the last couple of examples, the baby animals that come out of the grown female animal correspond to anger.

Now recall that one of the constituent mappings for the ANGER IS A HOT FLUID IN A CONTAINER metaphor was that the heat of the fluid corresponds to anger. In it, a basic element of the source (heat) is mapped onto a basic element of the target concept of anger (anger itself). However, there is a great deal of coherent knowledge that is associated with heat and its relationship to the fluid and the container. As the examples above indicate, the full and coherent entailment potential of this source is mapped onto the target of anger. This doesn't mean, however, that the concept of anger is fully described by this metaphor. That is a job that is performed jointly by this and several other metaphors. What it does mean, though, is that the potential metaphorical entailments of the source in relation to the target are fully exploited in the ANGER IS A HOT FLUID IN A CONTAINER metaphor.

This discussion of the entailment potential of source domains raises an important question for the entire theory: How do young children acquire conceptual metaphors? Do they also have to be "naive" physicists in order to learn conceptual metaphors such as ANGER IS A HOT FLUID IN A CONTAINER, as was suggested by some critics of the cognitive view of metaphor? Obviously not. It would be unreasonable to suggest that young children consciously learn conceptual metaphors by constructing coherent folk theories of source domains and applying the entailments of the source to the target. A more likely way for this learning to take place is that we subjectively experience our bodies as containers; we have the experience of a fluid inside the body; we experience heat or lack of heat in certain parts of the body; we also feel pressure when angry; and so on. These are unconscious experiences that we have very early on in our lives. In the cognitive view of metaphor, these experiences are assumed to play a crucial role in acquiring conceptual metaphors.

2.2. Complex Abstract Systems Are Plants

Unlike the metaphor discussed above, the COMPLEX ABSTRACT SYSTEMS ARE PLANTS metaphor takes several related target concepts. They include social organizations (such as companies), scientific disciplines, people, economic and political systems, human relationships, sets of ideas, and others. These are the major foci of the PLANT metaphor and all of them can be viewed as complex (abstract) systems. This explains why we have chosen to refer to this conceptual metaphor as COMPLEX ABSTRACT SYSTEMS ARE PLANTS. However, as we will shortly see below, this metaphor can also apply to things that are not, or are less easily, conceivable as complex systems, such as careers, youth, arguments, self-destruction, and so on. Nevertheless, on the whole it seems that the source concept of plant applies most naturally and most frequently to domains that we can readily regard as complex systems of some sort. This gives us justification to set up and use this particular conceptual metaphor.

The COMPLEX ABSTRACT SYSTEMS ARE PLANTS metaphor is based on a small number of constituent mappings, including the following:

(a) the plant is the complex system
(b) parts of the plant are parts of the complex system
(c) the biological growth of the plant is the abstract nonbiological development of the complex system

We can illustrate these mappings with such metaphorical sentences as these:

(1) Please turn to the local *branch* of the organization.
(2) She has *grown* a lot as a scholar lately.

Sentence (1) demonstrates mappings (a) and (b), whereas sentence (2) is a linguistic manifestation of mappings (a) and (c). The part of a plant can include several things, for example, a specialization in some discipline, as shown in sentence (3) below:

(3) Laser equipment is expensive but it can be used in many *branches* of surgery.

This sentence comes from *Cobuild English Guides 7: Metaphor*, which is a dictionary of English metaphors for learners of English as a foreign language. (We already made reference to this metaphor dictionary in the Preface.) The series is based on "the bank of English," a huge corpus of everyday English. Indeed, in our characterization of the COMPLEX ABSTRACT SYSTEMS ARE PLANTS metaphor below, we will rely exclusively on this source of information. This extensive corpus shows that many of the conceptual metaphors we have are very much alive and used all the time by everyday people.

As was noted earlier, in some cases we have a great deal of rich knowledge about the elements in the source, and consequently, we can make use of this knowledge in the comprehension of the target. Two such pieces of knowledge include the following: When plants grow, they become physically bigger, and plants are sometimes cut or pruned, which results in a smaller size. Now it seems that speakers make use of this additional information in understanding certain features of complex systems. We can represent these metaphorical entailments as submetaphors of COMPLEX ABSTRACT SYSTEMS ARE PLANTS as follows:

A COMPLEX SYSTEM BECOMING LARGER IS A PLANT GROWING BIGGER
Only now, 21 years since he established his distinctive women's line, is he *branching out into* men's clothing.

REDUCING COMPLEX SYSTEMS IS MAKING PLANTS SMALLER
   (PRUNING, CUTTING)
They selectively *pruned* the workforce.
Government and educational bureaucracies can and should be *ruthlessly pruned*.

The features of complex systems in question in these cases are (1) complex systems becoming physically larger, and (2) the reduction of complex systems. Additional rich knowledge concerning plants is utilized to capture these features.

However, most of the metaphorical entailments that derive from the PLANT metaphor in relation to complex systems have to do with mapping (c) above:

biological growth in the source corresponding to some abstract development in the target. As will be seen, a huge amount of detailed knowledge is carried over from plants to complex systems relative to this mapping. Here are the ones that stand out in *Cobuild English Guides 7: Metaphor*:

PREPARING THE DEVELOPMENT OF A COMPLEX SYSTEM IS PREPARING
   THE GROWTH OF A PLANT
The work *will prepare the ground for* future development.
Now they have signed agreements that *lay the ground for a huge growth* in trade and cooperation.

TO START OR CREATE A COMPLEX SYSTEM IS TO SOW A SEED
He had *the skill to plant the seed in* Jennifer's mind that her problem was not so important.
. . . debate that *sowed the seeds* of the welfare state.
By the time of his tragic murder in 1965, Malcolm X *had sown the seeds* of a new consciousness amongst African-Americans.

THE QUICK DEVELOPMENT OF A LARGE NUMBER OF THINGS IS THE
   QUICK GROWTH OF A LARGE NUMBER OF SHOOTS OR LEAVES
Concrete hotels and tourist villages are *sprouting* along the desert shore.
Across the land, shopping malls *sprout* like concrete *mushrooms*.
The number of managers *mushroomed* from 700 to 13,200.

POTENTIAL OR SOURCES OF FUTURE EVENTS ARE SEEDS; FUTURE
   EVENTS ARE THE FUTURE GROWTH OF A PLANT
He considered that there were, in these developments, the *seeds* of a new moral order.
The *seeds* of the future *lie in* the present.
He also *carries within* him *a seed* of self-destruction.

ORIGINS OR CAUSES LEADING TO EFFECTS ARE PARTS OF PLANTS FROM
   WHICH OTHER PARTS GROW
A good therapist will try *to find the root* of the problem.
Jealousy *has its roots in* unhealthy patterns of developments.
The controversy *stems from* an interview given by the mayor to Reuters news agency.
The beginning of an idea *took root in* Rosemary's mind.
They are fighting *deep-rooted* social and cultural traditions.

THE INITIAL STAGES OF DEVELOPMENT ARE THE BEGINNINGS
   OF GROWTH
Typically the *first green shoots* of recovery herald an increase in bankruptcy.
In this way, problems that can lead to depression and even illness *can be nipped in the bud*.
Our *budding* romance was over.
Another equally outstanding design *was germinating* at Bristol.

TO MAINTAIN OR TAKE CARE OF A COMPLEX SYSTEM IS
   TO CULTIVATE A PLANT
He always *cultivated* friendships with the ruling class.

This will make it more difficult *to weed out* people unsuitable for the profession.

THE FORCED DEVELOPMENT OF A COMPLEX SYSTEM IS
THE FORCED GROWTH OF A PLANT
The school has always had a *hothouse* atmosphere.

THE SUCCESSFUL OR APPROPRIATE DEVELOPMENT OF A COMPLEX
SYSTEM IS THE HEALTHY GROWTH OF A PLANT
Exports *flourished*, earning Taiwan huge foreign currency reserves.
His career *is flourishing* again.
. . . the ruins of a once *flourishing* civilization.

THE UNSUCCESSFUL OR INAPPROPRIATE DEVELOPMENT OF A COMPLEX
SYSTEM IS THE UNHEALTHY GROWTH OF A PLANT
They had been innocent sweethearts at a German university but their
romance *withered* when they came back to England.
I could see her happiness *withering*.
The sympathy made something in him *shrivel, shrink away*.
Tony looked at Momma, his smile *wilting*.

THE BEST STAGE IN THE PROGRESS OR DEVELOPMENT OF SOMETHING
IS THE FLOWERING OF A PLANT
The relationship *blossomed*. They decided to live together the following
year.
. . . a *blossoming*, diverse economy.
. . . the nation that had *briefly flowered* after 1918.
They remembered her as she'd been *in the flower* of their friendship.

THE BENEFICIAL CONSEQUENCES OF A PROCESS ARE
THE FRUITS OR THE CROP OF A PLANT
Now they've finished will they sit back and enjoy *the fruit* of their
labors?
American and Japanese firms are better at using *the fruits* of scientific
research.
Their campaign seems *to be bearing fruit*.
The plans finally *reached fruition*.
Unfortunately, a plan to reprint the play never *came to fruition*.
You have the capacity *to bring* your ideas *to fruition*.
Employers *reaped enormous* benefits from cheap foreign labor.
He began *to reap the harvest* of his sound training.

Apparently, then, the COMPLEX ABSTRACT SYSTEMS ARE PLANTS metaphor utilizes most of the metaphorical entailment potential associated with the concept of PLANT. This is everyday knowledge that we as ordinary people (as opposed to experts such as biologists) have about plants. The vast amount of rich knowledge focuses on one basic constituent mapping of the metaphor, the mapping according to which the natural, biological growth of plants corresponds to the (abstract) progress or development of complex systems. This elaborate knowledge about the growth of plants structures much of our knowledge about the "developmental" aspects of complex systems.

3. The Invariance Principle

In the previous section, we have seen cases where our everyday knowledge about plants and pressurized containers is fully exploited in comprehending the concept of complex systems, on the one hand, and that of anger, on the other. But what of cases where potential entailments are not metaphorically mapped from B to A? In those cases, the question arises: Why isn't everything carried over from B to A? What determines what is not carried over?

Let us take some examples where the mapping of entailments is blocked. Consider, first, sentences such as:

(a) She gave him a headache.
(b) She gave him a kiss.

These sentences are based on the metaphor CAUSATION IS TRANSFER (OF AN OBJECT) and can be explained with reference to such nonmetaphorical sentences as (c):

(c) She gave him a book.

In (c), the transfer (giving) of an object (book) takes place from a giver (she) to a recipient (he). This literal case entails certain things, one of them being that if I give you a book, you have it. Now this could be a metaphorical entailment when we apply the CAUSATION IS TRANSFER metaphor to produce (a) and (b). If the entailment is carried over, then we should be able to think and say that the "he" in both (a) and (b) has the metaphorical objects (the headache and the kiss) after they have been metaphorically handed over. But this does not seem to be the case, as shown by (a') and (b'):

(a') She gave him a headache, and he still has it.
(b') *She gave him a kiss, and he still has it.

(a') makes use of the potential metaphorical entailment that you have what has been given to you, while (b') does not. Why is it that one can be legitimately said to have the headache after it was given, whereas one cannot be said to have the kiss after it was given? In (a), a headache is a state and in (b) the kiss is an event. In both sentences "she" functions as the "cause" of the headache and the kiss, while "he" is the experiencer of an event and a state. In both cases, causation is expressed by the verb "give" (a form of transfer). Thus, we can paraphrase the sentences as "She caused him to experience a kiss/a headache." As we just saw, despite this similarity in interpretation, there is a difference in the metaphorical entailments that the sentences make use of.

Why is it then that the perfectly normal entailment in the source domain that if I give you something, you will have the thing applies to (a) but it does not apply to (b)? The answer is that kissing is an event and a headache is a state, which have different "shapes." Events do not last in time, are momentary, while states last for some time. In the target domain, we have CAUSA-TION OF AN EXPERIENCE; in the source domain, we have TRANSFER OF AN OBJECT. If the target experience that is caused is a state, the entailment of the source (you have the object that was given to you) will apply; if however, the target experience is a momentary event, the entailment of the source (you have the object that was given to you) will not apply. In this latter case, it can be suggested that the *schematic* or *skeletal* structure, or shape, of the target event rejects or overrides the entailment that arises from the source. Long-term states like having a thing after getting it cannot be imposed on momentary events like the experience of a kiss. The schematic structure of events (i.e., that they are momentary) does not accept an entailment from the source that contradicts this schematic structure. On the other hand, the same problem does not arise with headaches whose skeletal structure matches the metaphorical entailment of the source.

To handle cases such as this, scholars have proposed the **invariance principle** (or *hypothesis*). This states:

> Given the aspect(s) that participate in a metaphorical mapping, map as much knowledge from the source onto the target as is coherent with the image-schematic properties of the target.

Thus, the invariance principle blocks the mapping of knowledge that is not coherent with the schematic or skeletal structure of the target concept. For example, the generic structure of events is such that it prevents the mapping of some knowledge from the source domain of transferring things to the target domain of causation, given the CAUSATION IS TRANSFER metaphor.

The principle is called the **invariance principle** because the conceptual material that is mapped from the source preserves its basic structure in the mapping; it is *invariant*. When this basic structure of the source conflicts with that of the target, we get cases of *incoherence* between the two domains. Thus, the invariance principle consists of two parts: (1) the part that says what can be mapped from the source, and (2) the part that says what cannot and why.

It may be useful at this point to consider another example. Take LIFE IS A JOURNEY. In this metaphor, the fixity of the road in the source is not mapped onto the target. Alternative routes in the source correspond to choices in the target. Imagine that you come to a fork in the road and you start to walk in one direction. In the source domain, I can change my mind and walk back and go the other way in the fork. However, many choices in life are not like this. Once we have made a decision, we cannot "go back" and do the other thing. If we choose to go and see a certain movie at eight o'clock, we cannot go and see another movie at the same time. The choice was made in the target domain of life, and there is no possibility of "backtracking" and undoing what we have done. But this is precisely what we can do in the source domain of a journey. In the source domain of a journey, the road is preserved as I walk along it. This is why I can change my mind and backtrack and go the other way. But in the target of life, often the "road" is destroyed after I have made a choice, and I cannot undo what I previously chose to do. As a consequence, this feature of the source is prevented from being mapped onto the target. The reason is that the generic-level structure of the target domain of life is such that the mapping would import conflicting material from the source. Thus, the invariance principle would be violated.

However, it was suggested that the invariance hypothesis does not solve all the problems of "illegitimate transfer" from the source to the target. While it correctly handles metaphorical cases like giving someone a kiss or idea (as opposed to the literal case of giving someone a book), it cannot handle many other metaphorical cases. As Grady and his colleagues point out, there is no logical contradiction between a building having a window and a theory having a window; theories could have a window, just as much as they have a framework. But while the latter is metaphorically acceptable, the former is not. The invariance hypothesis does not offer a solution to this and many similar cases. The alternative solution, as we saw in chapter 7, was the one based on the notion of primary metaphor.

SUMMARY

Source domains are used to understand target domains. Only certain *aspects of sources* are utilized for this purpose. The various aspects of concepts consist of *conceptual elements*. We have a great deal of *everyday knowledge* about these elements.

When this rich knowledge about elements is mapped onto target domains, we have cases of *metaphorical entailment*. Each source concept has a *metaphorical entailment potential*; that is, it can potentially map extensive everyday knowledge onto the target. We call this everyday knowledge a *folk theory* or *folk understanding* of a domain.

The entailment potential of sources may be more or less fully utilized. In some cases, this utilization can be practically complete. We have seen two such cases: the ANGER IS A HOT FLUID IN A CONTAINER and COMPLEX ABSTRACT SYSTEMS ARE PLANTS metaphors.

The question arises: Given the metaphorical entailment potential of a source domain, how much of it is actually mapped onto the target and what is left out of the mapping? The answer is provided by the **invariance principle** which says that only those portions of the source can be mapped that do not conflict with the schematic structure of the target.

FURTHER READING

Metaphorical entailments were first treated in Lakoff and Johnson (1980). Lakoff and Kövecses (1987) introduce the idea that metaphorical entailments are based on coherent folk theories associated with some domains. They show this in detail in their study of anger. The notion of folk theory is discussed in Holland and Quinn (1987). Kövecses (1986, 1988, 1991b) works out several of the metaphorical entailments for some of the source domains of the concept of love. Ortony (1988) offers a criticism of Kövecses (1986) and the cognitive view of metaphor in general. The issue of the acquisition of metaphors is discussed by Chris Johnson (see, e.g., C. Johnson, 1997).

Ponterotto (2000) is a detailed study of the role of conceptual metaphor in discourse and conversation. Palmer (1996) looks at the issue from an anthropological perspective. Gibbs (1994) and Allbritton (1995) show experimentally that texts are often made coherent by the conceptual metaphors that underlie them.

The invariance hypothesis was first sketchily introduced by Lakoff and Turner (1989). It was refined, critically assessed, and modified by Lakoff (1990, 1993), Turner (1990, 1993, 1996), and Brugman (1990). Rudzka-Ostyn (1995), Ibarretxe-Antunano (1999), and Feyaerts (2000) are all attempts to refine the invariance principle. Grady, Taub, and Morgan (1996) offer an alternative solution to the kinds of problems that the invariance hypothesis was proposed to solve.

EXERCISES

1. Listen to the songs by the Beatles entitled (a) "Here We Go Again" and (b) "(Forgive me) My Little Flower Princess." Which metaphors do they evoke? What kind of entailments are mapped onto the targets?

2. We have seen in the chapter how the source domain of the CAUSATION IS TRANSFER metaphor is only partially mapped onto the target. Now let us take another CAUSATION metaphor: CAUSATION IS PROGENERATION (Turner 1987). Explain why it is possible to say that "Edward Teller was the *father* of the atomic bomb" but not that "Michael Jordan was the *father* of a beautiful slam-dunk in the last second of the game," although in both cases there is an individual who "causes an effect" (the atomic bomb and the ball in the basket, respectively).

9

The Scope of
Metaphor

Throughout this book we have seen cases in which a target domain was characterized by a number of source domains. For example, the concept of argument is understood in terms of metaphors such as:

AN ARGUMENT IS A JOURNEY: We will *proceed in a step-by-step* fashion.
AN ARGUMENT IS A BUILDING: She *constructed a solid* argument.
AN ARGUMENT IS A CONTAINER: Your argument has *a lot of content.*
AN ARGUMENT IS WAR: I couldn't *defend* that point.

Furthermore, it was pointed out in chapter 7 that there is a good reason why a single target concept is understood via several source concepts: one source just cannot do the job because our concepts have a number of distinct aspects to them and the metaphors address these distinct aspects. This was shown in detail for the concept of happiness, which is characterized by means of metaphors such as the following:

HAPPINESS IS UP: We had to cheer him *up.*
HAPPINESS IS LIGHT: When she heard the news, she *lit* up.
HAPPINESS IS VITALITY: That *put some life into* them.
HAPPINESS IS A FLUID IN A CONTAINER: The sight *filled* them with joy.
HAPPINESS IS AN OPPONENT: She was *overcome* by joy.
HAPPINESS IS A RAPTURE: It was a *delirious* feeling.
HAPPINESS IS INSANITY: They were *crazy* with happiness.
HAPPINESS IS A NATURAL FORCE: We were *carried away* with happiness.

Similarly, as we saw in chapter 2, many other abstract concepts have been shown to be characterized by a large number of distinct source domains. These abstract target domains include time, love, life, ideas, theories, morality, mind, anger, fear, politics, society, communication, religion, and many more.

1. The Scope of Metaphor

However, what has been less often observed is that a single source concept can characterize many distinct target domains. As a matter of fact, most of the specific source domains appear to characterize not just one target concept but several. For instance, the concept of WAR applies not only to argument but also to love; the concept of BUILDING not only to theories but also to societies; the concept of FIRE not only to love but also to anger, etc. This raises an interesting empirical and theoretical question: How many and what kind of target domains does a single source concept apply to? I will call this issue the question of the **scope of metaphor.** By the scope of metaphor I simply mean the range of cases, that is, the target domains, to which a given source concept applies.

To throw some light on this issue and to see why it is important, it seems best to go through a number of examples, where it is the case that a single source characterizes a number of targets. Consider the source domain of buildings again, as it applies to several targets. The following examples are based on *Cobuild's English Guide 7: Metaphor:*

THEORIES ARE BUILDINGS
Increasingly, scientific knowledge *is constructed* by small numbers of specialized workers.
McCarthy *demolishes* the romantic myth of the Wild West.
She lay back for a few moments contemplating the *ruins* of her idealism and her innocence.
Don't be tempted to skip the first sections of your programme, because they are the *foundations on which* the second half *will be built.*
. . . the advance that *laid the foundations* for modern science.
Our view, he said, is that these claims are entirely *without foundation.*
My faith was *rocked to its foundations.*
The second half of the chapter *builds on* previous discussion of change and differentiation in home ownership.

RELATIONSHIPS ARE BUILDINGS
Since then the two have *built a solid* relationship.
You can help *lay the foundations* for a good relationship between your children by preparing your older child in advance for the new baby.

CAREERS ARE BUILDINGS
Government grants have enabled a number of the top names in British sport *to build* a successful career.
Her career was *in ruins.*

A COMPANY IS A BUILDING
Ten years ago, he and a partner set up on their own and *built up* a successful fashion company.

ECONOMIC SYSTEMS ARE BUILDINGS
With its economy *in ruins,* it can't afford to involve itself in military action.
There is no painless way to get inflation down. We now have an excellent *foundation on which to build.*

SOCIAL GROUPS ARE BUILDINGS
He's about *to rock the foundations* of the literary establishment with his
   novel.
By early afternoon queues *were already building up*.

A LIFE IS A BUILDING
Now another young woman's life is *in ruins* after an appalling attack.

These are just some of the examples that were found by Alice Deignan,
the author of the *Cobuild Metaphor Dictionary*, in the Bank of English. In
real life, the whole range of "building terms" can apply to these target domains. Thus, both a company and a career can be said to have a *solid foundation*; one can *build* both a life and a social group with a *structure*; a relationship can be *in ruins*; and so on.

As these cases indicate, the source domain of buildings applies to a variety of targets. The target domains of theories, relationships, careers, economic
systems, companies, social groups, and life all appear to be complex abstract
systems—a concept that was introduced in the previous chapter. We can
generalize this observation by suggesting that the overarching metaphor that
includes all these cases is COMPLEX SYSTEMS ARE BUILDINGS. A diagram
might be helpful to illustrate this. See Figure 9.1.

As the examples above indicate, these target domains can all be structured
by the source domain of BUILDING. However, we will see in the next chapter
that this is not the only source that can apply to them.

2. The Main Meaning Focus of a
Conceptual Metaphor

The common thread that runs through these conceptual metaphors (i.e., THEO-
RIES ARE BUILDINGS, RELATIONSHIPS ARE BUILDINGS, etc.) is that they are
all concerned with certain specific features of complex systems; namely, the
creation of a strong and stable structure for a complex system. Most of the
metaphorical expressions capture these three interrelated features of complex
systems—their creation, their structure, and the stability of their structure.
This is clear from the preponderance of such expressions as *build, construct,
strong foundation, without foundation, rock the foundation, in ruins, solid,*

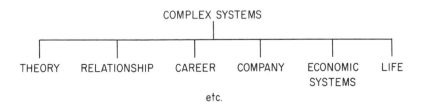

Figure 9.1. Complex systems.

lay the foundation in the examples above. I will say that these conceptual metaphors have a **main meaning focus**, a major theme, so to speak. What determines the main meaning orientation of a given source-target pairing, such as COMPLEX SYSTEMS ARE BUILDINGS? I will suggest that each source domain is designated to play a specific role in characterizing a range of targets to which it applies. This role can be stated as follows:

> Each source is associated with a particular meaning focus (or foci) that is (or are) mapped onto the target. This meaning focus is conventionally fixed and agreed-on within a speech community; it is typical of most cases of the source; and it is characteristic of the source only. The target inherits the main meaning focus (or foci) of the source.

What this statement says is that a source domain contributes not randomly selected but predetermined conceptual materials agreed upon by a community of speakers to the range of target domains to which it applies. Thus, the main meaning focus represents some basic knowledge concerning a source that is widely shared in the speech community, that can be found in most instances of the source, and that uniquely characterizes the source.

Let us take an example. In the present case of the complex systems-as-buildings metaphor, the main meaning focus is the creation of a stable structure for a complex system. These are also the mappings that predominate in Lakoff and Johnson's metaphor AN ARGUMENT (or A THEORY) IS A BUILDING:

AN ARGUMENT IS A BUILDING
We've got the *framework* for a *solid* argument.
If you don't *support* your argument with *solid* facts, the whole thing will *collapse*.
He is trying to *buttress* his argument with a lot of irrelevant facts, but it is still so *shaky* that it will easily *fall apart* under criticism.
With the *groundwork* you've got, you can *construct* a pretty *strong* argument.

Most of these examples have to do with the strength, structure, and the creation of an argument. Typically, buildings have a groundwork and foundation on which a framework or structure is built; the framework or structure stands above the ground; if the framework or structure is not solid and/or does not have a strong groundwork and foundation, it is likely to collapse. This knowledge is basic and central about buildings. Most people within a speech community possess it; it is characteristic of many instances of buildings; and it is knowledge that is most typical of buildings (but not of other things).

3. Central Mappings

Let us now see how this central knowledge is captured in the mappings that characterize the COMPLEX SYSTEMS ARE BUILDINGS metaphor. Given the linguistic examples, the mappings that constitute this metaphor are as follows:

COMPLEX SYSTEMS ARE BUILDINGS

(a) foundation ⇒ basis that supports the entire system
(b) framework ⇒ overall structure of the elements that make up the
    system
(c) additional elements to support the framework ⇒ additional
    elements to support the structure of the system
(d) design ⇒ logical structure of the system
(e) architect ⇒ maker/ builder of the system
(f) process of building ⇒ process of constructing the system
(g) strength ⇒ lastingness / stability of the system
(h) collapse ⇒ failure of the system

It should be pointed out here that in many cases one cannot avoid using metaphorical words (concepts) in the characterization of targets. For example, basis, support, stability, and structure are all metaphorical in relation to abstract targets, such as argument, mind, social and economic systems. This shows that abstract targets such as these cannot be conceived in other than metaphorical ways. This same point was made in connection with the concept of HAPPINESS in the previous chapter.

The eight mappings above can be reduced to three without any loss of information concerning the main meaning focus of the COMPLEX SYSTEMS ARE BUILDINGS metaphor. We can capture the main meaning focus with the help of the following mappings:

(1) building ⇒ creation or construction of the system (from mappings
    e and f)
(2) physical structure ⇒ abstract structure (from mappings a through d)
(3) physical strength (of the structure to stand) ⇒ abstract stability/
    lastingness (from mappings g and h)

These mappings can of course be recast as metaphors: CREATION/CONSTRUCTION OF AN ABSTRACT SYSTEM IS (THE PROCESS OF) BUILDING, ABSTRACT STRUCTURE OF A COMPLEX SYSTEM IS PHYSICAL STRUCTURE, and ABSTRACT STABILITY/LASTINGNESS IS PHYSICAL STRENGTH OF THE STRUCTURE TO STAND. What we get are primary metaphors—in the sense Joe Grady uses the term, as we saw in the previous chapter. To recapitulate, he used the primary metaphors ORGANIZATION IS PHYSICAL STRUCTURE (corresponding to (2) above) and PERSISTENCE IS REMAINING ERECT (corresponding to (3) above). What was added in this reanalysis is CREATION/CONSTRUCTION OF AN ABSTRACT SYSTEM IS BUILDING (corresponding to (1) above). These metaphors, however, do not only apply to ARGUMENTS or THEORIES; they also apply (at least potentially) to all or most of the COMPLEX ABSTRACT SYSTEMS as explained above. In Grady's terminology, the three primary metaphors are thus generalizations of the constituent mappings in (a) through (h).

As we just saw, the CREATION IS BUILDING, ABSTRACT STRUCTURE IS PHYSICAL STRUCTURE, and the ABSTRACT STABILITY IS PHYSICAL STRENGTH (OF STRUCTURE TO STAND) metaphors are mappings, or submetaphors, of

COMPLEX SYSTEMS ARE BUILDINGS. Since the main socially agreed-on meaning focus of the concept of BUILDING as a source is the making of a strong structure or framework, this will be mapped onto the target. Technically, this process takes place by means of a small number of mappings (i.e., those in 1, 2, and 3 above) from which all other mappings (i.e., those in a through h above) can be derived. Let us call generalized mappings from which other mappings derive **central mappings**. In the COMPLEX SYSTEMS ARE BUILDINGS metaphor, these are CONSTRUCTION IS BUILDING, ABSTRACT STRUCTURE IS PHYSICAL STRUCTURE, and STABILITY/LASTINGNESS IS STRENGTH (FOR THE PHYSICAL STRUCTURE TO STAND).

Characteristic of central mappings are the following: (a) conceptually, central mappings lead to the emergence of other mappings, either constituent basic mappings or metaphorical entailments; (b) culturally, central mappings reflect major human concerns relative to the source in question; (c) motivationally, they are the mappings that are most motivated experientially—either culturally or physically; (d) linguistically, they give rise to metaphorical expressions that dominate a metaphor. This last property of central mappings was especially clear in the case of another COMPLEX SYSTEMS metaphor that was discussed in the previous chapter: COMPLEX ABSTRACT SYSTEMS ARE PLANTS. Most of the metaphorical linguistic expressions dominating that metaphor were related to a mapping of this metaphor "physical growth ⇒ abstract development or progress of a complex system" in one way or another.

The notions of the scope of metaphor, main meaning focus, and central mapping(s) provide yet another answer to the question: What is and what is not mapped from the source to the target? Source domains are, on this view, characterized by a particular meaning focus (or foci). The main meaning focus that is associated with a source can be seen from the metaphorical linguistic expressions that dominate a metaphor. It is given or predetermined conceptual material in most sources (such as BUILDING or PLANT). It is this given or predetermined meaning focus attaching to a source that gets carried over to the target domains that are within the scope of this source. The central mappings carry over this conceptual material—and only this; they cannot carry over anything else.

4. The Case of Fire

Now let us see in another example how the three theoretical concepts developed above—scope of metaphor, main meaning focus, and central mapping—operate jointly. To do this, let us take the concept of FIRE, which is a common source domain for many target concepts. Again, the particular linguistic examples that demonstrate the application of fire as a source domain to a variety of targets will be taken from *Cobuild's English Guides 7: Metaphor*.

For most people, the related concepts of fire and heat are primarily associated with the metaphorical comprehension of emotions, such as anger, love,

desire, and so on. We can generalize this by assuming the metaphor EMO-
TION IS HEAT (OF FIRE). Here's a list of fire-related metaphors for these and
other emotions (the emotions involved are indicated in square brackets):

EMOTION IS HEAT (OF FIRE)
Behind his soft-spoken manner, *the fires* of ambition *burned*. [AMBI-
    TION-DESIRE]
Forstmann was a deeply angry man, *burning* with resentment. [RESENT-
    MENT-ANGER]
The young boy *was burning with* a fierce emotion. [EMOTION]
Dan *burned* to know what the reason could be. [CURIOSITY-DESIRE]
He gave his son a look of *burning* anger. [ANGER]
The trial left him with a *burning* sense of injustice. [INDIGNATION-
    ANGER]
As a boy my *burning* ambition was to become either a priest or a family
    doctor. [AMBITION-DESIRE]
. . . the *burning* desire to break free and express himself on his own
    terms. [DESIRE]
Marianne and I are both *fiery* people. [EMOTION]
The lady was ten years his senior. It was a *fiery* relationship. [RELA-
    TIONSHIP-LOVE]
As a child I had a real *hot* temper. [ANGER]

The emotion concepts of anger, love, curiosity, desire, ambition can all take
heat-fire as their source domain. Other examples reflect the many metaphorical entailments that are mapped from this source to the target of emotion:

THE HIGHEST DEGREE OF EMOTIONAL INTENSITY IS THE
    HIGHEST DEGREE OF FIRE
He got to his feet and his dark eyes *were blazing with* anger. [ANGER]
He *was blazing* with rage. [ANGER]

MAINTAINING THE INTENSITY OF THE EMOTION IS MAINTAINING
    THE FIRE
. . . keeping the flames of love alive. [LOVE]
. . . *fueling the flames* of hatred. [HATRED]

CONTROLLING THE INTENSITY OF THE EMOTION IS CONTROLLING
    THE FIRE
He'll have to keep his fiery temper *under control*. [ANGER]

LOW INTENSITY OF EMOTION IS A SMALL AMOUNT OF FIRE
Though we knew our army had been defeated, hope still *flickered* in our
    hearts. [HOPE]
For the first time she felt a *tiny spark* of hope. [HOPE]

A SUDDEN INCREASE IN EMOTION INTENSITY IS A SUDDEN INCREASE
    IN THE INTENSITY OF FIRE
Tempers *flared* and harsh words were exchanged. [ANGER]
It wasn't like Alex *to flare up* over something he had said about her
    looks. [ANGER]

CAUSATION IS LIGHTING AN OBJECT
Nicholas travelled to India which helped *spark* his passion for people and paintings. [PASSION-EMOTION]
By drawing attention to the political and social situation of their communities, they *sparked off* a renewed interest in Aboriginal culture. [INTEREST]

MAINTAINING MOTIVATION AT A HIGH INTENSITY IS MAINTAINING AN INTENSE FIRE
Jimmy was so enthusiastic and motivated when he was in high school. But some *spark has gone out of* him at college. [ENTHUSIASM]
Her eyes were like her mother's but lacked the *spark* of humor and the warmth. [HUMOR-JOY]

LATENT INTENSITY IS POTENTIAL OPEN FIRE
There is a *smouldering* anger in the black community throughout the country. [ANGER]
Baxter *smouldered* as he drove home for lunch. [ANGER]
Melanie Griffith seems *to smoulder* with sexuality. [SEXUALITY-LUST]

DECREASE IN INTENSITY IS A DECREASE IN THE DEGREE OF HEAT
Tempers *have cooled down* a bit and I hope we could sort things out between us. [ANGER]
You should each make your own lives, and when emotions *have cooled*, see if there's a possibility of friendship. [EMOTION]
You're angry, Wade, that's all. You ought to let yourself *cool off* for a few days. [ANGER]

LACK OF INTENSITY IS LACK OF HEAT
"Look here," I said, without *heat*, "all I did was to walk down a street and sit down." [ANGER]

As these entailments show, the main meaning focus of the metaphor is emotional intensity. Most of the entailments center around this particular aspect of the emotion concepts involved.

But the heat-fire source is not limited to the emotions, as indicated by the examples below. In other words, the scope of the metaphorical source of heat-fire extends well beyond the emotions. Consider the additional examples that follow:

They directed the full *heat* of their rhetoric against Mr. Bush. [ARGUMENT]
You need to perform well when the *heat is on*. [PRESSURE-EVENT]
Behind the next door a more *heated* discussion was taking place. [ARGUMENT]

As can be seen, the fire-heat metaphorical source domain applies to actions (argument) and events (pressure). It also applies to states of various kinds. In general, we can claim that the source domain has as its scope any intense situation (actions, events, states). The following examples arranged as metaphorical entailments amply illustrate this:

THE HIGHEST DEGREE OF INTENSITY IS THE HIGHEST DEGREE
   OF HEAT (FIRE)
His eyes *blazed* intently into mine. [LOOKING-ACTION]
The president launched his anti-drugs campaign *in a blaze* of publicity.
   [PUBLICITY-ACTION]
The career that began *in a blaze* of glory has ended in his forced
   retirement. [GLORY-STATE]
As soon as he walked in there was a *blazing* row. [ARGUMENT]

CHANGE OF INTENSITY IS A CHANGE IN HEAT
Then, in the last couple of years, the movement for democracy began *to
   heat up*. [POLITICAL MOVEMENT-ACTIVITY]
The battle for the Formula One Championship *hotted up*. [BATTLE-
   CONFLICT]
The debate *is hotting up* in Germany on the timing of elections.
   [ARGUMENT]
In a clear bid *to take the heat out of* the rebellion, he authorised an
   interest rate cut. [REBELLION-CONFLICT]
He has been advised to take a long family holiday *to take the heat off*
   the scandal. [SCANDAL-CONFLICT]
I think that the Scottish problem might *cool off*. [PROBLEM-CONFLICT]
The hope must be that the economy *has cooled* sufficiently to relieve
   inflationary pressures. [ECONOMIC ACTIVITY]

The metaphor CAUSATION IS LIGHTING can be given as:

CAUSE OF A SITUATION IS CAUSE OF HEAT (FIRE)
Many commentators believe that his resignation speech *ignited* the
   leadership battle. [CONFLICT]
Books can *ignite* the imagination in a way films can't. [IMAGINATION]
She has failed *to ignite* what could have been a lively debate.
   [ARGUMENT]
The strike was *sparked* by a demand for higher pay. [CONFLICT]
An interesting detail might *spark off* an idea. [THOUGHT]

MOTIVATION TO DO SOMETHING INTENSELY IS AN INTERNAL CAUSE
   OF HEAT (FIRE)
He said they were looking for someone with a bit of *spark* as the new
   technical director. [AGILITY IN ACTION]

CONTROLLING THE SITUATION IS CONTROLLING THE HEAT
This proved insufficient *to dampen the fires* of controversy. [ARGUMENT]

MAINTAINING INTENSITY IS MAINTAINING HEAT (OF FIRE)
The fact is that the very lack of evidence seems *to fan the flames* of
   suspicion. [SUSPICION-THOUGHT]
The president warned that this *will fuel the fires* of nationalism.
   [CONFLICT]

A SUDDEN INCREASE IN INTENSITY IS A SUDDEN INCREASE IN
   THE DEGREE OF HEAT (FIRE)
Dozens of people were injured as fighting *flared up*. [CONFLICT]

Dale stayed clear of the disease for six years until it *flared up* last
summer. [DISEASE-STATE]
I felt good but then this injury *flared up*. [INJURY-STATE]

LATENT INTENSITY IS POTENTIAL HEAT (OF FIRE)
The government was foundering on an issue that *had smoldered* for
years. [SOCIAL PROBLEM]
... the *smoldering* civil war. [WAR-CONFLICT]

INTENSITY CEASING IS THE HEAT (FIRE) GOING OUT
Some were simply *burnt out*, exhausted. [AGILITY IN ACTION]
... a *burnt-out* business executive. [AGILITY IN ACTION]

Thus, fire-metaphors have a wide scope; they apply to a variety of situations or states of affairs (actions, events, states). The main meaning focus of
this source domain appears to be the intensity of a situation. We can show
the basic constituent mappings for this metaphor as follows:

A SITUATION IS FIRE
Source		Target
the thing burning	⇒	the entity involved in the situation
the fire	⇒	the situation (action, event, state)
the heat of the fire	⇒	the intensity of the situation
the cause of the fire	⇒	the cause of the situation

These basic mappings account for the majority of the linguistic expressions above. Among them, it is "the heat of the fire ⇒ the intensity of the
situation" mapping that is central. The reason is, first, that most of the metaphorical entailments of this metaphor follow from or are based on this particular mapping (e.g., maintaining intensity, sudden increase in intensity, latent
intensity). Second, a major human concern with fire is its intensity; that is,
we ask whether we have a fire that is appropriate for the purpose at hand.
Third, the linguistic examples that dominate the various applications of this
source domain consist of metaphors that reflect intensity as a main meaning
focus. Finally, there is very clear experiential basis for this mapping. When
we engage in intense situations (actions, events, states), we produce body heat.
This is especially clear in the case of such emotion concepts as anger and love,
where many linguistic expressions capture this kind of bodily experience
associated with intense emotion.

5. The Relationship Between Simple and Complex Metaphors

This account gives rise to two distinct kinds of metaphor: **simple** and **complex**. It should be recalled that we have characterized the metaphors in which
the source concepts of building and heat-fire, respectively, participate as
COMPLEX SYSTEMS ARE BUILDINGS and A SITUATION IS HEAT (OF FIRE). But
we have also noted that given the central mappings of these metaphors, it is

reasonable to suggest that the same data can be accounted for by postulating four other metaphors: ABSTRACT CONSTRUCTION IS BUILDING, ABSTRACT STRUCTURE IS PHYSICAL STRUCTURE, and ABSTRACT STABILITY IS PHYSICAL STRENGTH (OF A BUILDING TO STAND) for complex systems, as well as IN-TENSITY (OF A SITUATION) IS HEAT (OF FIRE) for various states of affairs. These submetaphors come from generalized central mappings. This idea is obviously related to what was called "primary metaphor" in the previous chapter.

Abstract complex systems include theories, relationships, society, social groups, economic and political systems, life, and others. All of these can be individually conceived as buildings. The resulting metaphors THEORIES ARE BUILDINGS, SOCIETY IS A BUILDING, ECONOMIC SYSTEMS ARE BUILDINGS, RELATIONSHIPS ARE BUILDINGS, LIFE IS A BUILDING, etc. are complex meta-phors, in that they are constituted by the corresponding submetaphors AB-STRACT CREATION IS PHYSICAL BUILDING, ABSTRACT STRUCTURE IS PHYSI-CAL STRUCTURE, and ABSTRACT STABILITY IS PHYSICAL STRENGTH. The submetaphors will be said to be **simple,** in that they are the ones that make up **complex** metaphors, and they characterize an entire range of specific-level target concepts. One such case is the range of target concepts under the overarching concept of COMPLEX SYSTEMS.

Similarly, a large number of target concepts are characterized by the source concept of (heat of) fire. Various specific kinds of actions, events, and states are understood as fire. Correspondingly, there is a simple submetaphor IN-TENSITY IS HEAT (OF FIRE). This simple metaphor is a mapping in such com-plex metaphors as ANGER IS FIRE, LOVE IS FIRE, CONFLICT IS FIRE, or ARGU-MENT IS FIRE. In all of these, it is a central mapping that reflects the main meaning focus of the fire metaphors. The relationship between complex and simple metaphors can be shown in Figure 9.2.

In sum, simple metaphors constitute mappings in complex ones. The re-verse of this does not hold; complex metaphors like THEORIES ARE BUILD-INGS or ANGER IS FIRE do not constitute mappings in simple ones like AB-STRACT STABILITY IS PHYSICAL STRENGTH or INTENSITY IS HEAT. It is the simple submetaphors (or mappings) that provide the major theme of com-

complex metaphor:

e.g., ANGER IS FIRE

corresponding simple metaphor:

INTENSITY IS HEAT (OF FIRE)

from the mapping "the heat (of fire) → the intensity of the situation"

Figure 9.2. The relationship between complex and simple metaphors.

plex metaphors by means of the process of mapping the meaning focus of the source onto the target. Thus, for example, the various complex fire-metaphors, like ANGER IS FIRE, LOVE IS FIRE, ENTHUSIASM IS FIRE, CONFLICT IS FIRE will all be characterized by the mapping "the heat of fire ⇒ the intensity of a state or event." This mapping can be restated as a simple metaphor: THE INTENSITY (OF A SITUATION) IS THE INTENSITY OF HEAT. The complex metaphors contain as a mapping this simple metaphor.

SUMMARY

We can approach the study of conceptual metaphor in two additional ways. We can ask: (1) which source domains apply to a particular target and (2) which target domains does a particular source apply to? This chapter addressed the second issue.

Three theoretical notions were suggested: the scope of metaphor, main meaning focus, and central mapping. The **scope of metaphor** is the range of target concepts to which a given source domain applies. The **main meaning focus** of a metaphor is the culturally agreed-on conceptual material associated with the source that it conventionally imparts to its targets. A **central mapping** is one from which other mappings derive and which maps the main meaning focus of the source onto the target.

In addition to distinguishing metaphors according to conventionality, function, nature, and level of generality, we can distinguish them on the basis of their *complexity*. There are simple and complex metaphors. **Simple (or primary) metaphors** function as mappings within **complex metaphors**.

FURTHER READING

The analysis of the ARGUMENT (THEORY) IS A BUILDING metaphor is largely based on Joe Grady's (1997) paper on this metaphor. The issue of the scope of metaphor, together with that of the main meaning focus, is introduced by Kövecses (1995c) in relation to the discussion of the American conception of friendship. Kövecses (2000b) relates the notion of main meaning focus to Langacker's (1987) idea of "central knowledge." The distinction between simple and complex metaphors parallels, but is not equal to, Grady's distinction between primary or primitive and complex or compound metaphors (Grady, 1997; Grady, Taub, and Morgan, 1996).

EXERCISES

1. SPORT is a major source concept that applies to several target domains. Give the conceptual metaphors that have SPORT as their source domain in the following examples.

   (a) He tried to convince me but his argument was completely *off base*.
   (b) We went on a long holiday to get out of the *rat race* for a while.

(c) American businessmen ask for *a level playing field* when they compete with foreign companies.

(d) Politicians often employ *hardball tactics*.

(e) Life is not a *spectator sport*.

(f) America is not a party to the negotiations, yet it is *a key player*.

(g) I took her out to dinner last night but we didn't even *get to first base*.

(h) The election campaign was *a close race* because the presidential candidates had to *play it safe* for a long time to gain the support of the public.

2. Consider the following examples from the *Cobuild Metaphor Dictionary*. There is a single source concept, MACHINE, which can characterize several distinct target domains. Figure out what the conceptual metaphors are. Under which larger, overarching metaphor can the metaphors you have found be grouped?

(a) They affirmed their faith in the League of Nations and the *machinery* of international law.

(b) The *machinery* of democracy could be created quickly but its spirit was just as important.

(c) The National Party is edging toward agreement on the timing and *mechanics* of an election.

(d) The project might be kept *ticking over* indefinitely.

(e) The media are a commercial activity that *oils the wheels* of the economy.

(f) The wheels of justice *grind* slowly.

(g) For decades it was these people who *kept the wheels* of the British economy *turning*.

(h) As *cogs* in the Soviet *military machine*, the three countries' armies used to sit near their western borders.

3. We saw in this chapter that a single source concept can characterize many distinct target domains. Now it is your task (after reading the metaphorical linguistic examples below) to determine (a) the source concept that each of the examples share and (b) the various target domains.

(1) We couldn't get a room in any of the *top* hotels.

(2) She was feeling really *high*.

(3) He is young and *upwardly* mobile.

(4) It was an *uplifting* experience.

(5) Your *highness* is very moody today.

(6) After three months of exercise he was in *top* form.

(7) With this promotion she became a *top* dog.

(8) For the first time in months, my spirits *soared*.

(9) He is one of the world's *top* journalists.

(10) Only *top* politicians could attend this *top* secret meeting.

(11) This new invention is the *high* noon of his career.

(12) The *upper* class spend their time on the Riviera during high season.

(13) Sylvie's speech was the *highlight* of the conference.

4. Collect as many metaphorical expressions from a dictionary with the verb *fall* as you can, such as *fall in love*, *fall prey to*, and so on. (In this exercise, disregard cases of *falling* when it refers to some kind of decrease, as in *falling prices*.)

   (a) In all these cases we have physical falling as a source domain. Find the target domains of *falling*.

   (b) Given these target domains, try to see how wide the application of this source domain is, that is, try to identify the scope, and with this, the main meaning focus of *falling* as a source domain.

10

Metaphor
Systems

In the preceding chapters, we have seen overwhelming evidence for the view
that metaphorical linguistic expressions cluster together to form systems
that we called conceptual metaphors. What remains to be seen now is whether
the conceptual metaphors themselves form even larger systems. In other words,
in this chapter I will ask whether the conceptual metaphors are isolated from
each other, or whether they fit together to make up larger systematic groupings—that is, metaphor systems—that incorporate individual conceptual
metaphors.

In order to get clear about this issue, let us take the same list of English
metaphorical expressions from the *Cobuild Metaphor Dictionary* that we
already saw in the Preface:

(1) He was an *animal* on Saturday afternoon and is a disgrace to
British football.
(2) There is no painless way to get inflation down. We now have an
excellent *foundation on which to build*.
(3) Politicians are being blamed for the *ills* of society.
(4) The *machinery* of democracy could be *created* quickly but its spirit
was just as important.
(5) Government grants have enabled a number of the top names in
British sport *to build* a successful career.
(6) . . . a local *branch* of this organization.
(7) Few of them have the qualifications . . . *to put an ailing* company
back on its feet.
(8) The Service will continue *to stagger from* crisis *to* crisis.
(9) Her career was *in ruins*.
(10) How could any man ever understand the *workings* of a woman's
mind?
(11) Scientists *have taken a big step* in understanding Alzheimer's
disease.
(12) They selectively *pruned* the workforce.

(13) ... *cultivating* business relationships that can lead to major accounts.

(14) The coffee was perfect and by the time I was halfway through my first cup my brain *was ticking over much more briskly.*

(15) Let's hope he can *keep* the team *on the road to* success.

(16) Everyone says what a happy, *sunny* girl she was.

(17) It's going to be a *bitch* to replace him.

(18) The province is quite close to *sliding into* civil war.

(19) They remembered her as she'd been *in the flower* of their friendship.

(20) Vincent met his father's *icy* stare evenly.

(21) With its economy *in ruins*, it can't afford to involve itself in military action.

(22) ... French *sex kitten* Brigitte Bardot.

These metaphorical linguistic expressions suggest the existence of a number of conceptual metaphors in English:

THE MIND IS A MACHINE: (10) How could any man ever understand the *workings* of a woman's mind? (14) The coffee was perfect and by the time I was halfway through my first cup my brain *was ticking over much more briskly.*

ECONOMIC SYSTEMS ARE BUILDINGS: (21) With its economy *in ruins*, it can't afford to involve itself in military action. (2) There is no painless way to get inflation down. We now have an excellent *foundation on which to build.*

CAREERS ARE BUILDINGS: (9) Her career was *in ruins.* (5) Government grants have enabled a number of the top names in British sport *to build* a successful career.

SOCIAL ORGANIZATIONS (COMPANIES) ARE PLANTS: (6) ... a local *branch* of this organization. (12) They selectively *pruned* the workforce.

RELATIONSHIPS ARE PLANTS: (13) ... *cultivating* business relationships that can lead to major accounts. (19) They remembered her as she'd been *in the flower* of their friendship.

VIOLENT HUMAN BEHAVIOR IS ANIMAL BEHAVIOR: (1) He was an *animal* on Saturday afternoon and is a disgrace to British football.

SOCIETY IS A PERSON: (3) Politicians are being blamed for the *ills* of society.

SOCIETY IS A MACHINE: (4) The *machinery* of democracy could be *created* quickly but its spirit was just as important.

A COMPANY IS A PERSON: (7) Few ... have the qualifications *to put an ailing* company *back on its feet.*

PROGRESS IS MOTION FORWARD: (8) The Service will continue to *stagger from* crisis *to* crisis.

ACTION IS SELF-PROPELLED MOTION: (11) Scientists *have taken a big step* in understanding Alzheimer's disease.

MEANS ARE PATHS: (15) Let's hope he can *keep* the team *on the road to* success.

CHEERFUL IS SUNNY: (16) Everyone says what a happy, *sunny* girl she was.

DIFFICULT-TO-HANDLE THINGS ARE DOGS: (17) It's going to be a *bitch*
to replace him.

CHANGES ARE MOVEMENTS: (18) The province is quite close to *sliding
into* civil war.

UNFRIENDLY IS ICY: (20) Vincent met his father's *icy* stare evenly.

SEXUALLY ATTRACTIVE WOMEN ARE KITTENS: (22) . . . French *sex kitten*
Brigitte Bardot.

What is the relationship among these conceptual metaphors? Is it the case
that in order to account for the metaphorical linguistic expressions highlighted
above and many others we need to postulate several hundred (or maybe even
thousand) such conceptual metaphors that are independent of each other?
Or, perhaps, do the conceptual metaphors "hang together" in a coherent way
and form several (sub)systems in the conceptual system of speakers of English? It is this latter possibility that will be argued for below. I will suggest
that underlying these conceptual metaphors there are two large metaphor
systems. The two systems account for all the metaphorical expressions and
conceptual metaphors noted above and possibly hundreds of others.

How can we begin to see what the metaphorical system of English (or other
languages) looks like? So far, two large metaphor systems have been suggested:
The Great Chain of Being metaphor and the Event Structure metaphor. The
Great Chain metaphor system accounts for how objects, or things, in the world
are conceptualized metaphorically, while the Event Structure metaphor system
describes how events (and events as changes of states) are metaphorically understood. (I will present the two systems in some detail below in this chapter.)

The two systems (the Great Chain and Event Structure metaphors) can be
brought into correspondence with some other findings in cognitive linguistics. It has been suggested that the universal grammatical categories of noun
and verb reflect a structuring of the world into two kinds of basic conceptual
entities: things and relations. As cognitive grammarians define these terms,
conceptual entities denote any kind of mental unit; things are conceptual
entities that have stability in space and over time (such as house and tree);
and relations are conceptual links between two or more entities (such as bring,
laugh, into, because). See Figure 10.1.

In the clear cases at least, things appear in language (or, we can say, they
are linguistically coded) as nouns, while relations are coded as verbs, adjec-

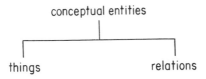

conceptual entities

things   relations

Figure 10.1. Two kinds of conceptual entities.

tives, prepositions, or conjunctions. Now we can observe an obvious correspondence between objects as described in the Great Chain metaphor and things
as conceptual entities in cognitive grammar, on the one hand, and between
events (and changes of states) described by the Event Structure metaphor and
relations as defined in cognitive grammar, on the other. In other words, the
Great Chain metaphor captures the metaphorical conceptualization of "things"
and the Event Structure metaphor that of "relations," including events and
changes of states. Setting up these parallels between the classification of conceptual entities and the two metaphor systems is not meant to imply that the
metaphorical conceptualization of *all* things and *all* relations is exhaustively
captured by the two metaphor systems. The claim is that the metaphorical
conceptualization of a large portion of what we view as things and what we
view as events can be successfully accounted for with the help of these systems.
In the following sections, I introduce the two systems in some detail.

1. The Great Chain of Being Metaphor

To begin, we may note that some of the metaphorical expressions on our list
above have to do with animals, that is, some of the metaphors employ source
domains that have to do with the concept of ANIMAL. These are the following:

> VIOLENT HUMAN BEHAVIOR IS ANIMAL BEHAVIOR: He was an *animal*
> on Saturday afternoon and is a disgrace to British football.
> DIFFICULT-TO-HANDLE THINGS ARE DOGS: It's going to be a *bitch* to
> replace him.
> SEXUALLY ATTRACTIVE WOMEN ARE KITTENS: . . . French *sex kitten*
> Brigitte Bardot.

We can arrive at larger generalizations if we look at more examples for
these metaphors. Much of human behavior seems to be metaphorically understood in terms of ANIMAL behavior, as is suggested by the examples below:

> HUMAN BEHAVIOR IS ANIMAL BEHAVIOR
> She *bitched* about Dan but I knew she was devoted to him.
> His mother was *catty* and loud.
> This is a research site. Not the best place for a couple of boys to be
> *horsing around.*
> Good friends *don't rat on* each other.
> The fact that the U.S. is saying these things makes it easier for the
> British Government *to weasel out.*
> They had been eating standing up, *wolfing* the cold food from dirty tin
> plates.
> The best British music isn't necessarily made with huge budgets or by
> *aping* the latest trends from across the Atlantic.
> He is sure as hell *going to go ape* that you didn't see Rocky yesterday.
> Not a day goes by without him getting in and *monkeying* with
> something.

Obviously, animals do not "complain," as suggested by *bitch*; they are not "impertinent," as suggested by *catty*; and they do not "behave foolishly," as suggested by *horse around*. How did these animal-related words acquire, then, their metaphorical meanings? The only way these meanings can have emerged is that humans attributed human characteristics to animals and then reapplied these characteristics to humans. That is, animals were personified first, and then the "human-based animal characteristics" were used to understand human behavior.

But it is not only human behavior that is metaphorically understood in terms of animal behavior; people themselves are also often described as animals of some kind. Thus, we have the conceptual metaphor PEOPLE ARE ANIMALS:

PEOPLE ARE ANIMALS
That man was a *brute*, he spent the little he earned on drink.
You are putting the men down and they don't like it, they think you are
    being a *bitch*.
. . . a bunch of *fat cats* with fast cars and too many cigars.
All I could hear was the producer screaming "What the hell does the
    silly *cow* think she is doing?"
"I've had my eye on her. Stupid *cow*, she thinks I don't know what goes
    on."
He is a complete *pig* to the women in his life.
Look at the things that have been done by these *swine*.
"Tell me what you did with the money, you *swine*."
The *vermin* are the people who rob old women in the street and break
    into houses.

The main meaning focus of the HUMAN BEHAVIOR IS ANIMAL BEHAVIOR and PEOPLE ARE ANIMALS metaphors seems to be 'objectionability' or 'undesirability.' This suggests that we can "rewrite" the metaphors as: OBJECTIONABLE BEHAVIOR IS ANIMAL BEHAVIOR and OBJECTIONABLE PEOPLE ARE ANIMALS. The notion of 'objectionability,' or 'undesirability,' as the main meaning focus of many animal metaphors is reinforced by the third metaphor below: DIFFICULT-TO-HANDLE THINGS ARE DOGS. It seems that most animal-related metaphors capture the negative characteristics of human beings. But some of them don't, as indicated by the metaphor SEXUALLY ATTRACTIVE WOMEN ARE KITTENS. We can generalize this observation by stating that we have in our conceptual system the highly general metaphor HUMAN IS ANIMAL which consists of at least the following conceptual metaphors:

HUMAN IS ANIMAL
OBJECTIONABLE HUMAN BEHAVIOR IS ANIMAL BEHAVIOR
OBJECTIONABLE PEOPLE ARE ANIMALS
DIFFICULT-TO-HANDLE THINGS ARE DOGS
SEXUALLY ATTRACTIVE WOMEN ARE KITTENS

Thus, we have a grouping of conceptual metaphors that fit together in that they all have human beings as their target and animals as their source domain. This is some type of a system but still not the complete system that underlies these examples.

Next consider two additional metaphors from our list:

> CHEERFUL IS SUNNY (HAPPY IS LIGHT): Everyone says what a happy, *sunny* girl she was.
> UNFRIENDLY IS ICY (AFFECTION IS WARMTH; LACK OF AFFECTION IS COLD): Vincent met his father's *icy* stare evenly.

Again, we can generalize and say that these conceptual metaphors point to a higher-level metaphor that we can state as HUMAN PROPERTIES ARE THE PROPERTIES OF INANIMATE THINGS. In addition to the examples given above, such other properties of (inanimate) objects as hard-soft, warm-cold, sharp-dull, big-small, tender-tough, clear-unclear, half-whole, etc. are utilized for the comprehension of human beings.

Given these generalizations, we can observe a more interesting kind of system of metaphors in English. As we just saw, humans are comprehended as animals and (inanimate) objects. This gives us what is called *The Great Chain of Being* metaphor, which is described in some detail in the cognitive literature by Lakoff and Turner. At the heart of the Great Chain metaphor is a certain folk theory of how "things" are related to each other in the world. This hierarchy of concepts is called the Great Chain of Being. What Lakoff and Turner call the "basic Great Chain" (which is a part of what they call the "extended Great Chain") looks like this:

> *THE GREAT CHAIN OF BEING*
> HUMANS: Higher-order attributes and behavior (e.g., thought, character)
> ANIMALS: Instinctual attributes and behavior
> PLANTS: Biological attributes and behavior
> COMPLEX OBJECTS: Structural attributes and functional behavior
> NATURAL PHYSICAL THINGS: Natural physical attributes and natural physical behavior

This folk theory of the relationship of things in the world, in the Jewish-Christian tradition, goes back to the Bible. But the folk theory can be found in many cultures and it may well be universal. The Great Chain of Being is not a metaphor yet; it is simply a hierarchy of things and corresponding concepts that is structured from the top to the bottom. The chain is defined by typical attributes and behavior. For example, humans are defined by rational thought, animals by instinct, plants by certain biological properties, and so on.

This system becomes a metaphorical system when a particular level of the chain (human, animal, etc.) is used to understand another level. This process can go in two directions (at least in the case of the basic Great Chain). It can go from a lower source to a higher target or from a higher source to a lower target. For example, as we saw above, humans can be understood metaphorically as animals and inanimate things. In this case, conceptualization proceeds from a lower source to a higher target in the basic Great Chain. More generally, animate beings are commonly comprehended in terms of inanimate things. The other direction of conceptualization goes from a higher source to a lower target. An example of this would be the case where humans are used to conceptualize complex physical objects, such as personifying a car.

The Great Chain metaphor explains why and how a number of seemingly unrelated conceptual metaphors fit together in a coherent fashion. Considering the large number of metaphorical expressions and conceptual metaphors that this metaphor system can account for in a natural way, we can regard it as a huge and important complex both in the mind of speakers of English and the description of English metaphors.

2. The Complex Systems Metaphor

But there are additional conceptual metaphors in the list with which we started the chapter and that can be accounted for as being a part of either the Great Chain or the Event Structure metaphor. The following conceptual metaphors from our list form a part of the Great Chain metaphor:

THE MIND IS A MACHINE
ECONOMIC SYSTEMS ARE BUILDINGS
CAREERS ARE BUILDINGS
SOCIAL ORGANIZATIONS (COMPANIES) ARE PLANTS
RELATIONSHIPS ARE PLANTS
SOCIETY IS A PERSON
SOCIETY IS A MACHINE
A COMPANY IS A PERSON

This seemingly heterogeneous set of target domains can be placed under the concept of *abstract complex systems*, a metaphor subsystem that we began to investigate in the previous two chapters. The mind, economic systems, careers, social organizations, relationships, society, and a company are all target domains that fit into the concept of (ABSTRACT) COMPLEX SYSTEMS. The targets referred to by this term are characterizable as typically abstract complex configurations of entities, where the nature and relationships of the entities vary from case to case. For example, political systems can be viewed as an abstract configuration of such entities as the people who participate in the political process, power, government, parties, ideologies, etc. that all interact with each other in complex ways. The other "systems" could be characterized in a similar way. Thus, abstract complex systems include those shown in Figure 10.2.

The major properties of these complex systems include the function, stability, development, and condition of the system. In other words, what we are most interested in concerning these systems are primarily four issues: (1) Do they function effectively?; (2) Are they long-lasting and stable?; (3) Do they develop as they should?; and (4) Are they in an appropriate condition?

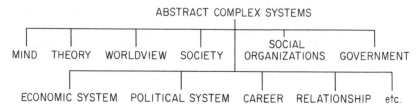

Figure 10.2. Abstract complex systems.

These four properties and issues come to the fore in the language we use about complex systems. If we look at the metaphorical linguistic expressions that reveal the above conceptual metaphors, we find that they address these issues. The properties of function, stability, development, and condition of abstract complex systems are primarily featured by four source domains: MACHINE, BUILDING, PLANT, and HUMAN BODY, respectively. The claim is not that these source domains focus *exclusively* on these aspects of abstract complex systems, but that these are their dominant foci. (I will discuss the details in the remainder of this section.) This claim yields the following generalized picture:

Target Domain	*Source Domains*
ABSTRACT COMPLEX SYSTEMS	MACHINE
	BUILDING
	PLANT
	HUMAN BODY

As will be seen below, these metaphors characterize and account for a huge portion of the language that we use about abstract complex systems. They all deal with different aspects of complex systems, such as function, stability, development, and condition.

But now let us ask in what sense can we claim that the conceptual metaphors in the list at the beginning of this section (and in a generalized form above) form a part of the Great Chain of Being metaphor? The short answer that I suggest is that abstract complex systems are part of the Great Chain and that machines (as complex objects), buildings (as complex objects), plants, and humans are also part of it, as we saw in the previous section. The question that remains to be answered is where abstract complex systems themselves are located in the Great Chain. To see this, we have to go beyond the basic Great Chain and consider what Lakoff and Turner call the "extended Great Chain," which looks like this:

GOD (at least in the Jewish-Christian tradition)
COSMOS/UNIVERSE
SOCIETY
HUMANS
ANIMALS
etc.

As we have seen above, society is a part of abstract complex systems. As a matter of fact, I want to suggest that the level that is above humans in the Great Chain is what I have been calling "abstract complex systems," and that it includes society as one of its categories. It should be noticed that all the cases of abstract complex systems involve human beings and their ideas, as well as a variety of other abstract and concrete entities and particular relationships among them.

Let us now look at the four major source domains that structure complex systems.

2.1. An Abstract Complex System Is the Human Body

Let us begin with those conceptual metaphors that have the concept of person as their source domain. As can be seen in our list above, they include such conceptual metaphors as SOCIETY IS A PERSON and A COMPANY IS A PERSON. But the range of target domains that the source domain of person takes is much wider than these two cases. As indicated by the evidence in *Cobuild's Metaphor Dictionary*, the scope of the metaphor includes, in addition, such target concepts as economic systems, industrial systems, worldviews (and sets of ideas in general), political systems, any kind of social organization, relationships, and, we can suggest, several others that are not mentioned in the Cobuild collection.

We can say, then, that abstract complex systems are conceptualized metaphorically as persons. But, as the examples below suggest, it is not really the entire person that serves as the source domain of this metaphor but only the body of the person. Therefore, if we slightly modify the conceptual metaphor, we get the more precise version: AN ABSTRACT COMPLEX SYSTEM IS THE HUMAN BODY. (To give a sense of the variety of possible target domains for this metaphor, after each example I indicate in small capital letters the specific target concept that is involved.)

> AN ABSTRACT COMPLEX SYSTEM IS THE HUMAN BODY
> . . . the world governing *body* in athletics [SOCIAL ORGANIZATION]
> Politicians are being blamed for all the *ills* of society. [SOCIETY]
> Few of them have the qualifications or experience *to put an ailing* company *back on its feet.* [COMPANY]
> The tour is the first visit to the country by a Jewish *head* of state. [POLITICAL SYSTEM]
> Observers here believe that the greatest difficulty before him is the *ailing* economy of the country. [ECONOMY]
> The *crippling disease* of state involvement in industry through nationalisation has not been *cured.* [INDUSTRY]
> . . . a three-star hotel in the *heart* of the Latin quarter. [SOCIAL ORGANIZATION]
> I have yet to meet a single American who automatically thinks any foreign product must be better than his own. The *disease* seems to be uniquely British. [WORLDVIEW]

I think it's a *symptom* of the rebellion and dissatisfaction of the young-
sters in our society who are growing up. [WORLDVIEW]
... at the very *heart* of our culture [CULTURAL SYSTEM]
The debate around the law is a *symptom* of a bigger problem. [A SET OF
PROBLEMS]
This behavior was *symptomatic* of a generally uncaring attitude towards
his wife. [RELATIONSHIP]
To some critics, the administration's troubles are *symptomatic* of
something deeper. [GOVERNMENT]
If we look at history, what has happened at NATO is not unusual; I call
it the rearview mirror *syndrome*. [SOCIAL ORGANIZATION]
Women are the church's *backbone* but rarely hold any positions of
leadership. [SOCIAL ORGANIZATION]

Given that this metaphor has abstract complex systems as its most natural scope, it seems that the main meaning focus of the metaphor is twofold:
(1) the appropriateness of the condition and (2) the structure of an abstract
system. This observation yields the simple or primary metaphors: for (1), AN
APPROPRIATE CONDITION IS A HEALTHY CONDITION and INAPPROPRIATE
CONDITIONS (DIFFICULTIES, PROBLEMS) ARE ILLNESSES and for (2), THE
STRUCTURE OF AN ABSTRACT COMPLEX SYSTEM IS THE PHYSICAL STRUC-
TURE OF THE HUMAN BODY. The simple, or primary, metaphors utilize these
particular aspects of the human body.

2.2. Abstract Complex Systems Are Buildings

But, as we saw above, the human body is not the only source domain in the
conceptualization of abstract complex systems. Another one is the concept
of building (that we already dealt with in the previous chapter). We can observe that many of the same abstract target domains that take the human body
also take the domain of buildings as their source. The following examples
suggest that there is a great deal of overlap between the targets of the human
body as a source and those of buildings as a source. This list shows that the
building metaphor also applies to complex systems as its target.

ABSTRACT COMPLEX SYSTEMS ARE BUILDINGS
Since then the two have *built a solid* relationship.
Government grants have enabled a number of the top names in British
sport *to build* a successful career.
Ten years ago, he and a partner set up on their own and *built up* a
successful fashion company.
The self-confidence that she *had built up* so painfully was still *paper-
thin*; beneath it hid despair and cold anger.
The truth is that standard economic models *constructed* on the evidence
of past experience are of little use.
Increasingly, scientific knowledge *is constructed* by small numbers of
specialized workers.
In his toughest speech yet on the economy, Mr. Major *demolished* his
critics.

McCarthy *demolishes* the romantic myth of the Wild West.
. . . citizens fleeing their country's economic *ruins*.
Her career was *in ruins*.
With its economy *in ruins*, it can't afford to involve itself in military
    action.
Now another young woman's life is *in ruins* after an appalling attack.
There is no painless way to get inflation down. We now have an
    excellent *foundation on which to build*.
You can help *lay the foundations* for a good relationship between your
    children by preparing your older child in advance for the new baby.
. . . the advance that *laid the foundations* for modern science.
Our view, he said, is that these claims are entirely *without foundation*.
As he candidly admitted, French fears were not *without foundation*.
He's about *to rock the foundations* of the literary establishment with his
    novel.
My faith was *rocked to its foundations*.

The main theme, or meaning focus, of the metaphor seems to be the creation of a well-structured and stable or lasting complex system. As we already
saw in chapter 9, this theme arises from the fact that most of the examples
have to do with these three interrelated aspects of buildings: construction (e.g.,
build, construct), structure (e.g., *foundation, lay the foundation, without
foundation, the foundation on which to build*), and strength (e.g., *solid, paper-
thin, in ruins*). We can summarize this observation in the form of the following mapping or metaphor: CREATING A WELL-STRUCTURED AND LASTING
ABSTRACT COMPLEX SYSTEM IS MAKING A WELL-STRUCTURED, STRONG
BUILDING, which consist of several simple metaphors, such as CREATING AN
ABSTRACT COMPLEX SYSTEM IS BUILDING, THE STRUCTURE OF AN ABSTRACT
SYSTEM IS THE PHYSICAL STRUCTURE OF A BUILDING, and A LASTING AB-
STRACT SYSTEM IS A STRONG BUILDING.

2.3. Abstract Complex Systems Are Machines

A third member of the complex systems metaphor group appears to be COM-
PLEX SYSTEMS ARE MACHINES. In this case, the target of complex systems
includes such abstract concepts as the legal system, the government, economic
systems, political parties, political systems, the family, the human mind, etc.
That is, there is again a great deal of overlap between this set of target concepts and those that we saw in the case of the body and building metaphors.
To see more clearly the main meaning focus of the metaphor, below I spell
out the metaphorical entailments of the concept of machine as a source in
relation to abstract complex systems as a target. Let us now look at some
examples again.

ABSTRACT COMPLEX SYSTEMS ARE MACHINES
The authorities now seem to be finally *setting in motion* the legal
    machinery to try and sentence those it regards as responsible for a
    counter-revolutionary rebellion.

The *machinery* of democracy could be *created* quickly but its spirit was just as important.

The National Party is edging toward agreement on the timing and *mechanics* of an election.

... the *mechanics* of running a family and home changed fundamentally.

The congress approved some modest changes, intended to make the party more democratic in its *workings*.

... the *workings* of the free market.

How could any man ever understand the *workings* of a woman's mind?

This metaphor has a number of metaphorical entailments:

THE REGULARITY OF THE OPERATION OF A COMPLEX SYSTEM IS
REGULARITY OF THE WORKINGS OF A MACHINE (CLOCKWORK)
He soon had the household *running like clockwork.*

Each day a howling wind springs up from the south with almost *clockwork* regularity.

INEFFECTIVE OR LESS THAN FULL OPERATION IS THE INEFFECTIVE OR
SLOW WORKING OF A MACHINE
The project might be kept *ticking over* indefinitely.

The coffee was perfect and by the time I was halfway through my first cup my brain *was ticking over much more briskly.*

The *wheels* of justice *grind slowly*, and it wasn't until eight years later that 13 people were convicted.

Mr. Major *has set the wheels in motion.* Now let's get on with it.

It's time everyone else started believing it and *put the wheels* of change *in motion.*

NOT ALLOWING THE SYSTEM TO STOP IS NOT LETTING THE
MACHINE STOP
If, however, it turns out that a lot more money is going to be needed *to keep the wheels turning* in eastern Germany, then another round of interest rate rise is expected.

... practical solutions which *would keep* the business *wheels turning.*

For decades it was these people who *kept the wheels* of the British economy *turning.*

TO MAINTAIN (THE EFFICIENT OPERATION OF) A COMPLEX SYSTEM IS
TO MAINTAIN (THE EFFICIENT WORKING OF) A MACHINE
The media are important to a healthy, *well-functioning* economy; they are a commercial activity that *oils the wheels* of the economy.

... keeping the wheels of business oiled.

Money-supply growth is currently inadequate to *grease the wheels* of recovery.

They *greased the wheels* of the consumer boom by allowing us to buy what we want, when we want.

UNKNOWN FACTORS IN THE OPERATION OF A SYSTEM ARE WHEELS
WITHIN WHEELS IN A MACHINE
There are *wheels within wheels.* Behind the actor's apparent freedom as a director or a producer may lie the interest of the studio subsidising the film.

UNIMPORTANT PARTS OF THE SYSTEM ARE SMALL COGS IN
   THE MACHINE

As *cogs* in the Soviet military *machine*, the three countries' armies used
   to sit mainly near their western borders.

They were *small*, totally insignificant *cogs in the great wheel* of the war.

. . . the great advertising *machine* in which they were *tiny cogs*.

As the bulk of the examples and the metaphorical entailments of the metaphor suggest, the key theme here is the functioning, or the operation, of an
abstract complex system. In several examples and entailments, we find a
concern not only with operation but also with *effective* operation. We can
capture this notion in the form of the simple metaphor: ABSTRACT FUNCTION-
ING IS PHYSICAL FUNCTIONING, or, in a more detailed way, THE (EFFECTIVE)
FUNCTIONING OR OPERATION OF A COMPLEX SYSTEM IS THE (EFFECTIVE)
FUNCTIONING OR WORKING OF A MACHINE.

Why should we use the source domain of machines to conceptualize the
functioning of abstract complex systems? The answer that lends itself most
naturally is that we possess fairly good and coherent (folk) knowledge about
the functioning of old-fashioned machines, such as machines with cogwheels,
that date back to the industrial revolution. It is noteworthy that other, more
recent machines, such as computers, do not appear to be used for the same
purpose. Possibly, knowledge concerning their functioning has not yet become conventionalized enough for a given linguistic community to use these
more sophisticated machines for understanding the functioning of abstract
complex systems. However, it is precisely the computer that serves as the
source domain to understand the functioning of the human mind (one abstract complex system) for some experts.

2.4. Abstract Complex Systems Are Plants

Finally, let us recall the metaphor discussed in chapter 8: ABSTRACT COMPLEX
SYSTEMS ARE PLANTS. As we saw there, the plant metaphor also involves such
more specific target concepts as organizations, economic and political systems,
relationships, our view of the future, as well as arguments and problems as
complex sets of ideas. Again, it is this large-scale overlap that entitles us to claim
that the major (though not the exclusive) focus of the plant metaphor is the
target concept of abstract complex systems. The key theme of the metaphor,
as we saw, is the development of an abstract complex system, which is conceptualized as the natural growth of a plant. This gives us the simple metaphor
ABSTRACT DEVELOPMENT OR PROGRESS IS NATURAL PHYSICAL GROWTH.

In sum, abstract complex systems are largely understood in terms of the
four metaphors we have discussed in this section:

AN ABSTRACT COMPLEX SYSTEM IS THE HUMAN BODY
AN ABSTRACT COMPLEX SYSTEM IS A BUILDING
AN ABSTRACT COMPLEX SYSTEM IS A MACHINE
AN ABSTRACT COMPLEX SYSTEM IS A PLANT

Together, the four metaphors form a subsystem of the (Extended) Great Chain metaphor, in which the target domain of abstract complex systems is high in the hierarchy of "things," while the source domains of human body, building, machine, and plant are all lower than the target.

The four conceptual metaphors that make up this subsystem are what have been called "complex metaphors." The "simple metaphors" on which the complex ones above are based are as follows:

> AN APPROPRIATE CONDITION IS A HEALTHY CONDITION; INAPPROPRI-
> ATE CONDITIONS ARE ILLNESSES; THE STRUCTURE OF AN ABSTRACT
> COMPLEX SYSTEM IS THE PHYSICAL STRUCTURE OF THE HUMAN
> BODY
> CREATING AN ABSTRACT COMPLEX SYSTEM IS BUILDING; THE STRUC-
> TURE OF AN ABSTRACT COMPLEX SYSTEM IS THE PHYSICAL STRUC-
> TURE OF A BUILDING; A LASTING ABSTRACT COMPLEX SYSTEM IS A
> STRONG BUILDING
> THE FUNCTIONING OF AN ABSTRACT COMPLEX SYSTEM IS THE WORK-
> ING OF A MACHINE
> ABSTRACT DEVELOPMENT IS NATURAL PHYSICAL GROWTH

These simple metaphors reveal the major human concerns that we have in connection with abstract complex systems, such as whether the systems are in an appropriate condition, whether they are well-structured and long-lasting, whether they function effectively, and whether they develop according to the standards we set for them. Furthermore, this analysis shows that the same simple metaphors (e.g., THE STRUCTURE OF AN ABSTRACT COM-PLEX SYSTEM IS THE PHYSICAL STRUCTURE OF THE HUMAN BODY) can participate in the constitution of several complex ones (e.g., AN ABSTRACT COM-PLEX SYSTEM IS THE HUMAN BODY and AN ABSTRACT COMPLEX SYSTEM IS A BUILDING).

3. The Event Structure Metaphor

The remaining conceptual metaphors that we still have to account for on our initial list in the chapter include the following:

> PROGRESS IS MOTION FORWARD: The Service will continue *to stagger from* crisis *to* crisis.
> ACTION IS SELF-PROPELLED MOTION: Scientists *have taken a big step* in understanding Alzheimer's disease.
> MEANS ARE PATHS: Let's hope he can *keep* the team *on the road to* success.
> CHANGES ARE MOVEMENTS: The province is quite close to *sliding into* civil war.

These conceptual metaphors seem to be unrelated at first glance, but they all have to do with events. They are conceptualizations of the structure of events, rather than conceptualizations of "things," as was the case with the Great Chain metaphor discussed in the previous sections.

George Lakoff and his colleagues describe a pervasive system of metaphors that involves all of these mappings, as well as others, called the "Event Structure Metaphor." The complete system of mappings as discussed by Lakoff is presented below (in a somewhat simplified form). (Most of the linguistic examples used for illustration come from Lakoff's work.)

STATES ARE LOCATIONS: They are *in* love.
CHANGES ARE MOVEMENTS: He *went* crazy.
CAUSES ARE FORCES: The hit *sent* the crowd into a frenzy.
ACTION IS SELF-PROPELLED MOTION: We've taken the first *step*.
PURPOSES ARE DESTINATIONS: He finally *reached* his goals.
MEANS ARE PATHS: She went from fat to thin *through* an intensive
  exercise program.
DIFFICULTIES ARE IMPEDIMENTS: Let's try *to get around* this problem.
EXTERNAL EVENTS ARE LARGE, MOVING OBJECTS: The *flow* of
  history . . .
EXPECTED PROGRESS IS A TRAVEL SCHEDULE: We're *behind schedule* on
  this project.
LONG-TERM, PURPOSEFUL ACTIVITIES ARE JOURNEYS: You should
  move on with your life.

The Event Structure metaphor has various aspects of events as its target domain. The aspects of events include states that change, causes that produce changes, change itself, action, purpose of action, and so on. These various aspects of events are understood metaphorically in terms of such physical concepts as location, force, and motion. We can represent this system diagrammatically in Figure 10.3.

In the following sections, I will exemplify only four of these mappings: CHANGES ARE MOVEMENTS, ACTION IS SELF-PROPELLED MOTION, PROGRESS

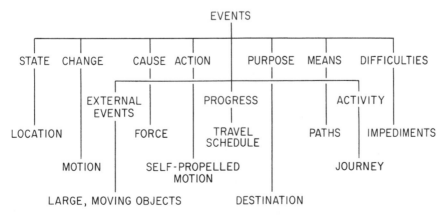

Figure 10.3. Event structure.

IS MOTION FORWARD, and MEANS ARE PATHS. I will continue to use examples from *Cobuild's Metaphor Dictionary*.

3.1. Changes Are Movements

We conceive of change in terms of movement. One linguistic example that is based on this is: "That is very low by the standards of the mid-1980s, when China's economy *galloped* ahead." Galloping is a form of motion. By its nature, it indicates that the change is happening at a good pace. (The "ahead" part of *gallop ahead* will be explained later in the section.)

The CHANGES ARE MOVEMENTS submapping within the Event Structure metaphor has some entailments. One entailment of the metaphor is that lack of control over change will be viewed as lack of control over movement:

> LACK OF CONTROL OVER CHANGE IS LACK OF CONTROL OVER MOVE-
> MENT: Decisive steps had to be taken to stop the country *sliding into*
> disaster.

It is this entailment that also explains the sentence on our initial list: "The province is quite close to *sliding into* civil war."

Another entailment of the metaphor is that accidental changes will be conceptualized as accidental movements such as stumbling.

> ACCIDENTAL CHANGES ARE ACCIDENTAL MOVEMENTS
> Many important scientific discoveries *have been stumbled across* by
> accident.
> The customs men were obviously hoping that they *had stumbled on* a
> major drug-trafficking ring.

In addition, the entailment provides a neat, clear explanation for why people *fall* in love, *fall* prey to something, *fall* into an error, and several others. In these cases, there is a change of state and the change is accidental. This then is conceptualized as accidental motion such as falling. (Thus, we get a natural solution to exercise 4 in the previous chapter.)

3.2. Action Is Self-Propelled Motion

This mapping involves linguistic examples such as:

> Scientists have *taken a big step* in understanding Alzheimer's disease.
> The setting up of stock-exchanges is *an important step on the road to* a
> free-market economy.
> If you feel that you have reason to be worried, *the first step* is to make
> an appointment to see your family doctor.
> Many salespeople have the mistaken belief that making a sale is *the last
> step* in the selling process.

Stepping is a kind of self-propelled motion. This is why it can be used for understanding actions in general. This metaphor has several entailments as well. Thus, the manner of motion can be utilized to conceptualize the manner of the action. This yields the entailment: MANNER OF ACTION IS MANNER OF MOTION. The entailment manifests itself in at least the following ways:

SPEED OF ACTION IS SPEED OF MOTION
Cooper *moved quickly into the fast lane* of Hollywood society.
He was still adapting to life *in the fast lane*.
. . . seven days of good food, fine wine, and living *in the slow lane*.

CAREFUL ACTION IS CAREFUL MOTION
It was a gradual process which could only be carried out *step-by-step*.
The book is full of facts, advice and *step-by-step* guides; it's just like
    having an expert at your side.

SIMILAR ACTION IS SYNCHRONIZED MOTION
Moscow is anxious *to stay in step with* Washington.
They have found themselves *out of step with* the Prime Minister on this
    issue.

3.3. Progress Is Motion Forward

As we saw above in Lakoff's system, progress is viewed as a travel schedule. But it is also understood metaphorically as motion forward: "That is very low by the standards of the mid-1980s, when China's economy *galloped ahead*."

Progress is a form a change, and as a result, it is conceptualized as movement. But it is also a special kind of change that is conceptualized as movement forward (or ahead). This metaphor also has an interesting entailment:

RATE OF PROGRESS IS RATE OF MOTION FORWARD
The Service will continue *to stagger from* crisis *to* crisis.
The marriage *staggered on* for a little while longer.
The state government *has lurched from* one budget crisis *to* another.
The company *stumbled* in the late 1980s when it rushed a new machine
    to market and allowed costs to soar.
He had a depressing three years, during which he *stumbled from* one
    crisis *to* another.

In all these examples, there is some difficulty involved in making progress. This difficulty is conceptualized as some kind of impediment that slows down motion forward.

3.4. Means Are Paths

Means in the Event Structure metaphor are comprehended as paths. The understanding of the word *through* requires the notion of path. In addition, there are distinct kinds of path and several of them are used metaphorically.

Most commonly, in English the words *route, road, avenue,* and the word *path* itself are employed for this purpose.

> By the time she was sixteen she had decided that education would be the best *route to* a good job.
> Marriage is not the *only route to* happiness.
> The *route toward* a market economy would be a very difficult one.
> Let's hope he can keep the team *on the road to* success.
> He must be well aware in private that the people need reassurance if they are *to travel along the road* of reform.
> She has explored all the *available avenues* for change.
> Allison made it clear that she was eager *to pursue other avenues.*
> This can prevent you from seeing which *path to take* in your career.
> A very long time ago, I decided on a change of career *path*—I was going to be a flight steward.
> The president said his country would continue *on its path to* full democracy.
> This job isn't a *path to* riches.

To sum up, then, the Event Structure metaphor provides metaphorical understanding for a large number of abstract concepts, such as state, cause, change, and so on. These abstract concepts converge on the superordinate concept of EVENT, of which they constitute various aspects. The constituent abstract concepts are metaphorically conceived as physical location, force, motion, and so on.

As some of the examples indicate, there can be an overlap between the Event Structure metaphor and the Great Chain metaphor. Concepts like relationship and career appear as both "things" and "events." That is, they serve as target domains of both event sources and thing sources. For example, we can conceptualize relationships both as things, such as a building (e.g., *building* a relationship) and as events, like a journey (e.g., The relationship is *foundering*). What this shows is that some target concepts can be viewed metaphorically both as events and things. This alternative metaphorical conceptualization of some target concepts depends on which aspect(s) of the target we are focusing on in particular communicative situations.

SUMMARY

We have found that seemingly isolated conceptual metaphors form coherently organized larger groupings called **metaphor systems**. In the present chapter, two such metaphorical systems and a subsystem have been presented in some detail; namely, the GREAT CHAIN METAPHOR, with one of its subsystems THE ABSTRACT COMPLEX SYSTEMS METAPHOR, and the EVENT STRUCTURE METAPHOR.

It may not be accidental that so far these two large systems have been found. In line with other findings in cognitive linguistics, the GREAT CHAIN metaphor represents a metaphorical understanding of "things" in the world, while the EVENT STRUCTURE metaphor is a way of understanding "relations," including states and events.

The two systems account for thousands of metaphorical linguistic expressions in English in an economical way that suggests an organization of linguistic and conceptual metaphors that is not simply an alphabetical list. In the GREAT CHAIN metaphor, there is a hierarchy of entities (things) and the entities higher in the hierarchy are understood via entities lower in the same hierarchy, but it can also be the case that entities lower in the hierarchy are conceptualized as entities higher up in the hierarchy (as when complex objects are personified in terms of humans). The COMPLEX SYSTEMS metaphor is a subsystem of the GREAT CHAIN metaphor, in which any kind of abstract complex system is comprehended in terms of the human body, buildings, machines, and plants. In the EVENT STRUCTURE metaphor, various kinds of events and their different aspects are conceptualized as location, force, and motion. Interestingly, the two large systems appear to be different as to their nature: in one, metaphorical processes apply to a hierarchy in both directions (Great Chain; though there is a dominant direction here as well), whereas in the other, various abstract concepts are invariably understood in terms of concrete ones (Event Structure). What other metaphor systems there are in English and how they interact with each other remain as issues to be determined by future research.

FURTHER READING

The "Event Structure metaphor" is presented by Lakoff (1990, 1993). An application of the Event Structure metaphor to the study of the verbs *come* and *go* is in Radden (1995). Lakoff and Turner (1989) describe the "Great Chain" metaphor. Hale (1971) provides an interesting history and analysis of the "body politic" in terms of the "Great Chain" metaphor on the basis of literary and philosophical works. Kövecses (1995c) contains a description of the "complex systems" metaphor.

EXERCISES

1. Read the quotations below from *The Home Book of Quotations* (selected and arranged by Burton Stevenson, 10th ed., 1967). Which metaphor (sub)system (COMPLEX SYSTEMS, GREAT CHAIN) do the following linguistic metaphors belong to?

    (a) Man is the only animal that blushes. Or needs to. (Mark Twain)
    (b) There is a cropping time in the generations of men, as in the fruits of the field; and sometimes, if the stock be good, there springs up for a time a succession of splendid men; and then comes a period of barrenness. (Aristotle)
    (c) Mankind is a tribe of animals. (George Santayana)
    (d) A man is the rope connecting animal and superman,—a rope over a precipice. . . . What is great in man is that he is a bridge and not a goal. (Nietzsche)

(e) I wonder what pleasure men can take in making beasts of themselves! (Samuel Johnson)

(f) A man is a bundle of relations, a knot of roots, whose flower and fruitage is the world. (Emerson)

(g) Man is a tool-making animal. (Benjamin Franklin)

2. Look at the following examples from the *Cobuild Dictionary of Metaphors*. Identify the target domains. What aspect of the human body is used here to understand target concepts?

(a) He has set up a *body* called security council.

(b) ... international meetings with *heads* of state and UN representatives.

(c) ... the acceptable *face* of Soviet foreign policy.

(d) ... Wall Street, the business and financial *heart* of the United States.

(e) The government feared a *hands-off* policy would bring still more unemployment and social tension in the East.

(f) ... the *skeleton* of his plan.

(g) in Britain small businesses are the *backbone* of the Asian community.

3. FRIENDSHIP is an abstract concept which is often understood in terms of less abstract concepts. Here are some proverbs focusing on friendship and friends. Try to analyze them and find which metaphor (sub)system they may belong to.

(a) An old friend is a new house.

(b) A man should keep his friendship in repair.

(c) The only rose without thorns is friendship.

(d) A broken friendship is never mended.

(e) There are many kinds of fruit that grow on the tree of life, but none so sweet as friendship.

(f) Soil and friendship must be cultivated.

(g) Water your friendships as you water your flowerpots.

(h) A broken friendship may be soldered but will never be sound.

(i) True friendship is a plant of slow growth.

(j) Flowers of true friendship never fade.

(k) Friendship, like persimmons, is good only when ripe.

4. The *Cobuild Metaphor Dictionary* gives the following information on bears and squirrels:

A *bear* is a large, strong animal with thick fur and sharp claws. Bears are not fierce, but they will fight and kill people if they think that they are threatening them or their young. Bears are associated with defensive behaviour.

A *squirrel* is a small furry animal with a long bushy tail and long sharp teeth. Squirrels live in trees, and they eat nuts and berries. In summer and autumn, squirrels bury supplies of nuts and berries so that they can dig them up and eat them in the winter. Squirrel is used metaphorically as a verb to talk about hiding or storing things secretly.

Now look at the last paragraph of the closing scene from John Osborne's play *Look Back in Anger* (Jimmy and Alison, the two protagonists, are on the stage):

We'll be together in our bear's cave, and our squirrel's drey, and we'll live on honey, and nuts—lots and lots of nuts. And we'll sing songs about ourselves—about warm trees and snug caves, and lying in the sun. And you'll keep those big eyes on my fur, and help me keep my claws in order, because I'm a bit of a soppy, scruffy sort of a bear. And I'll see that you keep that sleek, bushy tail glistening as it should, because you're a beautiful squirrel, but you're none too bright either, so we've got to be careful. There are cruel steel traps lying about everywhere, just waiting for rather mad, slightly satanic, and very timid little animals. Right?

Who is who here? How does our knowledge of these animals—based on the description above—enrich what we understand from this situation? Just from this segment of the play, how would you characterize Jimmy and Alison? (If you are familiar with the play, how does this relate to what happened in the rest of the story?)

5. Choose a newspaper article and underline the metaphorical expressions in it. Can you account for them and group them systematically with the help of the two metaphor systems (THE GREAT CHAIN OF BEING; EVENT STRUCTURE) discussed in the chapter?

11

Another

Figure:

Metonymy

M etaphor is not the only "figure of speech" that plays an important role in our cognitive activities. In this chapter, I will discuss an equally significant other "trope": metonymy. In addition to characterizing metonymy, I will also show that metaphor and metonymy, although clearly distinct, are related in several interesting ways.

1. What Is Metonymy?

Let us begin to answer the question in the section title by giving some metonymic linguistic expressions that might serve as examples (taken from Lakoff and Johnson's work).

(a) I'm reading *Shakespeare*.
America doesn't want another *Pearl Harbor*.
Washington is negotiating with *Moscow*.
Nixon bombed Hanoi.
We need a better *glove* at third base.

In the sentences above, the words in italics do *not* refer to the "things" that they would refer to in other, nonmetonymic applications, such as:

(b) Shakespeare was a literary genius.
We traveled to Pearl Harbor last year.
Washington is the capital of the United States.
Nixon is a former American president.
This glove is too tight for me.

Rather, the paraphrases of the sentences in (a) could be given as follows in (c):

(c) I'm reading *one of Shakespeare's works.*
America doesn't want another *major defeat in war.*
The American government is negotiating with *the Russian government.*
American bombers bombed Hanoi.
We need a better *baseball player* at third base.

This suggests that in metonymy we use one entity, or thing (such as *Shakespeare, Pearl Harbor, Washington, glove*), to indicate, or to provide mental access to, another entity (such as, *one of Shakespeare's works, defeat in war, the American government, baseball player*). We try to direct attention to an entity through another entity related to it. In other words, instead of mentioning the second entity directly, we provide mental access to it through another entity.

Similar to metaphor, most metonymic expressions are not isolated but come in larger groups that are characterized by a particular relationship between one kind of entity and another kind of entity. Thus, below, we find a number of additional metonymic linguistic expressions for each of the examples in (a). Furthermore, these additional examples can be given as instances of specific conceptual relationships between kinds of entities. The specific relationships, similar to metaphor, are stated in small capitals:

THE PRODUCER FOR THE PRODUCT (THE AUTHOR FOR THE WORK)
I'm reading *Shakespeare.*
She loves *Picasso.*
Does he own any *Hemingway?*

THE PLACE FOR THE EVENT
America doesn't want another *Pearl Harbor.*
Let's not let *El Salvador* become another *Vietnam.*
Watergate changed our politics.

THE PLACE FOR THE INSTITUTION
Washington is negotiating with *Moscow.*
The *White House* isn't saying anything.
Wall Street is in a panic.
Hollywood is putting out terrible movies.

THE CONTROLLER FOR THE CONTROLLED
Nixon bombed Hanoi.
Ozawa gave a terrible concert last night.

AN OBJECT USED FOR THE USER
We need a better *glove* at third base.
The *sax* has the flu today.

Thus, we can say that one kind of entity, such as the one referred to by the word *Shakespeare*, the AUTHOR or PRODUCER, "stands for" another kind of entity, such as the one referred to by the expression *one of Shakespeare's works*, the WORK or PRODUCT. In the same way, we get the PLACE for the EVENT, the PLACE for the INSTITUTION, the CONTROLLER for the CON-

TROLLED, etc. Metonymies, then, similar to metaphor, are conceptual in nature, and the conceptual metonymies are revealed by metonymic linguistic expressions. There are many other conceptual metonymies besides the ones above; for example, we have PART FOR WHOLE (as in, "We need some good *heads* on the project"); WHOLE FOR THE PART (as in, "*America* is a powerful country"); INSTRUMENT FOR ACTION (as in, "She *shampooed* her hair"); EFFECT FOR CAUSE (as in, "It's a *slow* road"); PLACE FOR ACTION (as in, "America doesn't want another *Pearl Harbor*"); DESTINATION FOR MOTION (as in, "He *porched* the newspaper"); PLACE FOR PRODUCT (as in, "Give me my *java/ mocca*"); TIME FOR ACTION (as in, "The 8:40 just arrived"); and many others.

We can call the entity that directs attention, or provides mental access, to another entity the *vehicle entity*, and the kind of entity to which attention, or mental access, is provided the *target entity*. Thus, in the examples above, *Shakespeare, Washington*, and *glove* would be vehicle entities, whereas *one of Shakespeare's works, the capital of the United States*, and *a baseball player* would be target entities. (This is not to be confused with "target domain" as used in connection with metaphor.)

It is a basic feature of metonymically related vehicle and target entities that they are "close" to each other in conceptual space. Thus, the producer is conceptually "close" to the product (because he is the one who makes it), the place of an institution is conceptually "close" to the institution itself (because most institutions are located in particular physical places), gloves are conceptually "close" to baseball players (because some baseball players wear gloves), and so on. In the traditional view of metonymy, this feature of metonymy is expressed by the claim that the two entities are contiguously related, or that the two entities are in each other's proximity. In the cognitive linguistic view, this claim is accepted and maintained but given a more precise formulation; namely, it is suggested that a vehicle entity can provide mental access to a target entity when the two entities belong to the same domain, or as Lakoff puts it, the same **idealized cognitive model** (ICM). For example, an author and his works belong to the ICM that we can call the PRODUCTION ICM, in which we have a number of entities including the producer (author), the product (the works), the place where the product is made, and so on. All of these form a coherent whole in our experience of the world as they co-occur repeatedly. Because they are tightly linked in experience, some of the entities can be used to indicate, that is, to provide mental access to, other entities within the same ICM.

Given the observations above, we can offer the following *definition of metonymy*:

> Metonymy is a cognitive process in which one conceptual entity, the
> vehicle, provides mental access to another conceptual entity, the target,
> within the same domain, or idealized cognitive model (ICM).

This way of thinking about metonymy raises two important issues: (1) What are the ICM's in which metonymies most commonly occur? (2) What are the entities that most commonly serve as vehicle entities to access targets? I will take up these issues in section 3.

2. A Comparison of Metaphor and Metonymy

Let us now review the major similarities and differences between metaphor and metonymy in light of how metaphor was characterized in this book and the description of metonymy above.

2.1. Similarity versus Contiguity

The two concepts participating in metaphor stand typically in the relationship of *similarity*. As we saw in chapter 6, there are many sources for similarity; it may emerge from real similarity, but also from perceived resemblance and correlations in experience. Thus, I am using similarity here in a deliberately vague and superficial way. Metonymy contrasts with metaphor in that it is based on the relationship of *contiguity*, in the sense in which it was discussed above. Given the difference between similarity and contiguity, Ray Gibbs suggests a good test to determine whether we have to do with a metaphoric or with a metonymic expression. It is the "is like" test. Consider two sentences—one metaphorical, the other metonymic:

> The *creampuff* was knocked out in the first round of the fight.
>   (metaphor)
> We need a new *glove* to play third base. (metonymy)

If we try to provide a nonliteral paraphrase for the comparison by making use of "is like," the comparison that is meaningful is metaphor; otherwise, it is metonymy (the * marks the sentence as unacceptable):

> The boxer is like a creampuff. (metaphor)
> *The third baseman is like a glove. (metonymy)

Obviously, this test has to be adjusted according to the grammatical category of the words and expressions that are involved in particular cases. If, for example, the metaphor is not a noun, unlike the case above, we have to make the appropriate adjustment in order for the test to be applicable. Consider a sentence like "He is *on cloud nine*." Here the test could not be applied without changing the sentence itself—"He is like on cloud nine" would not work. One possibility for adjustment is something like: "He feels as if he was on cloud nine." Thus, similarity characterizes metaphor, whereas contiguity is a feature of metonymy. It should be observed, however, that just as there are many different kinds of similarity, there are also many different kinds of contiguity, as we will see below.

2.2. Two Domains versus One Domain

The view that metonymy is a relationship based on contiguity has an important consequence for understanding the difference between metaphor and metonymy. Metaphor involves two concepts that are "distant" from each other in our conceptual system (although they are similar). The "distance" largely arises from the fact that one concept or domain is typically an abstract one, while the other is typically a concrete one. For instance, the concept of idea is distant from that of food (IDEAS ARE FOOD); the concept of love from that of a journey (LOVE IS A JOURNEY); the concept of social organization from that of plants (SOCIAL ORGANIZATIONS ARE PLANTS); the concept of action from that of physical motion (ACTION IS SELF-PROPELLED MOTION); and on and on for many others that we have seen in the previous pages. See Figure 11.1.

In metonymy, on the other hand, we have two elements, or entities, that are closely related to each other in conceptual space. For example, the producer is closely related to the product made (PRODUCER FOR PRODUCT); a whole is closely related to its parts (WHOLE FOR THE PART); effects are closely related to the causes that produce them (EFFECT FOR CAUSE); the controller is closely related to the thing controlled (CONTROLLER FOR THE CONTROLLED); the place is closely related to the institution that is located in that place (PLACE FOR THE INSTITUTION); and an instrument is closely related to the action in which it is used (INSTRUMENT FOR ACTION). See Figure 11.2.

In all these cases, we have a single domain or ICM (such as production, a whole entity, causation, control, institution, action) that involves several elements and the elements can stand metonymically for each other. The elements in a metonymic relationship form a single domain. By contrast, metaphor uses two distinct and distant domains or ICMs. I will refine this picture of potential metonymic relationships in section 3.

2.3. Understanding versus Directing Attention

The main function of metaphor is to understand one thing in terms of another. Understanding is achieved by mapping the structure of one domain onto another. There is a set of systematic mappings between elements of the source and the target. Metonymy, on the other hand, is used less for the

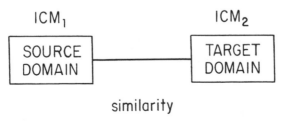

similarity

Figure 11.1. Metaphorical relationship.

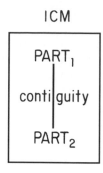

Figure 11.2. Metonymic relationship.

purposes of understanding, although this function is not completely ruled out. The main function of metonymy seems to be to provide *mental, cognitive access* to a target entity that is less readily or easily available; typically, a more concrete or salient vehicle entity is used to give or gain access to a more abstract or less salient target entity within the same domain. We can think of this process of affording access to a target as a kind of mapping. In metonymy, in contrast to metaphor, there is a single mapping—a mapping that takes the listener from one entity (the vehicle entity) to another (the target entity). (Of course, in so doing, it may evoke several other parts within the domain or the whole domain. But still, this will be less systematic than in the case of metaphor.)

2.4. Same Realm versus Distinct Realms

As has been shown throughout this book, the metaphoric process involves (two) conceptual domains (A and B). See Figure 11.3.

In other words, metaphor arises between concepts. The realm within which we find metaphor is that of concepts, that is, the conceptual realm (which is expressed through language). Typically, though as we will see not always, this is what characterizes metonymy as well, in that one conceptual entity stands for another conceptual entity (and this is also expressed through language). Thus, the metonymy that is most productive is the one where there are two concepts (conceptual entities) involved within the same domain or ICM. All the examples that we have dealt with so far in this chapter were of this kind.

Metonymy, however, occurs not only between concepts, that is, between two conceptual entities (within the same conceptual domain or ICM). Meto-

CONCEPTUAL DOMAIN$_1$ ——————— CONCEPTUAL DOMAIN$_2$

Figure 11.3. Possibilities for metaphor.

nymic relationships can also be found between word forms and real-world (nonlinguistic) referents and between word forms and corresponding concepts. This is because there are several kinds of relationships between the components of signs in general and those of the linguistic sign in particular. A (linguistic) sign is commonly viewed as being constituted by a word form, a concept, and a referent. This can be represented with the help of the well-known *semiotic triangle*. See Figure 11.4.

As the diagram shows, the possibility for metonymic processes to occur is not only between $concept_1$ and $concept_2$ (within the same ICM). In addition to $concept_1$ standing for $concept_2$ (a case not represented in the diagram), metonymy can occur also between $form_1$ and $concept_1$ or between $form_1$ and thing/$event_1$—that is, $form_1$ can stand for $concept_1$ or $form_1$ can stand for thing/$event_1$. While metaphor arises as an interaction between two concepts, metonymy can be produced by a more varied set of "things" (concepts, forms, and referents) belonging to different "realms." One example of this is when a form stands for a corresponding concept. The form-concept unity characterizes the form-meaning relationship of any sign. An example of this would be the sentence "That is a self-contradictory *utterance*." Here the word *utterance* is used metonymically, in that it refers to or denotes the content of a sentence. That is, what one actually "utters" is taken to refer to or denote the meaning of what one says. It is only the content, or meaning, of what one says that can be "self-contradictory." This is what Lakoff and Turner call the WORDS STAND FOR THE CONCEPTS THEY EXPRESS metonymy. In it, a word form (e.g., *utterance*) is used to indicate the meaning (concept) of that form (i.e. *utterance*).

In conclusion, it is important to note that domains that involve metonymy may and do cut across distinct realms (such as concept, word form, referent). In this respect, metonymy is different from metaphorical mappings, which only occur within the same realm (that of the concept) but across different and distant domains.

3. Typical Metonymic Domains and Typical Vehicle Entities

At the end of section 2, it was noted that two important issues arise from the cognitive linguistic definition of metonymy: (1) the issue of what are the ICM's

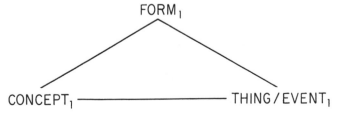

Figure 11.4. Possibilities for metonymy.

in which metonymy most commonly occurs and (2) the issue of which conceptual entities serve most naturally as VEHICLE entities, given an ICM. I will concentrate on the first issue, and, for lack of space, pay only marginal attention to the second in this chapter (but see "Further Reading").

A conceptual domain, or ICM, can be viewed as a whole that is constituted by parts; more specifically, the conceptual entities, or elements, are the parts that constitute the ICM that is the whole. Given this way of looking at ICM's, metonymies may emerge in two ways: (1) either a whole stands for a part or a part stands for a whole; (2) a part stands for another part. See Figure 11.5.

The parentheses around the various parts in (1) indicate that metonymy emerges between the whole and a part (PART₁)—not between a part and another part (but with the other parts being present in the background). See Figure 11.6.

The parentheses around the WHOLE ICM in (2) indicate that metonymy emerges between a part and another part—not between a whole and a part (but with the whole ICM being present in the background).

Version (1) may lead to metonymies in which we access a part of an ICM via its whole (e.g., THE WHOLE FOR THE PART) or a whole ICM via one of its parts (e.g., A PART FOR THE WHOLE); version (2) may lead to metonymies in which we access a part via another part of the same ICM (e.g., THE PRODUCER FOR THE PRODUCT).

It can be suggested that the two configurations, or versions, apply to two different sets of ICMs. The first configuration (i.e., version 1) applies to ICMs including the Thing-and-Part ICM, Constitution ICM, Complex Event ICM, Category-and-Member ICM, and Category-and-Property ICM. The second configuration (i.e., version 2) applies to ICMs including the Action ICM, Causation ICM, Production ICM, Control ICM, Possession ICM, Contain-

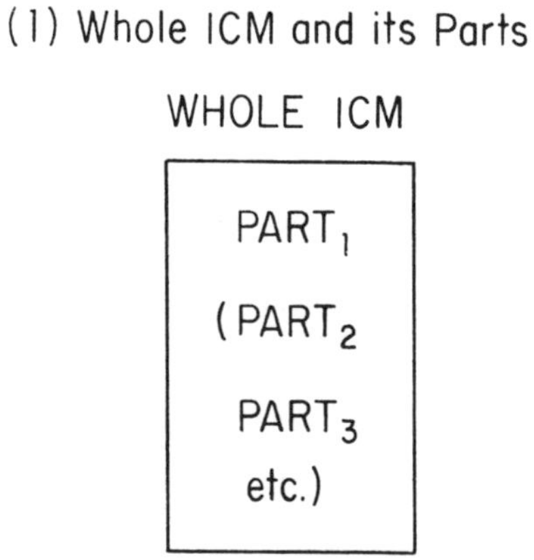

(1) Whole ICM and its Parts

WHOLE ICM

PART₁

(PART₂

PART₃

etc.)

Figure 11.5. Whole ICM and its parts.

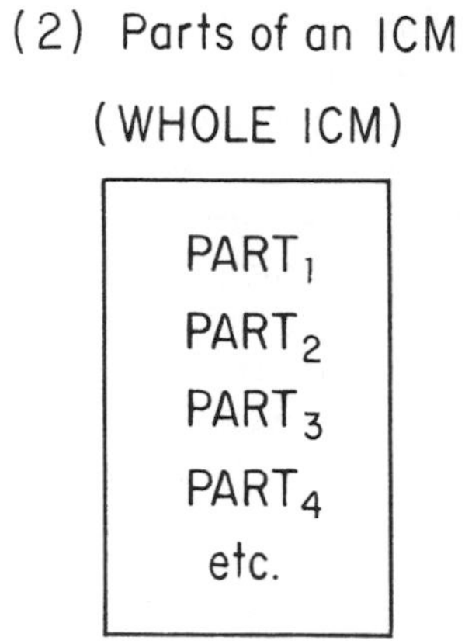

(2) Parts of an ICM

(WHOLE ICM)

| PART$_1$ |
| PART$_2$ |
| PART$_3$ |
| PART$_4$ |
| etc. |

Figure 11.6. Parts of an ICM.

ment ICM, and ICMs involving indeterminate conceptual relationships between a vehicle and a target.

3.1. Whole and Part

The relationship between a whole and a part typically applies to things, where the notion of *thing* is to be understood here in a maximally general, schematic sense—in the same way as in the previous chapter. Things, in particular physical objects, are typically conceived of as having well-delineated boundaries and as internally composed of various parts. Hence, the configuration of *Whole ICM and its Part(s)* mainly captures metonymies involving things.

3.1.1. The Thing and Its Parts ICM

There are basically two variants that belong here. Given the relationship between a whole and a part, either

THE WHOLE STANDS FOR A PART: *America* for "United States"
[or]
A PART STANDS FOR THE WHOLE: *England* for "Great Britain"

In speaking of *America* when we want to refer to the United States (as part of the whole continent), we are making use of a WHOLE-FOR-PART metonymy, and in speaking of *England* when we want to refer to Great Britain including Wales and Scotland, we are making use of a PART-FOR-WHOLE metonymy. (Actually, the former example may be confusing to some people. They can claim that the word form *America* is not used for the American continent, only the noun phrase *the Americas* is. I am here disregarding the article and the plural ending and concentrating only on the fact that the word form *America* is used in both. This usage then leads to a conceptual metonymy.)

The metonymy WHOLE THING FOR A PART OF THE THING is widely found in situations that Ronald Langacker describes as *active zone*. For example, in *He hit me* or *The car needs washing*, the whole things *he* and *the car* may be said to stand as a whole for the "active-zone" parts "his fist" and "the car's body," respectively. Also, abstract things such as the theater, democracy, or monarchy can have parts, which may be metonymically involved as active zones. Thus, in *Let's go to the theater tonight*, we have a "play" as a theater's active zone in mind, whereas in *This is the new Globe Theatre*, we are thinking of "building" as the active zone.

The other metonymic variant, PART OF A THING FOR THE WHOLE THING, has traditionally been given special status under the name of *synecdoche*. Parts which are used to stand for physical things include the well-known metonymies of *sail* for "sailboat" or body parts such as *hand*, *face*, *head*, or *leg* for the whole person.

Likewise, abstract things may be metonymically accessed via their parts as in *the ballot* for "democratic voting," *the bullet* for "force," the *stage* for "the theater," and *the crown* for "the monarchy." Thus, we can readily understand the part-for-whole metonymies in the sentence: "Most people prefer the *ballot* to the *bullet*."

3.1.1.1. Constitution ICM. Another ICM to which the relationship between a whole and a part may be said to apply is what can be called the "constitution ICM." Substances may be conceived of as parts that constitute or make up things, in particular, physical objects. The Constitution ICM gives rise to two metonymic variants:

> OBJECT FOR MATERIAL CONSTITUTING THAT OBJECT: "There was *cat* all over the road."
> THE MATERIAL CONSTITUTING AN OBJECT FOR THE OBJECT: *wood* for "the forest"

The relationship between an object and the material constituting it corresponds to the grammatical distinction between countable entities and mass entities.

3.1.1.2. Complex Event ICM. Since events evolve in time, subevents may occur in succession or they may occur simultaneously. Thus, in the case of PART OF AN EVENT FOR THE WHOLE EVENT, we have two more specific metonymies:

> SUCCESSIVE SUBEVENTS FOR COMPLEX EVENT: They *stood at the altar.*
> CO-PRESENT SUBEVENTS FOR COMPLEX EVENT: Mary *speaks* Spanish.

With successive events, initial, central, and final subevents may be conventionally used to stand for entire complex events. In "They *stood* at the altar," the initial subevent is used to stand for the whole wedding ceremony; in "Mother is *cooking* potatoes," the central subevent of cooking stands for the whole event of preparing food including, among other things, cleaning and peeling the potatoes and other ingredients, putting them in a pot and adding water; and in "I have to *grade* hundreds of papers," the final subevent describes the complex event of reading, correcting, and eventually grading students' papers. More specifically, we therefore have the submetonymies INITIAL SUBEVENT FOR COMPLEX EVENT, CENTRAL SUBEVENT FOR COMPLEX EVENT, and FINAL SUBEVENT FOR COMPLEX EVENT. In the case of "Mary *speaks* Spanish," the metonymy is based on the fact that speaking a language assumes several events and abilities other than speaking. Mary's command of speaking the language is, as a habitual event, copresent with other linguistic skills, such as comprehension, reading, and writing.

3.1.1.3. Category-and-Member ICM. Category-and-Member ICMs are instances of the Whole-and-Part configuration. The relationship between a category and one of its members may lead to reversible metonymies:

CATEGORY FOR A MEMBER OF THE CATEGORY: *the pill* for "birth control pill"
MEMBER OF A CATEGORY FOR THE CATEGORY: *aspirin* for "any pain-relieving tablet"

The member of a category that is used as a metonymic vehicle or target is an especially salient one. For example, aspirin is one of the best known pain-relievers, and it can, thus, be used easily to indicate pain-relievers in general.

3.1.1.4. Category and Property ICM. Properties may be seen as parts of a category. If categories are defined by a set of properties, these properties are necessarily part of the category. Categories typically evoke, and may metonymically stand for, one or more of their defining or otherwise essential properties and, conversely, a defining or essential property of a category may evoke, and stand for, the category which it defines:

CATEGORY FOR DEFINING PROPERTY: *jerk* for "stupidity"
DEFINING PROPERTY FOR CATEGORY: *blacks* for "black people"

3.1.2. Part and Part

Any type of possible relationship of one conceptual entity to another conceptual entity within an ICM will be understood as an instance of the PART-AND-PART metonymy. While the relationship between a whole and its parts typically applies to things (THING ICMS), the relationship between parts typically applies to conceptual entities within an event (EVENT ICMS).

3.1.2.1. Action ICM. Action ICM's involve a variety of participants, or entities, which may be related to an action (more precisely, the predicate expressing the action) or to each other. There are, thus, specific relationships such as between an INSTRUMENT and the ACTION, the RESULT of an action and the ACTION, an OBJECT INVOLVED in an action and the ACTION, the DESTINATION of a motion and the MOTION, all of which are parts of the Action ICM. The Action ICM, which is also taken to include events of motion, includes the following types of metonymic relationships:

> INSTRUMENT FOR ACTION: *to ski, to shampoo* one's hair
> AGENT FOR ACTION: *to butcher* the cow; *to author* a book
> ACTION FOR AGENT: *snitch* (slang: "to inform" and "informer")
> OBJECT INVOLVED IN AN ACTION FOR THE ACTION: *to blanket* the bed
> ACTION FOR OBJECT INVOLVED IN THE ACTION: Give me one *bite.*
> RESULT FOR ACTION: a *screw-up* (slang: "to blunder" and "blunder")
> ACTION FOR RESULT: a deep *cut*
> MEANS FOR ACTION: He *sneezed* the tissue off the table.
> MANNER OF ACTION FOR THE ACTION: She *tiptoed* to her bed.
> TIME PERIOD OF ACTION FOR THE ACTION: *to summer* in Paris
> DESTINATION FOR MOTION: *to porch* the newspaper, *to deck* one's
>   opponent
> TIME OF MOTION FOR AN ENTITY INVOLVED IN THE MOTION: The *8:40*
>   just arrived.

It should be noted that, in all the metonymic examples listed above, the forms of the words are the same, although their word classes may change. By choosing such examples, I deliberately avoid the issue of how derivational processes and inflections (such as the case of *America* vs. *Americas* above) affect metonymy. Examples of derivational changes would be *write-writer* (ACTION FOR AGENT), *fly-flight* (as in "The *flight* is waiting to depart": ACTION FOR OBJECT), and *beauty-beautify* (as in "to *beautify* the lawn": RESULT FOR ACTION).

3.1.2.2. Causation ICM. When one thing or event causes another, we have a Cause-and-Effect type of relationship. It can produce either CAUSE-FOR-EFFECT metonymies (*healthy* complexion for "the good state of health bringing about the effect of healthy complexion") or EFFECT-FOR-CAUSE metonymies (*slow road* for "slow traffic resulting from the poor state of the road" or *sad* book for "sadness resulting from reading a book"). The metonymic relationship EFFECT FOR CAUSE seems to be more widespread. Among EFFECT FOR CAUSE we find the special types:

> STATE/EVENT FOR THE THING/PERSON/STATE THAT CAUSED IT: She was a
>   *success*; He was a *failure*; She is my *ruin.*

The Action and Causation ICMs can combine and produce the metonymy

> SOUND CAUSED FOR THE EVENT THAT CAUSED IT: She *rang* the money
>   into the till.

This metonymy is particularly frequently found with motion events as in "The train *whistled* into the station," "The fire trucks *roared* out of the firehouse," or "The car *screeched* to a halt."

3.1.2.3. Production ICM. Production ICMs involve actions in which one of the participants, or entities, is a product. The production of objects seems to be a particularly salient type of causal action. The Production ICM gives rise to various metonymic relationships involving the thing produced:

PRODUCER FOR PRODUCT: a *Ford*.

Producers of highly outstanding "products" in a culture like artists, scientists, and inventors receive particular metonymic attention. As one of the subtypes of the PRODUCER-FOR-PRODUCT metonymy we have:

AUTHOR FOR HIS WORK: We are reading *Shakespeare*.

Certain food products are naturally associated with their place of origin and thus may be metonymically accessed via this place:

PLACE FOR PRODUCT MADE THERE: *mokka, java, china*.

Both metonymic relationships are, however, irreversible, that is, we do not seem to have either *PRODUCT FOR PRODUCER or *PRODUCT FOR PLACE.

3.1.2.4. Control ICM. The Control ICM includes a controller and a person or an object controlled. It gives rise to the reversible metonymic relationships:

CONTROLLER FOR CONTROLLED: *Schwarzkopf* defeated Iraq.
CONTROLLED FOR CONTROLLER: The *Mercedes* has arrived.

Possibly, the "use" relationship also belongs here, since, in it, the user controls the object used. Thus, we have THE OBJECT FOR THE USER OF THE OBJECT, as in Lakoff and Johnson's example *Mrs. Grundy frowns on blue jeans*, where the expression *blue jeans* stands for the people who wear blue jeans.

3.1.2.5. Possession ICM. The relationship of control blends into that of possession, in which a person is "in control" of an object. The Possession ICM may produce reversible metonymies; there is, however, a clear preference for choosing the Possessor as a vehicle:

POSSESSOR FOR POSSESSED: "This is *Harry*" for "Harry's drink"
POSSESSED FOR POSSESSOR: "He married *money*" for "someone who
   has money" and "She married *power*" for "someone who has power"

3.1.2.6. Containment ICM. The image-schematic relationship that holds between a container and the things contained in it is conceptually well entrenched and applies to many standardized situations, which may lead to metonymy. As a rule, we are more interested in the content of a container than in the mere container so that we commonly find metonymies that target the content via the container rather than the reverse metonymic relationship:

CONTAINER FOR CONTAINED: *glass* for "wine"
CONTAINED FOR CONTAINER: The *milk* tipped over.

The Containment ICM is widely extended metaphorically and also gives rise to metaphorically based metonymies. Places at large may be conceptualized as containers for people, so that we have as a containment metonymy PLACE FOR INHABITANTS, as in *the whole town* for "the people living in the town."

3.1.2.7. Assorted ICMs Involving Indeterminate Relationships. Unlike the cases discussed so far, not all metonymies are constituted by one clearly specifiable type of relationship. For example, the widely discussed metonymy *"The ham sandwich* wants a side dish of salad" does not occur on traditional lists of metonymic relationships. The reason may be that there does not appear to be a clearly specifiable type of conceptual relationship that obtains between a customer in a restaurant (i.e., the person indicated by the phrase *the ham sandwich*) and the dish ordered by him or her. The conceptual relationship might be specified as one of possession, part-whole, or control, but none of them seems to fully capture the "essence" of the kind of "contiguity" that we feel holds between a customer and his or her dish. The relationship is indeterminate within the set of general conceptual relationships, but it is clearly determinate within the specific restaurant ICM, with which the members of a culture are thoroughly familiar.

4. Metonymic Relationships and Metaphor

Given the metonymic relationships discussed in the previous section, it may not be unreasonable to suggest that many conceptual metaphors derive from conceptual metonymies. Take for example the metaphor ANGER IS HEAT. In the folk model of emotion, emotions are seen as resulting in certain physiological effects. Thus, anger can be said to result in increased subjective body heat (among other things). This case of a metonymic relationship between anger and body heat was called CAUSE AND EFFECT in this chapter. The kind of metonymy that applies to this example is EFFECT FOR CAUSE (BODY HEAT FOR ANGER). The conceptual metaphor ANGER IS HEAT arises from a generalization of body heat to heat. In this case, the metonymic vehicle (body heat) becomes the source domain of metaphor through the process of generalization. This again shows that metaphors are often based on correlations in experience—a topic to which we will return in the next chapter.

There are other metonymic relationships that may underlie conceptual metaphors. The essentially metonymic relationship that exists between a category and its members may be another case in point. Since, for instance, MOTION is a subcategory of ACTION and FORCE is a subcategory of CAUSE, the ACTION IS MOTION and CAUSES ARE FORCES metaphors described in chapter 10 may also be understood as ultimately deriving from such conceptual metonymies as MEMBER OF A CATEGORY FOR THE CATEGORY. If these observations are valid, they would suggest that many conceptual metaphors have a metonymic basis or motivation.

Let us try to take inventory of the possible metonymic relationships that might obtain between a source domain (S) and a target domain (T) in conceptual metaphor and on which metaphors may be built. What I am trying to do here is to see whether we can find a metonymic relationship for a particular metaphorical relationship between S and T. Obviously, the metonymic relationships mentioned in the previous section can be useful in this search. If a metonymic relationship can be found between a metaphorical source and target, then the metaphor can be said to be motivated by and derive from the metonymy in question.

Among the metaphors that I have examined, only two general metonymic relationships were applicable: CAUSE AND EFFECT (from the CAUSATION ICM) and WHOLE AND PART (from the THING ICM). That is, some metaphorical relationships can be said to be motivated by a CAUSE AND EFFECT type of metonymy, while some others by a WHOLE AND PART type of metonymy. As we will see, there are also metaphors to which no metonymic relationship applies. However, in addition to CAUSE AND EFFECT and WHOLE AND PART, other metonymic relationships are likely to characterize, and thus motivate, conceptual metaphors. The list of cases that follows is simply a beginning to study this issue in a serious way.

4.1. Causation

This case involves a source and a target domain that are causally (CAUSE AND EFFECT) related in a conceptual metaphor. The ICM in which this metonymic relationship emerges is CAUSATION; S causes T to occur and T causes S to occur. I will discuss three such cases.

4.1.1. Target Results in Source

There are conceptual metaphors in which the source domain can be seen as resulting from the target domain. A case in point is represented by the metaphor ANGER IS HEAT. In it, the source domain of HEAT arises from the common metonymic relationship that we put as EFFECT FOR CAUSE above. The "body heat produced by anger" can be viewed as a metonymy: BODY HEAT FOR ANGER. Thus, we have the following chain of conceptualization: ANGER produces BODY HEAT (metonymy); BODY HEAT becomes HEAT (generalization); HEAT is used to understand ANGER (metaphor). The metaphor ANGER IS HEAT is a case where the source domain of heat emerges from the target domain of anger through a metonymic process.

4.1.2. *Source Results in Target*

In some conceptual metaphors target domains may derive historically from source domains. For example, verbal arguments can be seen to derive from physical fighting or war in the sense that humans developed the verbal activity of argument to avoid physical conflicts. When this happens, the concept of argument may become the target domain of war, as in the well-established metaphor ARGUMENT IS WAR. In this case, the source results *in* the target. In this sense, the emergence of ARGUMENT IS WAR may be "reduced to" a metonymic process, in which the source (WAR) PRODUCES the target (ARGUMENT), which then "stands for" the source. This is a form of the metonymy EFFECT FOR CAUSE.

4.1.3. *Source Enables Target*

The relationship between some source and target domains in metaphor is such that the source enables the target to occur or to be the case. Here the source domain is a precondition for the event in the target to occur. Precondition is a "weak" kind of causation (unlike the two previous cases), in that it does not produce an effect but simply makes an effect possible. Examples of this include KNOWING IS SEEING and ANALYSIS IS DISSECTION. Seeing makes knowing possible in many cases, and dissection commonly enables us to perform analysis. Here the underlying metonymy is PRECONDITION (a kind of enabling cause) FOR RESULTING EVENT/ACTION (a kind of effect). Perhaps the metaphor (THE PASSING OF) TIME IS MOVEMENT (THROUGH SPACE) also belongs here. In this metaphor, however, it is the target domain of time that enables movement; that is, we would have a case in which a target enables the source. Without time, there is no movement (e.g., locomotion). Movement can only take place *in* time.

4.2. Part-Whole

In the previous section (section 3), we have seen a number of metonymic relationships characterizing "things." Things are viewed as wholes with parts. A metaphorical source and target domain may be related in such a way that one is a part and the other is a whole with respect to that part. We will look at two such cases below.

4.2.1. *Source Is a Subcategory of Target*

With some source domains we find that they are subcategories of the target domain. Thus, for example, motion is a subcategory of events. And physical forces are subcategories of causes, in that they produce effects, just like causes in general. Subcategorization is a metonymic relationship because, in it a subcategory stands for the category as a whole. This can, then, be considered as the basis of metaphor. Some metaphors that appear to have this kind of basis include:

EVENTS ARE ACTIONS
CHANGE IS MOTION
CAUSATION IS TRANSFER
CAUSES ARE FORCES
ACTION IS MOTION

4.2.2. Source and Target Are Subcategories of a Higher Category

An interesting special case of 4.2 involves cases where both the target and the source are subcategories of a higher, more inclusive category. An instance of this is the metaphor LUST IS HUNGER, where both lust and hunger are special cases of desire—desire for sex and desire for food.

4.3. Correlation in Experience

Correlation in experience was not mentioned in this chapter as a metonymic relationship. As a matter of fact, it is commonly taken to be the basis for metaphor. For example, in the well-known case of MORE IS UP (analyzed in chapter 6), it was suggested that this is a correlation-based metaphor because it involves two distinct and distant concepts: QUANTITY (i.e., more) and VERTI-CALITY (i.e., up) such that we understand one (quantity) through the other (verticality). In this metaphor, it can be claimed that QUANTITY and VERTICAL-ITY are very different concepts and that they are distant from each other in conceptual space. However, we can think of cases like this as being metonymic relationships. When we pour water into a glass or when we add more of something to a pile, we bring together two distant conceptual domains (i.e., quantity and verticality) in a single domain, in which the two can be found simultaneously. We perceive the pile go UP higher as we add MORE substance to it. In such cases, we bring together two previously distant conceptual domains into a single one in our perceptual experience, and because we now have the two concepts in a single domain, one can be used to stand for the other. This is what we find in UP being used for MORE, as in "*Fill* her *up*, please," said to a gas station attendant. This kind of metonymy is based on correlation in experience.

It should be noticed that this partial inventory of the metonymic basis of many metaphors is but a restatement of the experiential grounding of metaphor that was dealt with in chapter 6 (in particular, "correlations in experience" and "source as the root of the target"). This experiential grounding may be of various kinds, including bodily (ANGER IS HEAT), perceptual (MORE IS UP), cultural (ARGUMENT IS WAR), and category-based (CAUSES ARE FORCES). Most metaphors are based on one or several of these.

5. The Interaction of Metaphor and Metonymy

Particular linguistic expressions are not always clearly either metaphors or metonymies. Often, what we find is that an expression is both; the two figures blend in a single expression. In these cases, we have individual examples where metaphor and metonymy interact. This process is different from the one that was discussed above, where the relationship between conceptual metaphors and conceptual metonymies was examined. Let us see some examples of how metonymy and metaphor interact in particular linguistic expressions. This phenomenon was studied by Louis Goossens.

Consider the expression *to be close-lipped*. Literally, it means "to have one's lips close together." The expression has two nonliteral meanings: (1) "to be silent" and (2) "to say little." When it is used in the sense of "to be silent," we have a metonymic reading, in that having the lips close together results in silence. However, if we describe as *close-lipped* a talkative person who does not say what we would like to hear from him or her, we have a metaphoric reading. Given the saliency of the metonymic reading, we have a case here that can be described as "metaphor from metonymy."

Another type of interaction between metaphor and metonymy is the expression *to shoot one's mouth off*. We can call this case "metonymy within metaphor." A metaphor incorporates a metonymy within the same linguistic expression. In *to shoot one's mouth off*, we have the figurative meaning "to talk foolishly about something that one doesn't know much about or should not talk about." Metonymy within metaphor arises here in the following way. First, we have a metaphorical reading in which a source domain item, the gun, is mapped onto the target domain, speech, more precisely, onto the organ of speech, the mouth. In this way, the foolish use of a firearm is mapped onto foolish talk. "Buried" in this metaphor, so to speak, is a metonymy; namely, the mouth standing for the faculty of speech. Thus, we have the case of metonymy within metaphor.

SUMMARY

In this chapter, we have characterized the traditional and the cognitive linguistic view of metonymy. In the traditional view, metonymy is chiefly the use of a word in place of another in order to refer to some entity, where one word can be used for another if the meanings of the words are contiguously related. In the cognitive linguistic view, *metonymy is conceptual* in nature; its main function is to provide *mental access* through one conceptual entity to another; it is based on *ICMs* with specific conceptual relationships among their elements.

We have distinguished metaphor from metonymy in the following ways: (1) While metonymy is based on *contiguity*, that is, on elements that are parts of the same ICM, metaphor is based on *similarity*. (2) While metonymy involves a *single domain*, metaphor involves *two distant domains*. (3) While metonymy is largely used *to provide access* to a single target entity within a single domain, metaphor is primarily used to understand a whole system of entities in terms of another system. (4) While metonymy occurs between concepts, as well as between linguistic forms and concepts and between linguistic forms and things/events in the world, metaphor occurs between concepts.

Metonymy-producing relationships, such as PART OF A THING FOR THE WHOLE THING and AGENT FOR ACTION, are manifest in a variety of ICMs, such as THING ICM, CONSTITUTION ICM, COMPLEX EVENT ICM, as well as ACTION ICM, PERCEPTION ICM, CAUSATION ICM, etc. The relationships fall into two large *configurations*: Whole and Part and Part and Part.

Certain metonymic relationships form the *basis of many metaphors*. We have seen in this chapter several metonymic relationships that can lead to the development of conceptual metaphors. These include *causation, whole-part*, and *correlation*. There may well be other such metonymic relationships on which metaphors are based.

Metaphors and metonymies often *interact* in particular linguistic expressions. Some expressions can be interpreted as the mixed case of *metaphor from metonymy*, while others as mixes of *metonymy within metaphor*.

FURTHER READING

The traditional view of metonymy can be found in such works as Stern (1931), Ullmann (1962), and Waldron (1967). Lakoff and Johnson (1980) point out the conceptual nature of metonymy. Lakoff (1987), Lakoff and Turner (1989), and Langacker (1991, 1993) have placed the study of metonymy in a new light. The most detailed and the clearest discussion of metaphor and metonymy as distinct but related "tropes" is Gibbs (1994). Kövecses and Radden (1998) and Radden and Kövecses (1999) attempt to offer a new synthesis in the cognitive linguistic treatment of metonymy. Kövecses and Szabó (1996) examine metonymies relating to the concept of the human hand and attempt to place the study of metonymy and metaphor in the context of foreign language learning and teaching. Kövecses (1986, 1988, 1990, 2000a) examines the metonymic and metaphoric structure of emotion concepts. Croft (1993) discusses the role of domains in the interpretation of metaphors and metonymies. Taylor (1989), Dirven (1993), Barcelona (2000), Feyaerts (2000), Radden (2000), Ruiz de Mendoza (2000), and Turner and Fauconnier (2000) deal with the issue of the relationship between metaphor and metonymy. Goosens (1990) examines the way particular linguistic expressions can be both metaphors and metonymies in expressions of linguistic action. Norrick (1981) places the study of metonymy within a broader semiotic context. Gibbs (1994) and Panther and Thornburg, in a variety of publications (e.g., Thornburg and Panther 1997; Panther and Thornburg 2000), brought to our attention the essentially metonymic nature of speech acts. A volume edited by Panther and Radden (1999) offers a panoramic view of how metonymy is treated in cognitive linguistics.

EXERCISES

1. What metonymies are at work in the expressions below? What general conceptual metonymy underlies all of them?

   (a) Don't get *hot* under the collar.
   (b) He *blushed* with joy.
   (c) I was *petrified*.
   (d) He *stood tall* as he received the prize.

2. Look at the following metonymies. Try to group them under the conceptual metonymies discussed in the chapter.

    (a) Sylvia loves Van Gogh.
    (b) John wants to have an Opel.
    (c) The drum played awfully yesterday.
    (d) 10 Downing Street isn't saying anything.
    (e) Capitol Hill didn't ratify the new bill.
    (f) Clinton approved of the extension of NATO to Eastern European countries.

3. Decide which of the following is a metonymy and which is a metaphor with the help of the "is like" test.

    (a) The 10:50 was full.
    (b) The soccer player was an animal yesterday.
    (c) Susie is the joy of her parents.
    (d) You are the sunshine of my life.
    (e) He carries some heavy baggage in his life.
    (f) Our company wants good heads in top positions.
    (g) I am madly in love.
    (h) This scandal may become another Watergate.

4. As we saw, some metonymies make use of the "active zone" phenomenon. Interestingly, when the "active zone" is used directly, there is often a difference in meaning. What meaning difference do you recognize between the following sentences?

    (a) He hit me.
    (b) His fist hit me.

Find other such cases.

12

The Universality
of Conceptual
Metaphors

Are there any conceptual metaphors that can be found in all languages and cultures? This is an extremely difficult question to answer, considering that there are more than 4,000 languages spoken currently around the world. Our best bet to begin to understand this issue is to look at some conceptual metaphors that one can find in some language and then check whether the same metaphors exist in typologically very different languages. If they do occur, we can set up a hypothesis that they may be universal. With further research, we can then verify or disprove the universality of these metaphors.

In this chapter, I've chosen some conceptual metaphors from English and will check their occurrence in some genetically unrelated languages. In this way, certain hypotheses can be proposed concerning the universal or non-universal status of the metaphors.

If we find that the same conceptual metaphor does occur in several unrelated languages, we are faced with an additional question: *Why* does this conceptual metaphor exist in such different languages and cultures? This is one of the most interesting issues that the cognitive linguistic view of metaphor should be able to say something about.

1. Some Metaphors for HAPPINESS

Let us begin with some metaphors for happiness in English. We saw a number of these in a previous chapter. To recall, here they are again:

BEING HAPPY IS BEING OFF THE GROUND
BEING HAPPY IS BEING IN HEAVEN
HAPPY IS UP
HAPPINESS IS LIGHT
HAPPINESS IS VITALITY

HAPPINESS IS A FLUID IN A CONTAINER
HAPPINESS IS A CAPTIVE ANIMAL
HAPPINESS IS AN OPPONENT
HAPPINESS IS A RAPTURE
A HAPPY PERSON IS AN ANIMAL (THAT LIVES WELL)
HAPPINESS IS A PLEASURABLE PHYSICAL SENSATION
HAPPINESS IS INSANITY
HAPPINESS IS A NATURAL FORCE

Of these, three are especially important for conceptualizing happiness in English: the metaphors that employ the concepts of UP, LIGHT, and A FLUID IN A CONTAINER. In a study, the Chinese linguist Ning Yu checked whether these metaphors also exist in the conceptualization of happiness in Chinese. He found that they all do. Here are some examples that he described:

(Ning Yu used the following grammatical abbreviations: PRT = particle; ASP = aspect marker; MOD = modifier marker; COM = complement marker; CL = classifier; BA = preposition *ba* in the so-called *ba*-sentences.)

HAPPY IS UP
Ta hen gao-xing.
he very high-spirit
He is very high-spirited/happy.

Ta xing congcong de.
he spirit rise-rise PRT
His spirits are rising and rising./He's pleased and excited.

Zhe-xia tiqi le wo-de xingzhi.
this-moment raise ASP my mood
This time it lifted my mood/interest.

HAPPINESS IS LIGHT
Tamen gege xing-gao cai-lie.
they everyone spirit-high color-strong
They're all in high spirits and with a strong glow./They're all in great
    delight.

Ta xiao zhu yan kai.
he smile drive color beam
He smiled, which caused his face to beam./He beamed with a smile.

HAPPINESS IS A FLUID IN A CONTAINER
Ta xin-zhong chongman xiyue.
he heart-inside fill happiness
His heart is filled with happiness.

Ta zai-ye anna-buzhu xin-zhong de xiyue.
she no-longer press-unable heart-inside MOD happiness
She could no longer contain the joy in her heart.

It appears that the same metaphors also occur in Hungarian:

HAPPY IS UP
Ez a film feldobott.
this the film up-threw-me
This film gave me a high./This film made me happy.

Majd elszáll a boldogságtól.
almost away-flies-he/she the happiness-from
He/she is on cloud nine.

HAPPINESS IS LIGHT
Felderült az arca.
up-brightened the face-his/her
His/her face brightened up.

Derüs alkat.
he/she bright personality
He/she has a sunny personality.

HAPPINESS IS A FLUID IN A CONTAINER
Túlcsordult a szíve a boldogságtól.
over-flow-past the heart-his/her the happiness-from
His heart overflowed with joy.

Nem bírtam magamban tartani örömömet.
not could-I myself-in hold joy-my-ACC
I couldn't contain my joy.

(ACC means accusative.) English, Chinese, and Hungarian are three typologically completely unrelated languages and represent very different cultures of the world. The question arises: How is it possible for such different
languages and cultures to conceptualize happiness metaphorically in such
similar ways? Three answers to the question suggest themselves: (1) it has
happened by accident; (2) one language borrowed the metaphors from another; and (3) there is some universal motivation for the metaphors to emerge
in these cultures. I will opt for the third possibility, although the other factors cannot be ruled out completely either.

To see why this is a reasonable option, let us focus on variants of a single
conceptual metaphor that have been studied extensively in recent years. First,
I will show that there are metaphors that are at least near-universal. Second,
I will suggest that these near-universal metaphors share generic-level structure. Third, I will claim that their (near-)universality arises from universal
aspects of the human body.

2. The Case of the CONTAINER Metaphor for Anger

A metaphor that has received considerable attention in cross-cultural studies
is ANGER IS A HOT FLUID IN A CONTAINER that was first isolated and analyzed in English. Let us look at this metaphor and see whether researchers
have found something like it in a variety of unrelated languages, including
English, Hungarian, Japanese, Chinese, Zulu, Polish, Wolof, and Tahitian.

2.1. English

As we saw in chapter 8, in English the conceptual metaphor in question was characterized as ANGER IS A HOT FLUID IN A CONTAINER. To recapitulate, consider the following examples:

> You make my blood *boil*.
> *Simmer* down!
> Let him *stew*.

All of these examples assume a container (corresponding to the human body), a fluid inside the container, as well as the element of heat as a property of the fluid. It is the hot fluid or, more precisely, the heat of the fluid that corresponds to anger. That this is so is shown by the fact that lack of heat indicates lack of anger (as in "Keep *cool*").

Moreover, as we already saw in chapter 8, the HOT FLUID metaphor in English gives rise to a series of metaphorical entailments. This means that we carry over knowledge about the behavior of hot fluids in a closed container onto the concept of anger. Thus we get:

> WHEN THE INTENSITY OF ANGER INCREASES, THE FLUID RISES: His pent-up anger welled up inside him.
> INTENSE ANGER PRODUCES STEAM: Billy's just blowing off steam.
> INTENSE ANGER PRODUCES PRESSURE ON THE CONTAINER: He was bursting with anger.
> WHEN ANGER BECOMES TOO INTENSE, THE PERSON EXPLODES: When I told him, he just exploded.
> WHEN A PERSON EXPLODES, PARTS OF HIM GO UP IN THE AIR: I blew my stack.
> WHEN A PERSON EXPLODES, WHAT WAS INSIDE HIM COMES OUT: His anger finally came out.

Let us now see whether this metaphor, or something like it, can be found in other languages and if it can, how it is expressed and which entailments it gives rise to.

2.2. Hungarian

The Hungarian version of the CONTAINER metaphor also emphasizes a hot fluid in a container. The Hungarian metaphor ANGER IS A HOT FLUID IN A CONTAINER differs from the English one in only minor ways. (From here onward, I will only give the English translations—literal and/or idiomatic—of the non-English linguistic examples. The literal translations—if they are available—are in square brackets.)

> [boiled in-him the anger] Anger was boiling inside him.
> [seethe the anger-with] He is seething with anger.
> [almost burst the head-his] His head almost burst.

The only difference in relation to English seems to be that Hungarian (in addition to the body as a whole) also has the head as a principal container that can hold the hot fluid.

As can be seen from the examples below, most of the entailments of the HOT FLUID IN A CONTAINER metaphor also apply to Hungarian.

WHEN THE INTENSITY OF ANGER INCREASES, THE FLUID RISES
[up-piled in-him the wrath] Wrath built/piled up in him/her.
[up-welled in-him the wrath/anger] Anger welled up inside him/her.

INTENSE ANGER PRODUCES STEAM
[completely in-steamed-he/she] He was all steam.
[smoked in-himself/herself] He was fuming alone/by himself/herself.

INTENSE ANGER PRODUCES PRESSURE ON THE CONTAINER
[almost apart-burst-him/her the anger] His anger almost burst him/her.
[almost apart-exploded-he/she anger-in] He/she almost exploded with
    anger.
[hardly could-he/she himself/herself-in to hold anger] He/she could
    hardly hold his/her anger inside.

WHEN ANGER BECOMES TOO INTENSE, THE PERSON EXPLODES
[burst-he/she anger-in] He/she burst with anger.
[apart-exploded-he/she anger-in] He/she exploded with anger.
[not tolerate-I out-bursts-your] I do not tolerate your outbursts.

WHEN A PERSON EXPLODES, PARTS OF HIM GO UP IN THE AIR
[the ceiling-on is already again] He/she is on the ceiling again.

WHEN A PERSON EXPLODES, WHAT WAS INSIDE HIM COMES OUT
[out-burst from-inside-him/her the anger] Anger burst out of him/her.
[out-burst-he/she] He/she burst out.

2.3. Japanese

Keiko Matsuki observed that the ANGER IS A HOT FLUID IN A CONTAINER metaphor also exists in the Japanese language. One property that distinguishes the Japanese metaphor from both the English and the Hungarian ones is that, in addition to the body as a whole, the stomach/bowels area (called *hara* in Japanese) is seen as the principal container for the hot fluid that corresponds to anger. Consider the following Japanese examples:

The *intestines* are *boiling*.
Anger *seethes* inside the body.
Anger *boils* the bottom of the stomach.

Some of the metaphorical entailments are also the same as in English and Hungarian:

WHEN THE INTENSITY OF ANGER INCREASES, THE FLUID RISES
[anger in my mind/inside me was getting bigger] My anger kept building
    up inside me.

INTENSE ANGER PRODUCES STEAM
[she with steam/steaming up was angry] She got all steamed up.
[out of his head smoke was coming/pouring out] Smoke was pouring
    out of his head.

INTENSE ANGER PRODUCES PRESSURE ON THE CONTAINER
To be unable to suppress the feeling of anger.
[I anger suppressed] I suppressed my anger.
Blood rises up to the head.

WHEN ANGER BECOMES TOO INTENSE, THE PERSON EXPLODES
My mother finally exploded.
["patience bag" tip/end was cut/broken/burst] His patience bag burst.
[anger exploded] My anger exploded.

The entailments that do not carry over in the case of Japanese are "when a
person explodes, parts of him go up in the air" and "when a person explodes,
what was inside him comes out." This finding may be due to insufficient linguistic evidence. What is clear, though, is that Japanese does have the first
four of the entailments, the fourth being "the explosion corresponding to loss
of control over anger." Indeed, the others that follow this entailment in the
sequence may be regarded as mere embellishments on the notion of loss of
control.

2.4. Chinese

Chinese offers yet another version of the CONTAINER metaphor for the Chinese counterpart of anger (*nu* in Chinese). The Chinese version makes use of
and is based on the culturally significant notion of *qi*. *Qi* is energy that is
conceptualized as a gas (or fluid) that flows through the body and that can
increase and then produce an excess. This is the case when we have the emotion of anger. Brian King isolated the "excess *qi*" metaphor for anger on the
basis of the following examples:

    (King uses the following grammatical abbreviations: POSS = possessive,
NEG = negative.)

ANGER IS EXCESS QI IN THE BODY
[heart in POSS anger qi] the anger qi in one's heart
[deep hold qi] to hold one's qi down
[qi well up like mountain] one's qi wells up like a mountain
[hold back one stomach qi] to hold back a stomach full of qi
[pent up at breast POSS anger qi finally explode] the pent up anger qi in
    one's breast finally explodes
[NEG make spleen qi start make] to keep in one's spleen qi

First, it may be observed that in Chinese anger *qi* may be present in a variety
of places in the body, including the breast, heart, stomach, and spleen. Second, anger *qi* seems to be a gas or fluid that, unlike in English, Hungarian,
and Japanese, is not hot. Its temperature is not specified. As a result, Chinese

does not have the entailment involving the idea of steam being produced. Third, anger *qi* is a gas or fluid whose build-up produces pressure in the body or in a specific body organ. This pressure typically leads to an explosion that corresponds to loss of control over anger.

2.5. Zulu

The Zulu version of the CONTAINER metaphor was described by John Taylor and Thandi Mbense. They offer the following examples:

(Taylor and Mbense use the following grammatical abbreviations: SC = subject concord; PERF = perfect (recent past); PAST = (remote) past; LOC = locative morpheme; MIDDLE = middle-forming (detransitivizing) morpheme; APPL = applicative morpheme; ASP = aspectual marker; FUT = future marker; IMP = imperative; INF = infinitive (nominalizing morpheme).)

ANGER IS IN THE HEART
[this-person SC-with-heart long] This person has a long heart, i.e., "He is tolerant, patient, rarely displays anger."
[he-with-heart small/short] He has a small/short heart, i.e. "He is impatient, intolerant, bad-tempered, prone to anger."
[heart SC-say-PERF xhifi I-him-see] My heart went 'xhifi' when I saw him, i.e., "I suddenly felt hot-tempered when I saw him."
[it.PAST-say 'fithi' heart-LOC] It went 'fithi' in the heart, i.e., "I suddenly felt sick/angry."
[I.PAST-him-tell then he.PAST-inflate-MIDDLE] When I told him he inflated.
[he-PAST-be.angry he.PAST-burst] He was so angry he burst/exploded.

The Zulu CONTAINER metaphor is somewhat "deviant," in that it is primarily based on the heart, and that the things that cause pressure in the container are the variety of emotions that are produced by the events of daily life. When there is too much of these emotions in the heart, people are "inflated" and are ready to "burst." A person with a "small/short heart" is more likely to lose control than one with a "long heart," as the first two examples show.

2.6. Polish

Although marginally, the CONTAINER metaphor is present in Polish as well. Agnieszka Mikolajczuk offers the following examples (in transcribing the Polish examples, I have left out special Polish diacritic marks):

(Mikolajczuk uses the following grammatical abbreviations: NOM = nominative; LOC = locative; INSTR = instrumental; GEN = genitive)

ANGER IS A HOT FLUID IN A CONTAINER
[bile/anger-NOM itself in him-LOC boil] he is boiling with rage
[burst exasperation-INSTR] to burst with anger

As the second example indicates, the notion of pressure is also a part of this metaphor in Polish.

2.7. Wolof

Pamela Munro notes that in Wolof, an African language spoken in Senegal and Gambia, the word *bax* means "to boil" in a literal sense. It is also used metaphorically in the sense of "to be really angry." The existence of this metaphor indicates that Wolof has something like the CONTAINER metaphor as a possible conceptualization of the counterpart of anger.

2.8. Tahitian

Tahitian can serve as our final illustration of a culture, where anger is conceptualized as a force inside a container. For example, Robert Levy quotes a Tahitian informant as saying: "The Tahitians say that an angry man is like a bottle. When he gets filled up he will begin to spill over." This saying again indicates that the concept of anger is conceptualized in Tahitian as being a fluid in a container that can be kept inside the container or that can spill out.

3. The Structure of the PRESSURIZED CONTAINER Metaphor for Anger

Notice that what is common to these CONTAINER metaphors is that the container is a pressurized container, either with or without heat. The major correspondences, or mappings, of the metaphor include:

(1) the container with the substance in it ⇒ the angry person's body

(2) the substance (fluid, gas, objects) in the pressurized container ⇒ the anger

(3) the physical pressure in the container ⇒ the potentially dangerous social or psychophysiological force of the anger

(4) the cause of the pressure ⇒ the cause of the dangerous force

(5) the control of the physical pressure ⇒ the control of the social or psycho-physiological force

(6) the inability to control the physical pressure ⇒ the inability to control the dangerous social or psycho-physiological force

These are the mappings that play a constitutive role in the construction of the basic structure of the folk understandings of anger and its counterparts in different cultures. Without these mappings (i.e., imposing the schematic structure of how the force of a fluid or gas behaves in a container onto anger), it is difficult to see how anger and its counterparts could have acquired the structure they seem to possess: a situation producing a force inside a person and then the force causing the person to act in certain ways that should be suppressed. The 'cause, force, forced expression' structure remains a mystery and a completely random occurrence without evoking the PRESSURIZED CONTAINER metaphor. Through its detailed mappings, the metaphor provides a coherent structure for the various "anger-like" concepts in the different languages.

But now a new question arises: How does the PRESSURIZED CONTAINER metaphor come into the picture in all these different languages and cultures in the first place?

4. The Emergence of the Same CONTAINER Metaphor for Anger

How do such different languages and cultures as English, Hungarian, Japanese, Chinese, Zulu, Polish, Wolof, and Tahitian produce a remarkably similar shared metaphor—the PRESSURIZED CONTAINER metaphor for anger and its counterparts? The reason is that, as linguistic usage suggests, English-speaking, Hungarian, Japanese, Chinese people appear to have very similar ideas about their bodies and seem to see themselves as undergoing the same physiological processes when in the state of *anger, düh, ikari, nu*, and so forth. They all view their bodies and body organs as containers. And, also as linguistic evidence suggests, they respond physiologically to certain situations (causes) in the same ways. They seem to share certain physiological processes including body heat, internal pressure, and redness in the neck and face area (as a possible combination of pressure and heat). The claim here is a conceptual one and is based on the linguistic examples that follow. The examples cluster together and reveal the following underlying conceptual metonymies:

BODY HEAT STANDS FOR ANGER

English
Don't get hot under the collar.
Billy's a hothead.
They were having a heated argument.

Chinese
My face was pepperily hot with anger.

Japanese
[my head get hot] My head got hot.
[head cool should] You should cool down.

Hungarian
hotheaded
heated argument

Polish
[white fever] 'high fever'
[gall itself in sb-LOC boils] sb's blood boils

Zulu
[he.PAST-be.hot-INTENSIFIER] He was really hot.
[I.PAST-feel it-become.hot blood] I felt my blood getting hot.

Wolof
[to be hot] to be bad-tempered
[he heated my heart] He upset me, made me angry.

Tahitian [*no data for body heat*]

INTERNAL PRESSURE STANDS FOR ANGER

English
Don't get a hernia!
When I found out, I almost burst a blood vessel.

Chinese
[qi DE brain full blood] to have so much qi that one's brain is full of
    blood
[break stomach skin] to break the stomach skin from qi
[lungs all explode] one's lungs explode from too much qi

Japanese
[he due to blood pressure to keep going up] My blood pressure keeps
    going up because of him.
[like that get angry blood pressure to go up] Don't get so angry; your
    blood pressure will go up.

Hungarian
[cerebral-hemorrhage gets] will have a hemorrhage
[up-goes in-him the pump] pressure rises in him
[up-went the blood-pressure-his] His blood pressure went up.

Polish
[heart oneself] to storm
[explosion-NOM anger-GEN] blaze of anger

Zulu
[heart my SC-fill.up-PERF blood] My heart is full of blood.
[he.PAST-be.angry he.PAST-choke] He was so angry he choked.

Tahitian [*no data*]

Wolof [*no data*]

REDNESS IN FACE AND NECK AREA STANDS FOR ANGER

English
She was scarlet with rage.
He got red with anger.

Chinese [he face all red eyes emit fire come] His face turned red and his
    eyes blazed.

Japanese [he red to be get angry] He turned red with anger.

Hungarian [red became the head-his] His head turned red.

Polish [scarlet out rage-GEN] scarlet with rage

Zulu [chief he.PAST-redden he.PAST-be-red] The chief went red (with anger).

Tahitian [*no data*]

Wolof [*no data*]

English, Hungarian, Japanese, Zulu, Polish, Wolof, and, to some degree, Chinese as well seem to share the notion of an increase in body heat in anger, and they also talk about it metonymically. The notion of subjective body heat, perhaps together with the idea of the felt warmth of blood, seems to be the cognitive basis for the heat component of the English, Hungarian, Japanese, and Wolof CONTAINER metaphors. The fact that Chinese does not have a large number of metonymies associated with body heat may be responsible for the Chinese CONTAINER metaphor *not* involving a *hot* fluid or gas.

Internal pressure is present in English, Chinese, Japanese, Hungarian, Polish, and Zulu. We do not have data for internal pressure in Tahitian and Wolof. The physiological response "redness in the face and neck area" can be taken to be the result of both body heat and internal pressure. This response seems to characterize English, Chinese, Japanese, Hungarian, Polish, and Zulu. There is no data for Tahitian and Wolof, although the Wolof word *boy* "to be red hot (of charcoal)" also means "to be really angry."

Since the word for human blood is present in many of the linguistic examples we have seen, it is reasonable to assume that it is mainly blood (but also some other body fluids) that accounts for the fluid component in many of the CONTAINER metaphors. Many of the examples suggest that blood is often seen as producing an increase in blood pressure when angry, and this, together with muscular pressure and pressure in the lungs, may be responsible for the pressure element in the CONTAINER metaphors. All the languages seem to have the image of a pressurized container, with or without heat.

I propose then that conceptualized physiology (i.e., the conceptual metonymies) provides the cognitive motivation for people to conceptualize the angry person metaphorically as a PRESSURIZED CONTAINER. Put in linguistic terms, the conceptual metonymies make this particular conceptualization natural for people. If conceptualized physiological responses include an increase in internal pressure as a major response in a given culture, people in this culture will find the use of the PRESSURIZED CONTAINER metaphor natural.

P. Ekman, R. Levenson, and their colleagues provide ample evidence that anger does indeed go together with objectively measurable bodily changes such as increase in skin temperature, blood pressure, pulse rate, and more intense respiration and that other emotions, like fear and sadness, go together with a different set of physiological activities. These studies were conducted with American subjects only. However, Levenson and his colleagues extended their research cross-culturally and found that emotion-specific ANS (autonomic nervous system) activity is the same in Americans and the Minangkabau of West Sumatra. For example, an increase in skin temperature is attributable to anger in both Americans and the Minangkabau. These findings give us reason to believe that the actual physiology might be universal. The universality of actual physiology might be seen as leading to the similarities (though not equivalence) in conceptualized physiology (i.e., the conceptual metonymies) that might then lead to the similarity (though again not equivalence) in the metaphorical conceptualization of anger and its counterparts (i.e., the CONTAINER metaphor).

A major implication is that the embodiment of anger appears to constrain the kinds of metaphors that can emerge as viable conceptualizations of anger. This seems to be the reason why very similar CONTAINER metaphors have emerged for this concept and its counterparts in a variety of different cultures. It is on the basis of this similarity that the metaphors in different cultures can be viewed as forming a category of metaphors, a category that we have called the CONTAINER metaphor. Without the constraining effect of embodiment, it is difficult to see how such a surprisingly uniform category (of CONTAINER metaphors) could have emerged for the conceptualization of anger and its counterparts in very different languages and cultures.

But how general can this explanation be? Anger, it can be suggested, is a concept that is deeply rooted in the human body. It is thus not surprising that it is characterized by at least one near-universal metaphor at the generic level. What about other concepts that are less likely to be grounded in the kind of physiological experience that anger is? We will now turn to one such case.

5. Event Structure in Chinese

In chapter 10, we looked at the Event Structure metaphor in some detail. It was pointed out that different aspects of events, such as state, change, cause, action, purpose, are comprehended via a small set of physical concepts: location (bounded region), force, and movement. Let us recall this metaphor complex in English:

STATES ARE LOCATIONS: They are *in* love.
CHANGES ARE MOVEMENTS: He *went* crazy.
CAUSES ARE FORCES: The hit *sent* the crowd into a frenzy.
ACTION IS SELF-PROPELLED MOTION: We've taken the first *step*.
PURPOSES ARE DESTINATIONS: He finally *reached* his goals.
MEANS ARE PATHS: She went from fat to thin *through* an intensive
    exercise program.
DIFFICULTIES ARE IMPEDIMENTS: Let's try *to get around* this problem.
EXTERNAL EVENTS ARE LARGE, MOVING OBJECTS: The *flow* of
    history . . .
EXPECTED PROGRESS IS A TRAVEL SCHEDULE: We're *behind schedule* on
    this project.
LONG-TERM, PURPOSEFUL ACTIVITIES ARE JOURNEYS: You should
    move on with your life.

Ning Yu investigated the possibility of the existence of the English Event Structure metaphor in Chinese. He read the leading Chinese daily newspaper and made note of the cases where he found something like the metaphors above in English. He discovered that the entire system works for Chinese as well! In his book, he richly documents the Chinese version of Event Structure. We will take just one or two of his examples to illustrate that the Event Structure metaphor really exists in Chinese and also to offer the hypothesis that it may actually be found in many, if not all, languages of the world. Here are some examples from Chinese:

STATES ARE LOCATIONS: [state-owned enterprises be located in fine state] The state-owned enterprises are in a fine state.

CHANGE IS MOTION FROM ONE LOCATION TO ANOTHER
[this project enter into motion] This project got into motion (i.e., got started).
[basic industries construction step into good state] The construction of basic industries stepped into a good state.

CAUSES ARE FORCES (CONTROLLING MOVEMENT TO OR FROM LOCATIONS) [these prop industries MOD formation bring-move ASP overall economy MOD development] The formation of these prop industries brought into motion (i.e., gave impetus to) the development of the overall economy.

ACTIONS ARE SELF-PROPELLED MOVEMENTS: [China quicken wipe-out poverty steps] China quickened steps toward wiping out poverty.

PURPOSES ARE DESTINATIONS (DESIRED LOCATIONS): [China PRT toward build new system realize modernization MOD goal advance] China is advancing toward the goal of building up a new system and realize modernization.

MEANS ARE PATHS TO DESTINATIONS: [Tongzhou open-up new technology break new road] Tongzhou opened up new technology to break a new path.

DIFFICULTIES ARE IMPEDIMENTS TO MOTION: [we should remove Hong Kong smooth transition road on MOD any obstacles] We should remove any obstacles on the road of Hong Kong's smooth transition.

EXPECTED PROGRESS IS A TRAVEL SCHEDULE (a schedule is a virtual traveler, who reaches prearranged destinations at prearranged times): [import foreign intelligence make this province only use eight-year time finish-walking ASP convention need forty year then can finish-walking MOD way] Importing foreign intelligence enables this province to use only eight years to finish walking over the way that conventionally requires forty years' walking.

EXTERNAL EVENTS ARE LARGE MOVING OBJECTS: [reform to China countryside bring-come ASP huge change] The reform brought tremendous change to the countryside in China.

LONG-TERM, PURPOSEFUL ACTIVITIES ARE JOURNEYS: [I always follow ASP his artistic steps PRT his very-long MOD artistic careers in zigzags ups-and-downs very many but he march-forward-bravely chop-thorns-cut-brambles remove one-after-another roadblocks walk out oneself MOD unique MOD artistic path] I was always following his artistic steps closely. In his very long artistic career, there were so many zigzags and ups-and-downs, but he marched forward bravely, chopping thorns and cutting brambles, removing roadblocks one after another, and he walked out a unique artistic path of his own.

Intuitively, the concept of EVENT is a very different kind of concept than anger in that it seems to have a much less obvious physiological basis. This would suggest that the potential universality of the Event Structure metaphor could not be motivated by such direct bodily experience as was the case for anger above. What, then, enables speakers of English and Chinese to metaphorically conceive of events and its dimensions in such similar ways as they do?

In chapter 6, in the discussion of the experiential basis of conceptual metaphors, it was mentioned that conceptual metaphors are often based on physical and cultural connections between two kinds of experience. In the previous chapter, we added that these connections amount to "contiguities" in human experience and suggested that we can regard (many of) them as conceptual metonymies that have, or presuppose, ICMs (idealized cognitive models) in the background. The ICMs can be for actions, causation, categories, etc. In the case of the CONTAINER metaphor for anger that we saw above, the ICM in the background is that of causation, with a cause and effect structure. The physiological effects of anger can stand metonymically for the emotion of anger as such, which is seen as the cause in the ICM.

Obviously, this motivation does not apply to the Event Structure metaphor, in which events are conceptualized as location, force, and movement. Simply, there is no causal link between events, on the one hand, and location, force, and movement, on the other. However, what can be suggested is that the major submetaphor (or central mapping) in this metaphor system is EVENTS ARE MOVEMENTS and that movement is a subcategory of events. Recall that this is a metonymic relationship, and in it, a subcategory (movement) stands for the category as a whole (event). We can, then, claim that there is a metonymic basis for the Event Structure metaphor, similar to many other cases. This kind of contiguity in experience, though not a bodily one, was called a "category-based" metonymic relationship in the previous chapter. And similarly for all the other mappings in the Event Structure metaphor: We find that they are all individually motivated in some way. This finding would provide a great deal of cognitive motivation for this metaphor complex. Given this relationship between the sources and the targets of the Event Structure metaphor, it would not be surprising to find that the metaphor occurs in most languages of the world.

SUMMARY

It has been argued in this chapter that some conceptual metaphors may be **universal**. These include such metaphors as HAPPINESS IS UP, HAPPINESS IS LIGHT, HAPPINESS IS A FLUID IN A CONTAINER, ANGER IS A PRESSURIZED

FLUID OR GAS IN A CONTAINER, and the EVENT STRUCTURE metaphor.

We showed in the case of ANGER IS A PRESSURIZED CONTAINER that the universality of this metaphor can be found at the **generic level**. Anger seems to be conceptualized in a variety of unrelated languages as some kind of internal pressure inside a container.

The hypothetical universality of the PRESSURIZED CONTAINER metaphor for anger and its counterparts appears to derive from certain universal aspects of *human physiology*. When a metaphorical concept has such an experiential basis, it can be said to be *embodied*. However, not all metaphorical concepts have such clear *bodily motivation* (in the sense of physiological) as in the case of the PRESSURIZED CONTAINER metaphor for anger. It can be suggested that there are other kinds of correlations in experience that can motivate other metaphors, including perceptual, cultural, category-based, etc. correlations. We saw that the Event Structure metaphor may also be motivated by correlations in experience, which can be viewed as metonymic in character. The universality of such metonymic correlations may explain the universality of many conceptual metaphors.

FURTHER READING

Geeraerts and Grondelaers (1995) criticize the Lakoff and Kövecses (1987) study of anger and discuss the relationship of the present-day model of anger to the medieval "humoral" theory. Kövecses (1995d) replies to this challenge. Kövecses (1991b) analyzes the concept of happiness in English.

Ekman, Levenson, and Friesen (1983) deal with the issue of how autonomic nervous system activity distinguishes among emotions. Levenson, Carstensen, Friesen, and Ekman (1991); Levenson, Ekman, and Friesen (1990); Levenson, Ekman, Heider, and Friesen (1992) deal with various aspects of the physiology of emotion, including the issues that physiology may distinguish among emotions and that this emotion-specific physiology may be universal.

King (1989) is a doctoral dissertation that describes in detail the Chinese conception of some emotion concepts from a cognitive linguistic perspective, including anger. Levy (1973) is a study of Tahitian culture, including the emotions. Kusumi (1996) provides psychological evidence for the universality of anger metaphors. Lutz (1987, 1988) approaches emotions from a cognitive-anthropological perspective. Matsuki (1995) looks at the Japanese conception of anger, using metaphor analysis. Mikolajczuk (1998) describes anger in Polish. Munro (1991) provides valuable linguistic data on anger in Wolof. Ning Yu (1995, 1998) contrasts the metaphorical conception of anger, happiness, time, and Event Structure in English with their counterparts in Chinese. Emanatian (1995) provides a description of lust in Chagga. Taylor and Mbense (1998) contrast the Zulu conception of anger with that found in English. Lakoff and Johnson (1999) provide the most systematic and comprehensive statement on how meaning in general is embodied in human sensorimotor experience, as well as in the brain.

In a series of fascinating studies, Heine and his colleagues examine the metaphorical conceptualization of several concepts and basic grammatical constructions in, literally, hundreds of languages. See, for example, Heine, Claudi, and Hunnemeyer (1991), Heine (1995, 1997).

EXERCISES

1. Look at the following proverbs about love which are taken from various languages. Can you find any common conceptual metaphors underlying them?

   (a) *French:* One grows used to love and fire.
   Swedish: Love or fire in your trousers is not easy to conceal.
   English: Love can melt the ice and the snow of the coldest regions.

   (b) *Italian:* It is all one whether you die of sickness or of love.
   Japanese: For lovesickness there is no medicine.
   English: No herb will cure love.
   Philippine: Too much love causes heartbreak.

2. On the basis of Michele Emanatian's study of the concept and the metaphors of SEX in Chagga, it can be inferred that there are certain congruities between English and Chagga in the conceptualization of lust, since both languages make use of similar source domains. Figure out the similar metaphors present in both English and Chagga.

English

   (a) He has quite a sexual appetite.
   The thought of Gina in that black skirt made him even hungrier.
   He is quite a piece of meat.
   You look juicy.

   (b) I've got the hots for her.
   He was burning with desire.
   She's frigid.
   Don't be cold to me, baby.

Chagga

   (i) *ngi'kúndiimlya* [I want to eat her] > to have intercourse with her
   ngi'ichuo njáa (ia mndu mka) [I feel hunger (for a woman)] > be desirous
   ngi'ndépfúlá wundo wóó lýo [I am going to look for a little something to eat] > to find a sexual partner
   napfú'lié mruwa [She is searching for milk] > desirous of sex

   (ii) *nékehá* [She burns] > sexually desirable
   náwo(é ·mrike [She has warmth] > sexually desirable
   kyambúya rikó lílya [Look at that oven] > sexy woman
   nékechólóliá [She's cold] > lacks desirable sexual attributes

3. The following are literal translations of metaphorical linguistic expressions used in Chinese, English, Hungarian, Japanese, Polish, and Zulu to describe anger. Read them carefully; then fill in the table according to the instructions in (a), (b), and (c) below.

Chinese
   (1) Don't provoke me to shoot fire.
   (2) You're adding oil to the fire.
   (3) You're gassing/pumping me up.

(4) He is inflated with gas.
(5) To possess anger qi in one's heart.
(6) To hold one's qi down.
(7) To restrain one's anger.
(8) He was submerged by anger.

English
(9) He was battling his anger.
(10) He was growling with rage.
(11) She was brimming with rage.
(12) When he gets angry, he goes bonkers.
(13) Your insincere apology just added fuel to the fire.
(14) I had reached the boiling point.
(15) You're beginning to get to me.
(16) He's a pain in the neck.

Hungarian
(17) His blood is boiling.
(18) He got all steamed up.
(19) He was seething/fuming with anger.
(20) I almost burst from anger.
(21) There's a great storm inside.
(22) He is foaming at the mouth.
(23) She's raging mad.
(24) She couldn't control her anger.
(25) He is angry like a hamster.
(26) He is always roaring like the sea.

Japanese
(27) Anger spreads all over the body like violent waves.
(28) To get angry and crazy.
(29) Anger gradually flows out.
(30) The intestines are boiling.
(31) Anger starts burning.
(32) To fight against the rising anger.
(33) Terrible anger crawls around the eyebrows.
(34) I feel light after having expressed my anger.

Polish
(35) He looks as if a wasp had stung him.
(36) To pour out all bile/ exasperation on somebody.
(37) He was seized with a fit of rage.
(38) Venomous remarks.
(39) She was angry like a wasp.
(40) Anger overcomes somebody.
(41) Somebody flings thunderbolts of anger.
(42) There is an angry flame on his face.
(43) Bile/anger is boiling in him.
(44) A surge of anger flooded him.

Zulu
(45) This person is full of anger.
(46) His heart has anger in it.

Table 12.1

METAPHORS	LANGUAGES					
	English	Hungarian	Chinese	Japanese	Polish	Zulu
THE BODY IS A CONTAINER FOR THE EMOTIONS						
ANGER IS FIRE						
ANGER IS THE HEAT OF A FLUID IN A CONTAINER						
ANGER IS INSANITY						
ANGER IS AN OPPONENT IN A STRUGGLE						
ANGER IS A DANGEROUS ANIMAL						
THE CAUSE OF ANGER IS PHYSICAL ANNOYANCE						
CAUSING ANGER IS TRESPASSING						
ANGER IS A BURDEN						
ANGER IS A NATURAL FORCE						

(47) I felt my blood getting hot.
(48) He is burning with roaring flames.
(49) He was raving mad with anger.
(50) The chief changed into a ferocious (carnivorous) animal.
(51) He suddenly darkened/became overcast like the sky before a storm.
(52) Why did he blow a gale?
(53) You are sticking your finger into my eye.

(a) Use the translations above to fill in Table 12.1: put a plus (+) sign if you have found a linguistic example for the metaphors, e.g., ANGER IS FIRE.
(b) What do you think is the reason that some metaphors exist in *all* of the languages above?
(c) What do you think is the reason that some metaphors exist in only *some* of the languages?

13

Cultural Variation in Metaphor and Metonymy

It is to be expected that, in addition to universality, there will also be cultural variation in metaphor and metonymy. How does this happen precisely and why? Given a particular abstract target domain, what kind of variation can we expect in the metaphorical conceptualization of that domain? I suggest that the following are likely possibilities for **cultural variation**:

(1) variation in the *range* of conceptual metaphors and metonymies for a given target;

(2) variation in the particular *elaborations* of conceptual metaphors and metonymies for a given target;

(3) variation in the *emphasis* on metaphor versus metonymy associated with a given target, or the other way around.

In general, we can distinguish between two kinds of cultural variation: (a) *cross-cultural (intercultural)* and (b) *within-culture (intracultural)*. As a limiting case of within-culture variation, there will also be individual variation. In the present chapter, I will consider each of these possibilities.

Since I mainly used emotion concepts to demonstrate universal aspects of metaphor and metonymy, it will be reasonable and convenient to deal with cultural variation by continuing to use mostly emotion concepts. Emotions constitute an area where a considerable amount of research has been done on cultural variation in cognitive linguistics.

1. Cross-Cultural Variation

1.1. Range of Conceptual Metaphors

There can be differences in the *range* of conceptual metaphors that languages and cultures have available for the conceptualization of particular target domains. This is what commonly happens in the case of emotion concepts as targets.

Matsuki observes that all the metaphors for anger in English as analyzed by Lakoff and Kövecses can also be found in Japanese. At the same time, she also points out that there is a large number of anger-related expressions that group around the Japanese concept of *hara* (literally, "belly"). This culturally significant concept is unique to Japanese culture, and so the conceptual metaphor ANGER IS (IN THE) HARA is limited to Japanese.

Zulu shares many conceptual metaphors with English. This does not mean, however, that it cannot have metaphors other than the ones we can find in English. One case in point is the Zulu metaphor that involves the heart: ANGER IS (UNDERSTOOD AS BEING) IN THE HEART. When the heart metaphor applies to English, it is primarily associated with love, affection, and the like. In Zulu it applies to anger and patience-impatience, tolerance-intolerance. The heart metaphor conceptualizes anger in Zulu as leading to internal pressure since too much "emotion substance" is crammed into a container of limited capacity. The things that fill it up are other emotions that happen to a person in the wake of daily events. When too many of these happen to a person, the person becomes extremely angry and typically loses control over his anger.

As we saw, Chinese shares with English all the basic metaphor source domains for happiness: UP, LIGHT, FLUID IN A CONTAINER. A metaphor that Chinese has, but English does not, is HAPPINESS IS FLOWERS IN THE HEART. According to Ning Yu, the application of this metaphor reflects "the more introverted character of Chinese." He sees this conceptual metaphor as a contrast to the (American) English metaphor BEING HAPPY IS BEING OFF THE GROUND, which does not exist in Chinese at all and which reflects the relatively "extroverted" character of speakers of English.

1.2. Elaborations of Conceptual Metaphors

In other cases, two languages may share the same conceptual metaphor, but the metaphor will be elaborated differently in the two languages. For example, English has ANGER IS A HOT FLUID IN A CONTAINER. One metaphorical elaboration of this metaphor in English is that the hot fluid produces steam in the container (cf. "He's just *blowing off steam*.") Now this particular elaboration is absent in, for instance, Zulu.

Hungarian shares with English the conceptual metaphors THE BODY IS A CONTAINER FOR THE EMOTIONS and ANGER IS FIRE. The body and the fire inside it are commonly elaborated in Hungarian as a pipe, where there is a burning substance inside a container. This conceptual elaboration seems to be unique to Hungarian.

Hungarians also tend to use the more specific container of the head (with the brain inside) for the general body container in English in talking about anger, and a number of Hungarian expressions mention how anger can affect the head and the brain. Linguistic expressions in English do not seem to emphasize the head (or brain) to the same degree (except the expression *to lose one's head*).

Both English and Zulu have FIRE as a source domain for anger, but Zulu elaborates the metaphor in a way in which English does not. In Zulu you can *extinguish* somebody's anger by pouring water on them. This possible metaphorical entailment is not picked up by the English fire metaphor in the form of conventionalized linguistic expressions. Notice, however, that the metaphorical entailment is perfectly applicable to enthusiasm in English, as when someone is said to be a *wet blanket* at a party.

Anger has desire (to harm) as a component, which can be found in the DESIRE IS HUNGER metaphor. The metaphor appears to exist in Zulu as well, but Zulu elaborates it in unique ways. We can interpret Taylor and Mbense's description in such a way as to suggest that in Zulu an angry person's appetite can be so voracious that he eats food that is not even prepared or he does not even separate edible from inedible food. This aspect of the metaphor is obviously missing from English, at least as judged by the conventionalized linguistic expressions.

In both English and Zulu, anger can be comprehended as A NATURAL FORCE. But speakers of Zulu go much further in making use of this metaphor than speakers of English. In Zulu you can say of an angry person that "the sky became dark with thunderclouds," "the sky (= lightning) almost singed us," or "why did he blow a gale?" These elaborations do not exist in English in conventionalized form, but speakers of English may well understand them given the shared conceptual metaphor.

1.3. Range of Metonymies

Not only conceptual metaphors but also conceptual metonymies can participate in producing cross-cultural variation. One language-culture may have metonymies that the other does not have in a conventionalized linguistic form. In the case of emotion concepts, conceptual metonymies are the linguistic descriptions of the physiological and expressive responses associated with an emotion. As was observed in the previous chapter, the major conventionally verbalized conceptual metonymies for anger in English include body heat, internal pressure, agitation, and interference with accurate perception. Now these certainly exist in, for example, Zulu, but speakers of Zulu use in addition nausea, interference with breathing, illness, perspiration, crying (tears), inability to speak. Most of these can also be found in English for some target domains, but not in association with anger.

1.4. Elaborations of Metonymies

But even the same conceptual metonymies vary cross-culturally in terms of their elaboration and the importance given to them. As we saw in chapter 12, Chinese culture appears to place a great deal more emphasis on the increase in internal pressure due to anger than on body heat. Brian King's and Ning Yu's data suggest that Chinese abounds in metonymies relating to pressure, but not to heat. The conceptual metonymy of heat is recognized, but it is not emphasized and elaborated. This seems to result in a particular kind of CON-TAINER metaphor, one in which the component of pressure is emphasized to the exclusion of heat.

While the eyes are commonly viewed as the "window to the soul" in many cultures, languages vary in the ways in which they make use of the eyes in the conceptualization of emotion. English, for example, employs primarily the intensity of the "light" of the eyes as a metonymic indicator of happiness: the verbs *gleam*, *glint*, *shine*, *sparkle* can all be used to describe a happy person. Chinese, however, elaborates primarily on the eyebrows to talk about happiness. Eyebrows in Chinese, as Ning Yu notes, "are regarded as one of the most obvious indicators of internal feelings."

1.5. Metonymy versus Metaphor

Cultural-linguistic variation may arise from whether a language emphasizes metaphors or metonymies in its conceptualization of emotion. For example, Taylor and Mbense note that English uses primarily metaphors to understand the concept of anger, while Zulu predominantly uses metonymies. In addition, metonymic processes appear to play a bigger role in the understanding of emotions in Chinese than in English, as the work of King and Yu indicates.

2. Causes of Cross-Cultural Variation

There appear to be two large categories of causes that bring about cultural variation in metaphor and metonymy. One is what we can call the *broader cultural context*; by this I simply mean the governing principles and the key concepts in a given culture. The other is the *natural and physical environment* in which a culture is located. Let us briefly look at these in turn.

2.1. Broader Cultural Context

The governing principles and key concepts will differ from culture to culture or from cultural group to cultural group. To demonstrate the effect of these differences on metaphor, let us consider in some detail the near-universal PRESSURIZED CONTAINER metaphor for anger in a variety of cultures. We saw in the previous chapter that at a generic level, this metaphor is very similar across cultures. However, at a specific level we can notice important differences in this metaphor across certain culture groups.

Geeraerts and Grondelaers note that in the Euro-American tradition (including Hungarian), it is the classical-medieval notion of the *four humors* from which the Euro-American conceptualization of anger (and that of emotion in general) is derived. But they also note that the application of the humoral doctrine is not limited to anger or the emotions. The humoral view maintains that the four fluids (phlegm, black bile, yellow bile, and blood) regulate the vital processes of the human body. They were also believed to determine personality types (such as sanguine, melancholy, etc.) and account for a number of medical problems, together with cures for them (like blood-letting). Obviously, then, the use of the humoral view as a form of cultural explanation extends far beyond anger and the emotions. In addition to being an account of emotional phenomena, it was also used to explain a variety of issues in physiology, psychology, and medicine. In other words, the humoral view was a key component of the classical-medieval cultural context.

In Japan, as Matsuki tells us, there seems to exist a culturally distinct set of concepts that is built around the concept of *hara*. Truth, real intentions, and the real self (called *honne*) constitute the content of *hara*. The term *honne* is contrasted with *tatemae* or one's social face. Thus, when a Japanese person keeps his anger under control, he is hiding his private, truthful, innermost self and displaying a social face that is called for in the situation by accepted standards of behavior.

King and Yu suggest that the Chinese concept of *nu* (anger) is bound up with the notion of *qi*, that is, the energy that flows through the body. *Qi* in turn is embedded not only in the psychological (i.e., emotional) but also the philosophical and medical discourse of Chinese culture and civilization. The notion and the workings of *qi* is predicated on the belief that the human body is a homeostatic organism, the belief on which traditional Chinese medicine is based. And the conception of the body as a homeostatic organism seems to derive from the more general philosophical view that the universe operates with two complementary forces, *yin* and *yang*, which must be in balance to maintain the harmony of the universe. Similarly, when *qi* rises in the body, there is anger (*nu*), and when it subsides and there is balance again, there is harmony and emotional calm.

Thus, the four emotion concepts, *anger* in English, *düh* in Hungarian (the two representing European culture), *ikari* in Japanese, and *nu* in Chinese, are in part explained in the respective cultures by the culture-specific concepts of the *four humors, hara,* and *qi*. What accounts for the distinctiveness of the culture-specific concepts is the fact that, as we have just seen, the culture-specific concepts that are evoked to explain the emotion concepts are embedded in very different systems of cultural concepts and propositions (as pointed out, e.g., by Lutz). It appears then that the broader cultural contexts account for many of the specific-level differences among the four emotion concepts and the PRESSURIZED CONTAINER metaphor.

2.2. Natural and Physical Environment

The natural and physical environment shapes a language, primarily its vocabulary, in an obvious way; consequently, it will shape the metaphors as well. Given a certain kind of habitat, speakers living there will be attuned (mostly subconsciously) to things and phenomena that are characteristic of that habitat; and they will make use of these things and phenomena for the metaphorical comprehension and creation of their conceptual universe.

A good test case of this suggestion is a situation in which a language that was developed by speakers living in a certain kind of natural and physical environment was moved by some of its speakers to a new and very different natural and physical environment. If this happens, we should expect to find differences between metaphorical conceptualization by speakers of the original language and that used by people who speak the "transplanted" version.

One case in point can be Dutch and its derivative language Afrikaans Dutch, spoken in some parts of South Africa. René Dirven analyzes and describes this situation in his 1994 book *Metaphor and Nation*. Dirven examined some Afrikaans newspapers and collected the common metaphors in them. He wanted to see to what extent these metaphors are shared by Dutch. His study is a systematic comparison of common stock Dutch and new, Afrikaans metaphors. In the description of "nature" metaphors, he points out that the shared metaphors include images of water, light and shadow, lightning, earthquake, sand, stars, wind, and clouds and that "this is a picture of the typical natural setting of the Low Countries or any other more northern European country" (p. 70). A curious feature of Dutch nature metaphors is that they almost completely lack metaphors based on animals. In contrast to this relatively calm and serene natural atmosphere, he finds metaphors in new, Afrikaans Dutch that are based on both animals of various kinds and forceful images of nature. Dirven writes:

> ... Afrikaans not only seems to have developed many more expressions based on the domain of nature, but the new metaphors also depict a totally different scenery; this may contain mountains, heights and flattened or levelled-off rises or it may be a flat or hilly landscape, used as grazing or farming land (= veld); there are no permanent clouds or shadows, but the "clouds bulge heavily downwards"; all sorts of familiar animals provide the stereotypical images for human behaviour or appearances. (1994, p. 73)

Another example is provided by English. The English spoken in Britain was carried to North America by the settlers. The freshness and imaginative vigor of American English has been noted by many authors. Among them, Baugh and Cable provide a useful comment:

> He [the American] is perhaps at his best when inventing simple homely words like *apple butter*, *sidewalk*, and *lightning rod*, *spelling bee* and *crazy quilt*, *low-down*, and *know-nothing*, or when striking off a terse metaphor like *log rolling*, *wire pulling*, *to have an ax to grind*, *to be on the fence*. . . . The American early manifested the gift, which he continues to show, of the imaginative, slightly humorous phrase. To it we owe *to bark up the wrong tree*, *to face the music*, *fly off the handle*, *go on the warpath*, *bury the hatchet*, *come out at the little end of the horn*, *saw wood*, and many more, with the breath of the country and sometimes of the frontier about them. In this way, the American began his contributions to the English language, . . . (1983, p. 365)

Many of these and other metaphorical expressions in American English owe their existence to the new landscape the settlers encountered, the many new activities they engaged in, and the frontier experience in general.

3. Within-Culture Variation

In this section, I will be concerned with variation in the conceptualization of emotion that occurs within a culture. This is a much more difficult task than handling cross-cultural variation because there has been practically no work done on this aspect of emotion from a cognitive linguistic point of view.

We know from the research outside linguistics that the conceptualization of emotion is not the same, not homogeneous within a culture or society. Individual usage may vary, and there is variation according to social factors and through time. How can this within-culture variation be captured with the same conceptual machinery that was used to make generalizations about cross-cultural differences?

3.1. Metonymy versus Metaphor

As was pointed out above, the language of emotion may emphasize metaphoric or metonymic understanding of a given emotion, and different cultures may prefer one way of understanding emotional experience rather than the other. The same can apply to a single culture through time. There can be a shift from one to the other, probably typically from metonymic to metaphoric understanding. It is worth quoting in full what the historian Peter Stearns has to say about such a process in connection with the United States:

> Prior to the nineteenth century, dominant beliefs, medical and popular alike, attached anger, joy, and sadness to bodily functions. Hearts, for example, could shake, tremble, expand, grow cold. Because emotions were embodied, they had clear somatic qualities: people were gripped by rage (which could, it was held, stop menstruation), hot blood was the essence of anger, fear had cold sweats. Emotions, in other words, had physical stuff. But during the nineteenth century, historians increasingly realize, the humoral conception of the body, in which fluids and emotions alike, could pulse, gave way to a more mechanistic picture. And in the body-machine emotions were harder to pin down, the symptoms harder to convey. Of course physical symptoms could still be invoked, but now only metaphorically. (1994, pp. 66–67)

In other words, Victorian Americans used the "pressurized container" metaphor for anger, which emphasized less the bodily basis (the metonymic conceptualization) of anger (although it was obviously motivated by it), but allowed them to conceptualize their anger metaphorically as something in a container that could be channeled for constructive purposes.

3.2. Conceptual Metonymy

If it is true that conceptual metonymies of emotions reflect, at least for the most part, real universal physiology, then it should not be the case that they vary a whole lot either cross-culturally or within a culture (either through time or at the same time). Indeed, we saw some evidence for this in chapter 12 as regards cross-cultural variation. The metonymies appear to remain roughly the same through time in a given culture, as Stearns's study shows. Analyzing descriptions of Victorian anger, he writes:

> Another angry wife almost dies herself: her face reddens with rage, every vein swells and stands out, every nerve quivers, foam covers her lips, and finally she falls as blood gushes from her nose and mouth. (1994, p. 24)

Despite the exaggerated character of the description, we can easily identify aspects of the folk theory of the physiological effects of anger that is prevalent today: REDNESS IN THE FACE, INTERNAL PRESSURE, PHYSICAL AGITATION, and INSANE BEHAVIOR. As we would expect, physiological responses associated with anger in the nineteenth century must have coincided largely with the ones that characterize the folk model today. Moreover, in their experimental studies of the emotions, Ekman and Levenson and their colleagues found consistently that American men and women, young and old, exhibit the same responses when in intense emotional states.

3.3. Alternative Conceptual Metaphors

3.3.1. Friendship

The conceptual metaphors for a given emotion can change through time within a given culture. For example, in Victorian times what we would identify today as romantic love was part of the concept of friendship between males. This came through clearly in the contemporary letters and journals that Peter Stearns studied: "In letters and journals they described themselves as 'fervent lovers' and wrote of their 'deep and burning affection'" (p. 81–82). In general, the FIRE metaphor characterizes passions, like romantic love, while affection today is more commonly thought of in terms of WARMTH than (the heat of) FIRE. Indeed, in some interviews my students conducted in the United States, where people talked about love in relation to friendship, it was always a more subdued, less intense form of love (affection) conceptualized as warmth that occurred. This change shows that a metaphor that was conventionally associated with male friendship as fire (through love) for the Victorians was dropped and replaced by a metaphorical source domain (warmth) indicating less intensity.

3.3.2. Love

Alternative conceptual metaphors may also be available for a given emotion simultaneously in a culture. This seems to be the case with two very prevalent metaphors of love today: LOVE IS A UNITY and LOVE IS AN ECONOMIC EXCHANGE. Importantly, these are the two metaphors that play a central role in the constitution of two major cultural models of love: "ideal love" and "typical love." The ideal version of love is mainly characterized by the UNITY metaphor, whereas the typical version mainly by ECONOMIC EXCHANGE. The ideal version reflects more traditional ideas about love, while the typical model more recent ones. Stearns notes in this connection that after the Victorian period "[t]he sexual emphasis also tended, if only implicitly, to highlight the rewards an individual should get from a relationship rather than the higher unity of the relationship itself" (p. 173). Obviously, talk about "higher unity" and "the rewards an individual should get from a relationship" correspond to the UNITY and EXCHANGE metaphors, respectively. In her study of American love in the 1970s, Ann Swidler reaches a similar conclusion:

> In a *successful exchange* each person is enhanced so that each is more complete, more autonomous, and more self-aware than before. Rather than becoming *part of a whole, a couple, whose meaning is complete only when both are together*, each person becomes stronger; each *gains* the skills he was without and, thus strengthened, is *more "whole."* If we enter love relationships to complete the missing sides of ourselves, then in some sense when the *exchange* is successful we have learned to get along without the capacities the other person had *supplied*. (Bellah et al. 1988, p. 119) [italics added]

In the passage, as in the two metaphors, love is viewed in two possible ways: In one, there are two parts and only the unity of the two makes them a whole. This essence of the traditional conception of love, was recognized but not accepted by, for instance, Margaret Fuller as early as 1843. The second more recent metaphor takes two wholes that are each not as complete as they could be, but in the process of the exchange they both become stronger, complete wholes. In Swidler's words: "The emerging cultural view of love . . . emphasizes exchange. What is valuable about a relationship is 'what one gets out of it'" (p. 119). Apparently, the EXCHANGE metaphor has become a prevalent metaphor in American culture. This does not mean, however, that the UNITY metaphor is completely forgotten. There are many people in the United States who still use the UNITY metaphor as well.

3.4. Broader Cultural Context

But why did all these changes occur in the conceptualization of anger, friendship, and love in American culture? The explanation comes from nonlinguistic studies of the broader cultural context.

3.4.1. Anger

As Peter Stearns notes in connection with Victorian emotionology, anger was not a permissible emotion in the home, but, for men, it was actually encouraged at the workplace and in the world of politics. Women were supposed to be "anger-free," and men, while calm at home, were expected to make good use of their anger for purposes of competition with others and for the sake of certain moral ends. But why did this "channeled anger" give way to the ideal of "anger-free" people or to the ideal of suppressing anger under all circumstances? Why did anger become a completely negative emotion? There were a variety of specific reasons, as Stearns argues, including the following:

> New levels of concern about anger and aggression followed in part from perceptions of heightened crime, including juvenile delinquency, and the results of untrammeled aggression in Nazism and then renewed world war. It was difficult, in this context, to view channeled anger as a safe or even useful emotional motivation. (1994, p. 195)

As a result, the attacks on any form of anger, which started around the 1920s, continued throughout the Depression period and the Second World War, leading to a global rejection of the emotion by the 1960s in mainstream culture. The new metaphoric image that became prevalent was that of the "pressure cooker waiting to explode." This fully mechanical metaphor depicted anger as something completely independent of the rational self, the angry person as incapable of any rational judgment, and the resulting angry behavior as extremely dangerous. The process (that started in the eighteenth century) of the separation of the emotion from the self and the body, that is, the "mechanization" of anger, was now completed.

3.4.2. Friendship

To turn to friendship, we can ask why in addition to the view of friendship in the Victorian period, as almost love-like, there emerged a very different, less intense form of friendship called "friendliness" in American culture? Again, the causes are numerous and we can't go into all of them. One of them, however, is that there were demands for a "new emotionology" from outside the "private sphere," especially the world of business and large corporations. Again, Stearns explains:

> American language continued to reflect incorporation of a pleasant but nonintense emotionality. "Niceness" became a watchword for sales clerks and others in casual contact. "Have a nice day" struck many foreigners—even neighboring Canadians—as a remarkably insincere phrase. At the same time though, they noted that Americans did seem "nice," an attribute that includes unusual discomfort with emotional outbursts on the part of those raised in different cultures where displays of temper might be more readily accepted. In American culture, "nice" did have a meaning—it connoted a genuine effort to be agreeably disposed but not deeply emotionally involved while expecting pleasant predictability from others. (1994, pp. 292–293)

Furthermore, the new emotionology considerably "reduced tolerance to other people's intensity." Although friendship for many Americans is an opportunity to talk out their problems, "intense emotion was also a sign of immaturity, and it could be shunned on that basis." (1994, p. 245)

3.4.3. Love

Finally, why did the conception of love change? But even before that happened, why was romantic love so intense in the Victorian period to begin with? According to Stearns: "Hypertrophied maternal love increased the need for strong adult passion to aid products of emotionally intense upbringing in freeing themselves from maternal ties" (p. 66). In addition, "in intense, spiritualized passion, couples hoped to find some of the same balm to the soul that religion had once, as they dimly perceived, provided. . . . more concluded that true love was itself a religious experience" (p. 69). Now, in the wake of increasingly loosening family ties and the ever-weakening importance of religion, the intensity of romantic love also declined. Romantic love ceased to be regarded "as the spiritual merger of two souls into one" (p. 172). Rationality was emphasized in all walks of life, possibly due to the influence of business and the rational organization of large corporations. By 1936, marriage manuals stressed the idea of "rational, cooperative arrangements between men and women. Soaring ideals and spirituality were largely absent. . . . Companionship, not emotional intensity, was the goal" (pp. 175–176). And after the 1960s, relationships were regarded as "exchange arrangements in which sensible partners would make sure that no great self-sacrifice was involved" (p. 180).

According to Stearns, the overall result was that "[t]wentieth-century culture . . . called for management across the board; no emotion should gain control over one's thought processes" (p. 184). The rational culture of the computer was in place, together with the new and highly valued emotional attitude of staying "cool."

3.5. Individual Variation

Do metaphors vary from person to person? We know from everyday experience that they do. Since there hasn't been much work done on this issue, I try to offer some speculations about how and why individuals differ with respect to the metaphors they use.

3.5.1. Human Concern

One source of individual variation seems to be what can be termed *human concern*. We can often observe that people use metaphors that derive from their major concerns in life. For example, in listening to doctors talk about nonprofessional topics, we notice that they often employ metaphors that come from their professional lives. They have certain general concerns and interests (their professional activities as doctors), and they will apply these to domains that call for source-to-target mappings. What is interesting about this process is that expertise of whatever kind may lead to the exploitation of this expert knowledge. At the same time, a negative consequence may be that people who are not doctors may not be able to gain much from these metaphors because they do not have the necessary expertise to make sense of the doctor's metaphors based on their professional activities as a revealing source domain.

3.5.2. Personal History

Another source for individual variation in the use of metaphor is *personal history*. This simply means the salient events and experiences in people's lives. Thus, for example, certain salient experiences in childhood or as students may influence the kinds of metaphors we use later on as adults.

Consider as an example some of the metaphors that were used by American politicians in the course of their election campaigns in 1996, as pointed out by an American journalist in *Time* magazine. It is well known that Americans have a great liking for sports. It comes as no surprise then that all the candidates running for office in the 1996 campaign used sports metaphors—that is, conceptualizations of a variety of issues in terms of the source domain of SPORTS. Here are some instances of this from a 1996 issue of *Time:*

> Bill Clinton: "Let's don't *take our eye off the ball*. I ask for your support, not on a partisan basis, but to rebuild the American economy."

> Bob Dole: "Everything before has been a *warm-up lap*, a *trial heat*. . . . In San Diego the real *race* begins."

> Al Gore: "[Progress] takes *teamwork*. . . . It's *three yards* and a cloud of dust."

> Jack Kemp: "You're the *quarterback* and I'm your *blocker*, and we're *going all the way*."

As was observed above, the fact that these politicians used sports metaphors is not particularly surprising for anyone who knows that most American politicians "live by" the POLITICS IS SPORTS metaphor. The interesting issue, though, is why they use so many different ones. In light of our hypothesis above, we can provide an answer. Personal history may, and often does, influence the choice of metaphors. As it turns out, according to *Time*, Clinton has for a long time been an enthusiastic golfer; Dole did track, football, and basketball and was a record-holder in Russell, Kansas, in the half-mile; Gore was the captain of his high school football team; Kemp was a professional football player (playing quarterback) with the Los Angeles Chargers and Buffalo Bills. Now if we match these activities with the actual metaphors used by the politicians, we find a remarkable fit that indicates a close correlation between personal history and the metaphors used by individuals.

SUMMARY

In sum, conceptual metaphors and metonymies and their *cultural context* can all be put to useful work in the study of **cultural variation** in the conceptualization of target concepts, such as the emotions. They enable us to see with considerable clarity precisely where and how cultural variation occurs both *cross-culturally* and *within a culture*. Most cultural variation in conceptual metaphor occurs at the *specific level*, whereas, as we saw in the previous chapter, universality in metaphor can be found at the generic level. Moreover, given the cultural context and its influence on conceptualization, we can see why the changes take place in the cultural models and the conceptual metaphors.

FURTHER READING

Matsuki (1995) studied the Japanese concept of anger. King (1989) and Yu (1995, 1998) deal with various emotion concepts, such as anger, happiness, sadness, and worry in Chinese. Bokor (1997) describes several differences in the language and conceptualization of anger in English and Hungarian. The study of Zulu anger was done by Taylor and Mbense (1998). Geeraerts and Grondelaers (1995) describe the origin of the present-day conception of anger in English and point out that it derives from the classical-medieval humoral theory. Emanatian (1995) provides a description of lust in English and Chaga. Lutz (1988) studied various emotion concepts in Ifaluk, a Micronesian atoll. Dirven (1994) is a book-length study of the relationship of language and social-geographical environment in South Africa, investigating the Afrikaans language. Baugh and Cable (1983) is a history of English and offers insightful observations on American English metaphors. Stearns (1994) is a detailed study of the social history of emotions in the United States. Kövecses (1988) is a detailed analysis of the most common love metaphors in everyday English. Bellah et al. (1985) is a large-scale study of the American worldview, including the conception of love and marriage. Fuller (1843) is one of the early feminist studies of love in the United States, containing an interesting metaphorical argument based on the LOVE IS A UNITY metaphor. Gibbs (1999) discusses the relationship between the conceptual and cultural worlds in connection with the role of conceptual metaphors in both. Boers (1999) shows how body-related metaphors we use for the socioeconomic domain may change with the season in which we use them. Balaban (1999) deals with the issue of which factors might play a role in the selection of metaphors related to knowledge. In addition to these studies, most of the works cited in the previous chapter offer important observations concerning the issue of cultural variation in metaphorical conceptualization.

EXERCISES

1. In the previous chapter, you have already encountered the examples showing the similar metaphors for sex in English and Chagga, which make use of the source domains of EATING, HUNGER, and HEAT as the most important domains. Nevertheless, there are other metaphors in these two languages as well, which make use of similar domains, like ANIMALS, but in different ways: the mappings, or correspondences, and entailments may be different in these languages. Consider the following examples and discuss the differences. (You can make use of what you already know about the Great Chain of Being metaphor as well):

   English
   (1) He is a wolf.
   (2) She is a real tigress.
   (3) He is a beast.
   (4) She is always so horny.
   (5) That guy preys on young women.

   Chagga
   (6) *ní kíte* [She's a dog] > promiscuous
   (7) *kiambúya úlu(óí lyo* [Look at that rooster] > sexy young guy
   (8) *apáá 'táwó ngíleyetsi* [Wow, a fattened heifer] > sexy young woman
   (9) *nái chá ndoro* [She is like a bushbaby] > soft, small, delicate, shapely
   (10) *nái chá ndoro* [She's like a colobus monkey] > soft, smooth

2. Now consider other metaphors for the conceptualization of lust that are only present in English and were not mentioned above in connection with the Chagga understanding of sex (Emanatian's examples). On the basis of the examples, identify the new conceptual metaphors that you can find only in English.

   (a) When she grows up, she's gonna be a knockout.
   (b) She is driving me insane.
   (c) I can't believe the electricity between us.
   (d) We were drawn to each other.
   (e) What a sweet surrender it was.
   (f) That guy is a sex-maniac.

3. An example of within-culture variation is provided by the differences between the major metaphors that are present in various genres, like romance novels and pornographic magazines, which make use of various linguistic expressions for lust. Below are some examples of metaphorical expressions of lust from romance novels on the one

hand, and from pornographic magazines on the other hand. The examples are arranged in the order of frequency of the conceptual metaphors and thus illustrate the most often-used conceptual metaphors of the genres.

(a) Identify the conceptual metaphors.
(b) Find the metaphors that are present only in romance novels.
(c) Find the metaphors that are present only in pornographic magazines.
(d) What do the most frequent conceptual metaphors focus on in both genres?

Examples from romance novels
   (i) his eyes smoldered with desire
  (ii) he prepared to satisfy their sexual hunger
 (iii) something exploded inside her at his kiss
  (iv) he lost the battle against his passion
   (v) she tried to hold on to her fleeing sanity
  (vi) she felt a delicious stirring of her senses
 (vii) she lost the battle
(viii) he gave her a drugging kiss

Examples from pornographic magazines
  (ix) he dipped a finger into her honey pot
   (x) she told him not to bother eating her pussy
  (xi) he grunted and groaned like an animal
 (xii) she pressed her hot lips to his
(xiii) he found her overflowing
 (xiv) the scent of her heat drew him to it like a magnet
  (xv) a good fuck got her going

14

Metaphor, Metonymy, and Idioms

Of the many potential applications of the cognitive linguistic view of metaphor and metonymy to the study of language, we single out one in this chapter: the treatment of *idioms*. We have chosen idioms because this is a notoriously difficult area of *foreign language learning and teaching*. If the cognitive linguistic view can significantly contribute to this area, it would clearly show the practical and applied linguistic potential of the theory of metaphor and metonymy I am outlining in this book. In the next chapter, I will take up the issue of the theoretical and descriptive implications of the theory for the study of language in general.

1. The Traditional View of Idioms

The class of linguistic expressions that we call idioms is a mixed bag. It involves metaphors (e.g., *spill the beans*), metonymies (e.g., *throw up one's hands*), pairs of words (e.g., *cats and dogs*), idioms with *it* (e.g., *live it up*), similes (e.g., *as easy as pie*), sayings (e.g., *a bird in the hand is worth two in the bush*), phrasal verbs (e.g., *come up*, as in "Christmas is *coming up*"), grammatical idioms (e.g., *let alone*), and others. Most traditional views of idioms agree that *idioms consist of two or more words and that the overall meaning of these words cannot be predicted from the meanings of the constituent words.*

In the *traditional view*, idioms are regarded as a special set of the larger category of words. They are assumed to be a matter of language alone; that is, they are taken to be items of the lexicon (i.e., the mental dictionary) that are independent of any conceptual system. According to the traditional view, all there is to idioms is that, similar to words, they have certain syntactic properties and have a meaning that is special, relative to the meanings of the forms that comprise it. Although there are some notable exceptions to this general characterization, the core conception of idioms, in what we term the traditional view, can be represented in diagrammatic form in Figure 14.1.

Moreover, idioms are also taken to be independent of each other which follows from the previous view that idioms are simply a matter of language. If they are just a matter of language, then we just need to characterize their syntactic properties and meanings one by one. Words are characterized in the lexicon one by one according to their syntactic properties and meaning, and the same is assumed to apply to idioms. Certain relationships between words are recognized, but these are only certain sense relations, such as homonymy, synonymy, polysemy, and antonymy. Idioms may be seen as standing in the same relationships. It should be noticed, however, that these are relations of linguistic meanings, not relations in a conceptual system. In the traditional view, linguistic meaning is divorced from the human conceptual system and encyclopedic knowledge that speakers of a language share.

I would like to suggest that one major stumbling block in understanding the nature of idioms and making use of this understanding in the teaching of foreign languages is that they are regarded as linguistic expressions that are independent of any conceptual system and that they are isolated from each other at the conceptual level.

2. The Cognitive Linguistic View of Idioms

To see that the traditional view is mistaken, consider the following examples that all involve an idiom with the word *fire*:

He was *spitting fire*.
The *fire* between them finally *went out*.
The painting *set fire to* the composer's imagination.
Go ahead. *Fire away!*
The killing *sparked off* riots in the major cities.
He was *burning the candle at both ends*.
The bank robber *snuffed out* Sam's life.
The speaker *fanned the flames* of the crowd's enthusiasm.

special idiomatic meaning	'die'
the meanings of the linguistic forms linguistic forms and their syntactic properties	'kick,' 'the,' 'bucket' kick the bucket (no passive, etc.)

Figure 14.1. Idioms in the traditional view. (As in the diagram, meanings will be given in single quotation marks.)

In this set of examples, we have idioms that are related to various aspects of the phenomenon of fire, including its beginning (*spark off*), its end (*snuff out*), how it makes use of an energy source (*burn the candle at both ends*), how it can be made more intense (*fan the flames*), and the danger it presents (*fan the flames, spit fire*). As the examples suggest, in addition to the word *fire*, several other words are used from the domain of fire, such as *burn, candle, snuff, flame,* etc. These and many other examples suggest that it is the conceptual domain (the concept) of fire—and not the individual words themselves—that participates in the process of creating idiomatic expressions. The individual words merely reveal this deeper process of conceptualization. (The metaphor *fire away* above is not an idiom which belongs to the domain of fire as such; it is an example of the ARGUMENT IS WAR metaphor.)

Given this analysis, an important generalization can be made: Many, or perhaps most, idioms are products of our conceptual system and not simply a matter of language (i.e., a matter of the lexicon). An idiom is not just an expression that has a meaning that is somehow special in relation to the meanings of its constituting parts, but it arises from our more general knowledge of the world embodied in our conceptual system. In other words, idioms (or, at least, the majority of them) are conceptual, and not linguistic, in nature.

If this is the case, we can rely on this knowledge to make sense of the meanings of idioms; hence, the meanings of idioms can be seen as motivated and not arbitrary. The knowledge provides the motivation for the overall idiomatic meaning. This goes against the prevailing dogma which maintains that idioms are arbitrary pairings of forms (each with a meaning) and a special overall meaning. **Motivation** is to be distinguished from **prediction**. When it is suggested that the meaning of an idiom is motivated, no claim is made that its meaning is fully predictable. In other words, no claim is made that, given the nonidiomatic meaning of an idiom (e.g., 'emit sparks' for the expression *spark off*), we can entirely *predict* what the idiomatic meaning (e.g., 'begin') will be that is associated with the words (e.g., *spark* and *off*). As we saw in chapter 6, motivation is a much weaker notion than prediction. In some cases, we do not have conceptual motivation for the meaning of idioms at all (as in the case of the well-worn idiom *kick the bucket*). Understandably, these latter kinds of idiomatic expressions are the most celebrated examples of idioms in the standard views.

The motivation for the occurrence of particular words in a large number of idioms can be thought of as a cognitive mechanism that links domains of knowledge to idiomatic meanings. The kinds of mechanisms that seem to be especially relevant in the case of many idioms are metaphor, metonymy, and conventional knowledge as shown in Figure 14.2.

I would like to suggest that the implication of these ideas for teaching idioms is that this kind of motivation should facilitate the teaching and learning of idioms. By providing the learners of foreign languages with cognitive motivation for idioms, learners should be able to learn the idioms faster and retain them longer in memory. This commonsensical view is also shared by some applied linguists, like Irujo, who states:

Idiomatic meaning:

> the overall special meaning of an idiom

Cognitive mechanisms:

> metaphor, metonymy, conventional knowledge (= domain(s) of knowledge)

Conceptual domain(s):

> one or more domains of knowledge

Linguistic forms and their meanings:

> the words that comprise an idiom, their syntactic properties, together with their meanings

Figure 14.2. The conceptual motivation for many idioms.

> Teaching students strategies for dealing with figurative language will help them to take advantage of the semantic transparency of some idioms. If they can figure out the meaning of an idiom by themselves, they will have a link from the idiomatic meaning to the literal words, which will help them learn the idiom. (1993, p. 217)

I have used the term *motivation* for what Irujo calls *semantic transparency* throughout this chapter. What Irujo does not discuss, however, is what the precise nature of semantic transparency is in the case of idioms. My proposal is that the transparency, or motivation, of idioms arises from knowledge of the cognitive mechanisms (metaphor, metonymy, conventional knowledge) I will describe below, and that these link idiomatic meanings to literal ones. I believe that this more specific concept of semantic transparency has important implications for teaching idioms. I will return to this issue in section 2.2.

2.1. Idioms Based on Metaphor

As has been seen throughout this book, conceptual metaphors bring into correspondence two domains of knowledge. In the examples above, the domain of fire is used to understand a varied set of abstract concepts. But how do conceptual metaphors provide semantic motivation for the occurrence of particular words in idioms? To see this, let us again take some of the examples we have seen earlier.

In the expression *spit fire*, the domain of fire is used to understand the domain of anger. That is, anger is comprehended via the ANGER IS FIRE conceptual metaphor. In the case of the sentence "The *fire* between them finally *went out*," the conceptual metaphor underlying the idiom is LOVE IS FIRE; in "The painting *set fire to* the composer's imagination," it is IMAGINATION IS FIRE; in "The killing *sparked off* riots," it is CONFLICT IS FIRE; in the case of *burning the candle at both ends*, it is ENERGY IS FUEL FOR THE FIRE; in the case of *snuff out*, it is LIFE IS A FLAME; in the case of *fan the flames*, it is ENTHUSIASM IS FIRE. These idioms are not isolated linguistic expressions, as the examples below will show.

It may be observed that some of the examples given below consist of only one word (e.g. *burn, ignite, kindle*), and given that idioms are multiword expressions by definition, they do not count as idioms at all. I have listed these examples to be able to make the point that it is not claimed that *all* metaphorical linguistic expressions based on conceptual metaphors are idioms. The class of metaphorical expressions generated by conceptual metaphors is larger than that of metaphorical idioms. Nevertheless, as will be shown shortly, the number of metaphorical idioms produced by conceptual metaphors is quite large. Although strictly speaking not idioms (since they violate the condition that idioms are multiword expressions), I have included some one-word metaphorical expressions in the examples.

ANGER IS FIRE
After the row, he *was spitting fire*.
Smoke was coming out of his ears.
He is *smoldering* with anger.
She was *fuming*.
Boy, am I *burned up*!

LOVE IS FIRE
The *fire* between them finally *went out*.
I am *burning* with love.
She *carries a torch for* him.
The *flames are gone* from our relationship.

IMAGINATION IS FIRE
The painting *set fire to* the composer's imagination.
His imagination *caught fire*.
Her imagination is *on fire*.
The story *kindled* the boy's imagination.

CONFLICT IS FIRE
The killing *sparked off* the riot.
The *flames* of war *spread* quickly.
The country was *consumed* by the *inferno* of war.
They extinguished the *last sparks* of the revolution.

ENERGY IS FUEL FOR THE FIRE
Don't *burn the candle at both ends*.
I am *burned out*.
I need someone *to stoke my fire*.

ENTHUSIASM IS FIRE
The speaker *fanned the flames* of the crowd's enthusiasm.
The team played so well that the crowd *caught fire*.
He was *burning* with excitement.
Don't be a *wet blanket*.
Her enthusiasm was *ignited* by the new teacher.

These conceptual metaphors can be seen as conceptually motivating the use of words such as *spark off, fire, go out, burn the candle, fan the flames,* and so on in the idioms in which they occur. Given these conceptual metaphors, we can see why the idioms have the general meaning that they do; that is, why they have to do with anger, love, imagination, etc., respectively. The reason is that these conceptual metaphors exist and serve as links between two otherwise independently existing conceptual domains. Because of the connections they make in our conceptual system, the conceptual metaphors allow us to use terms from one domain (e.g., fire) to talk about another (e.g., anger and love). The idioms that employ these terms (such as those of fire) will be about certain target domains (such as anger) as a result of the existence of conceptual metaphors (such as ANGER IS FIRE). Now we are in a position to provide a specific illustration of Figure 2 in the previous section. To do this, I will take the idiomatic expression *to spit fire* as an example:

Special idiomatic meaning:	'be very angry'
Cognitive mechanisms:	metaphor: ANGER IS FIRE
Conceptual domain(s):	FIRE and ANGER
Linguistic forms:	spit fire
Meanings of forms:	'spit,' 'fire'

(To be sure, the meaning of *spit fire* is more complex than just 'be very angry.' I will come back to some of the complexities concerning its meaning later.) Our ability to see many idioms as being conceptually motivated (i.e., as having the general meaning they do) arises from the existence of conceptual metaphors. The general meaning of many idioms (i.e., what concepts they are about) remains completely unmotivated, unless we take into account the interplay between meaning and our conceptual system as comprised by conceptual metaphors to a large extent. It is claimed that the meaning of many (though not all) idioms depends on, and is inseparable from, the (metaphorical) conceptual system.

What has to be shown now is that the conceptual metaphors really exist in the minds of speakers, that is, they have psychological validity. There is independent (i.e., nonlinguistic) evidence to show that conceptual metaphors exist for speakers, and that they have conceptual reality. American psycholinguist, Ray Gibbs, has found that conceptual metaphors have *psychological reality* and that they motivate idiomatic expressions. The results of Gibbs's studies show that people have tacit knowledge of the metaphorical basis for many idioms. This tacit knowledge is easiest to recover if we examine speakers' mental images for idioms in detail. For example, Gibbs and O'Brien investigated the conventional images and knowledge that people have when asked to form mental images of idioms. They looked at five sets of idioms with similar nonliteral meanings—idioms that have to do with revelation (e.g., *spill the beans, let the cat out of the bag, blow the whistle*); anger (e.g., *blow your stack, flip your lid, hit the ceiling*); insanity (e.g., *go off your rocker, lose your marbles, go to pieces*); secretiveness (e.g., *keep it under your hat, button your lips, hold your tongue*); and exerting control (e.g., *crack the whip, lay down the law, call the shots*). Participants in the experiments were asked to form mental images of idioms and were asked a series of questions about their images. There was a remarkable degree of consistency in people's images and responses to the questions. This consistency in people's understanding of idioms is a result of conceptual metaphors. For example, in the case of anger, it is the MIND IS A CONTAINER and the ANGER IS A HOT FLUID IN A CONTAINER metaphors that guarantee the consistency. Gibbs explains:

> When imagining Anger idioms people know that pressure (that is, stress or frustration) causes the action, that one has little control over the pressure once it builds, its violent release is done unintentionally (for example, the blowing of the stack) and that once the release has taken place (i.e., once the ceiling has been hit, the lid flipped, the stack blown), it is difficult to reverse the action. Each of these responses are based on people's conceptions of heated fluid or vapor building up and escaping from containers (ones that our participants most frequently reported to be the size of a person's head). We see that the metaphorical mapping of a source domain (for example, heated fluid in a container) into target domains (for example, the anger emotion) motivates why people have consistent mental images, and specific knowledge about these images, for different idioms about anger. (1990, p. 434)

If it were not the case that people's tacit knowledge about idioms is structured by (different) conceptual metaphors, there would be very little consistency in people's understanding of idioms with similar nonliteral meanings. Anger idioms like *blow your stack, flip your lid, hit the ceiling* (which all have the nonliteral meaning 'to get angry') are understood by people in terms of the same general image and specific knowledge (like cause, action, consequence, etc.) because conceptual metaphors like the MIND IS A CONTAINER and ANGER IS A HOT FLUID IN A CONTAINER exist in the conceptual system of speakers of English.

So far we have talked only about the general meaning of idioms. Now I will say something about the more precise meaning of particular idiomatic expressions that involves the structure of the source domain and the corresponding structure of the target domain. As has been seen throughout this book, a conceptual metaphor is a set of mappings, or correspondences, between two domains—the source and the target. Many of the fire-metaphors listed above, such as ANGER IS FIRE, LOVE IS FIRE, etc., are constituted by the following conceptual mappings or correspondences:

the thing burning is the person in a state/process
the heat of fire is the state (like anger, love, imagination)
the cause of the fire is the cause of the state
the beginning of the fire is the beginning of the state
the existence of the fire is the existence of the state
the end of the fire is the end of the state
the intensity of the fire is the intensity of the state

This set of mappings goes a long way in explaining the more precise meaning of a large number of idioms based on the domain of fire. It will explain why, for example, "*setting fire to* one's imagination" means 'causing one's imagination to function'; why "*extinguishing the last sparks* of the uprising" means 'ending the uprising'; why *spitting fire* and *smoke coming out of your ears* mean 'more intense anger' than merely "*burning with* anger"; and why *to carry a torch for someone* has as a large part of its meaning 'for love to exist for someone,' or, more simply, 'to love someone' (although the complete meaning of this idiom includes more).

The conclusion that we can draw from what has been done so far is that in many cases what determines the general meaning of an idiom (i.e., what concept it has to do with) is the target domain of the conceptual metaphor that is applicable to the idiom at hand, and that the more precise meaning of the idiom depends on the particular conceptual mapping that applies to the idiom. For example, the general meaning of the idiom *spit fire*, which has to do with anger, depends on the existence of the conceptual metaphor ANGER IS FIRE, and its more precise meaning, which is 'be very angry,' depends on the conceptual mapping "intensity of fire is intensity of anger" between the source domain (fire) and the target domain (anger). The specific meaning of the other idioms can also be explained by recourse to the mappings that characterize the FIRE metaphors.

2.2. Pedagogical Implications of Metaphor Research

The pedagogical implications of the line of research I have described are obvious. Metaphorical conceptualization is an intrinsic feature of discourse. In addition to, and underlying, what Danesi calls *conceptual fluency*, people have a *metaphorical competence*. Danesi explains:

> the programming of discourse in metaphorical ways is a basic feature
> of native-speaker competence. It underlies what I have designated
> conceptual fluency. As a "competence," it can be thought about
> pedagogically in ways that are parallel to the other competencies that
> SLT has traditionally focused on (grammatical and communicative).
> (1993, p. 493)

Kövecses and Szabó report on an experiment that gives us a way of building up metaphorical competence in learners of English as a foreign language. We conducted an informal experimental study in which one group learned idioms merely through memorization (i.e., without motivation) and another through conceptual metaphors (i.e., with motivation). The study involved idioms that are motivated by a special type of metaphor—metaphors based on "up-down" orientation, such as the phrasal verbs *cheer up* and *break down*. The results showed that learners who learned idioms in a motivated way performed roughly 25% better in an idiom-related task than those who did not. Thus, the results of the experiment give us real evidence for the claim that idiom learning can be greatly aided with the help of the ideas that have been developed in this study.

2.3. Idioms Based on Conventional Knowledge and Metonymy

Conceptual metaphor is not the only cognitive mechanism that can motivate idioms. To see how two further mechanisms—**conceptual metonymy** and **conventional knowledge**—are also involved in this process, I turn now to another conceptual domain: that of the human hand.

My students and I have collected a large number of idioms that have to do with the human hand from a variety of sources, especially from some standard dictionaries. My goal in this section is to present the major cognitive mechanisms that play a role in a cognitivist account of these idiomatic expressions. We have found that, in addition to conceptual metaphor, a cognitive linguistic account may also require (often nonmetaphorical) conventional knowledge as well as conceptual metonymies. The specific cognitive mechanisms required for an account of the idioms we have collected relating to the human hand include the following:

> general conventional knowledge about the USE OF THE HAND
> specific knowledge about the CONVENTIONAL GESTURES INVOLVING
>   THE HAND
> the metonymy THE HAND STANDS FOR THE ACTIVITY
> the metonymy THE HAND STANDS FOR THE PERSON
> the metaphor FREEDOM TO ACT IS HAVING THE HANDS FREE
> the metonymy THE HAND STANDS FOR THE SKILL
> the metonymy THE HAND STANDS FOR CONTROL
> the metaphor CONTROL IS HOLDING SOMETHING IN THE HAND
> the metaphor POSSESSING SOMETHING IS HOLDING SOMETHING IN THE
>   HAND
> the metaphor ATTENTION IS HOLDING SOMETHING IN THE HAND

I will only deal with some of these cognitive mechanisms in what follows.

The cognitive mechanisms listed above and their combinations take us a long way in accounting for, and motivating, the meanings of a large number of idiomatic expressions that have to do with the human hand.

2.3.1. Conventional Knowledge

By **conventional knowledge** as a cognitive mechanism, I simply mean the shared knowledge that people in a given culture have concerning a conceptual domain like the human hand. This shared everyday knowledge includes standard information about the parts, shape, size, use, and function of the human hand, as well as the larger hierarchy of which it forms a part (hand as a part of the arm, etc.).

Let us begin with general conventional knowledge. Consider the expression *have one's hands full* (= 'to be busy'). What is the explanation for the particular meaning of this idiomatic expression? If we hold things in the hand already, we cannot easily pick up other things with it and use the hand for another activity. We are busy with the things already in the hand, and we are not in a position to engage in any other activity. This is perhaps not the only explanation one can come up with for the idiom, but it is this kind of conventional (nonmetaphoric and nonmetonymic) knowledge that underlies and thus motivates its meaning.

Consider now the expression *with an open hand* meaning 'generously,' as in "She gives her love to people *with an open hand*." The image of a person physically giving objects to another with an open hand implies the knowledge that nothing is held back and everything can be taken. This image stands in marked contrast to the knowledge about the image of a person who gives with his fist held tight. As a matter of fact, it is hard to imagine how this person can hand over anything at all. Indeed, the expression *tight-fisted* indicates just the opposite of giving *with an open hand*. The latter suggests willingness and the former reluctance in giving. Here again it is conventional knowledge that motivates idiomatic meaning.

2.3.2. Metonymy

Now let us turn to idioms involving the hand where idiomatic meaning is largely based on *metonymy*. The particular metonymy that seems to provide motivation for the following idiomatic expressions is THE HAND STANDS FOR THE ACTIVITY. The basis for this conceptual metonymy is that many prototypical human activities are performed with the hands. (This metonymy may be a special case of the more general metonymy THE INSTRUMENT USED IN AN ACTIVITY STANDS FOR THE ACTIVITY. Thus, the hand may be viewed as an instrument.) Consider, as an example, the idiom *hold one's hand* meaning 'wait and see.' This particular meaning arises in large measure as a result of the metonymy THE HAND STANDS FOR THE ACTIVITY. We can guess that the expression is about an activity because of this metonymy. But we also appear to have further knowledge associated with holding one's hand. When we hold our hands (i.e., when we arrest the movement of the hand), we have temporarily stopped an activity. We are waiting to see whether to continue or how to continue the activity we are engaged in. Thus, the metonymy THE HAND STANDS FOR THE ACTIVITY and some further conventional knowledge jointly produce a large part of the motivation for the idiomatic meaning of the expression *hold one's hand*. Other idioms that behave in a similar way include:

> sit on one's hands ('deliberately do nothing')
> put one's hands in one's pockets ('deliberately do nothing')
> turn one's hand to something ('tackle some project')
> be able to do something with one hand behind one's back ('be able to
>   do something very easily')
> join hands with somebody ('cooperate with a person')

One of the best known metonymies in English is THE HAND STANDS FOR THE PERSON (an instantiation of the more general metonymy THE PART STANDS FOR THE WHOLE). In a sentence like "We need more *hands*," the word *hands* refers to persons. Disregarding the possibility of cannibalism, speakers of English would take the meaning of the sentence to be 'we need more people'. The same metonymy can be used to account for the meaning of some additional expressions:

a factory hand ('a factory worker')
from hand to hand ('directly, from one person to another')
all hands on deck ('everybody ready for action, duty, etc.')

THE HAND STANDS FOR THE PERSON metonymy seems to be based on the metonymy THE HAND STANDS FOR THE ACTIVITY. The prototypical person is an ACTIVE person and since we have the metonymy THE HAND STANDS FOR THE ACTIVITY, it is natural that we also have THE HAND STANDS FOR THE PERSON.

Several of the idioms involving the human hand have to do with the notion of control. We find some form of control or authority in all of the following examples:

gain the upper hand ('attain an advantage over another person')
rule with an iron hand ('keep strict discipline')
with a heavy hand ('in an oppressive fashion')
with an iron hand in a velvet glove ('with a hard attitude made to seem soft')
keep a strict hand upon a person ('keep under total control')

The meaning of all these examples somehow involves 'control.' Thus, it seems sensible to suggest that the conceptual metonymy that underlies, and thus provides the basis for, all the expressions is THE HAND STANDS FOR CONTROL. A more general metonymy that underlies this may be THE INSTRUMENT STANDS FOR CONTROL.

While in the previous examples the notion of control is indicated via a metonymy, it is also understood metaphorically, as shown by the examples below:

hold the power to do something in the hollow of one's hands ('have the right to make crucial decisions')
be in hand ('be under control')
be out of somebody's hands ('be out of one's control')
be in someone's hands ('be being dealt with by someone with the necessary authority')
take something in hand ('assume control over something')
get out of hand ('get out of control')
have the situation well in hand ('have the situation well under control')
fall into the hands of somebody ('unintentionally come under the control of somebody')

These idioms all have to do with control and employ the act of holding something in the hand which suggests the conceptual metaphor CONTROL IS HOLDING (SOMETHING IN THE HAND). If we hold an object in the hand, we can do whatever we wish to do with it. Thus, the ability or possibility of directly manipulating an object as we wish can be regarded as the basis for this metaphor.

3. Multiple Motivation for Idioms

We have seen throughout the discussion that not just one but several cognitive mechanisms can contribute to the motivation of a particular idiomatic expression. What has not been explained so far is how parts of expressions that are not directly related to the hand receive their conceptual motivation. Let us take the expression *gain the upper hand*. As we have seen, the use of the word *hand* is motivated by the metonymy THE HAND STANDS FOR CONTROL. But what of the word *upper*? The most likely motivation for this word seems to be the CONTROL IS UP conceptual metaphor (which is also manifest in other examples like "I'm *on top of* the situation," "He's the *under*dog," etc.). Thus, we have an idiomatic expression that consists of a word (*hand*) that is motivated by a conceptual metonymy relating the hand to the notion of control and another word (*upper*) that is based on the conceptual metaphor CONTROL IS UP that is completely independent of the system constituted by the concept of hand. Another example could be the expression *to do something in an underhanded way*. In this case, the word *under* is motivated by the ETHICAL/MORAL IS UP and UNETHICAL/AMORAL IS DOWN metaphor complex. (On orientational metaphors such as these, see chapter 3.)

Other idioms also interact with conceptual metaphors and metonymies that make use of the human hand. Take the idiom *have clean hands*. The expression means 'be innocent or act ethically' and this meaning is partly based on the metonymy THE HAND STANDS FOR THE ACTIVITY. Another part of the meaning is motivated by the structural metaphor ETHICAL IS CLEAN (which also shows up in a number of other linguistic expressions such as *have blood on one's hand*). When the word *blood*, an "unclean" substance on the hand, appears in conjunction with the hand in an idiom, we have another example of a cognitively complex situation. This is because in addition to the metonymy THE HAND STANDS FOR THE ACTIVITY and the metaphor MORAL/ETHICAL IS CLEAN, we also make use of some conventional knowledge concerning blood and the human hand. Idioms based on the joint functioning of these cognitive mechanisms also include *catch somebody red-handed* ('apprehend a person in the course of committing a crime') and *have blood on one's hand* ('be the person responsible for someone else's predicament').

SUMMARY

According to the *traditional view*, idioms consist of two or more words and the overall meaning of these words is unpredictable from the meanings of the constituent words. A major assumption of the traditional view is that *idiomatic meaning* is largely *arbitrary*.

The *cognitive linguistic view of idioms* shares with the traditional view that the meanings of idioms are not completely *predictable*, but it suggests that a large part of an idiom's meaning is *motivated*. There are at least three *cognitive mechanisms* that make the meanings of idioms motivated:

(1) **metaphor**, (2) **metonymy**, and (3) **conventional knowledge.** *Psycholinguistic experiments* show that many idioms have *psychological reality* and many idioms are based on these cognitive devices.

When it is the case that an idiom is motivated by metaphor, the more *general meaning of the idiom* is based on the **target domain** *that is applicable to the idiom* in question. The more precise aspects of an idiom's meaning are based on the *conceptual mapping* that is relevant to the idiom.

A major practical advantage of the cognitive linguistic view is that it facilitates the *teaching and learning of idioms* in the context of *foreign language teaching*.

FURTHER READING

Classifications of idioms can be found in the *Longman Dictionary of Idioms* (1979) and the *Oxford Dictionary of Idiomatic English*, Vol. 1 (1975), Vol. 2 (1973), and more recently, Alexander (1987) and Lattey (1986). For the standard or traditional views of idioms, see, for example, Gairns and Redman (1986), Carter and McCarthy (1988), McArthur (1992), and the idiom dictionaries cited above.

Lakoff (1987) provided much of the impetus for the study of idioms in cognitive linguistics. Most of the psycholinguistic research into idioms from a cognitive perspective was done by Gibbs and his colleagues (e.g., 1990, 1994; Gibbs and O'Brien 1990). Idiom comprehension is a huge topic and Gibbs (1994) surveys the relevant literature. In one recent development, Giora (1997) offers what she calls the "graded salience hypothesis."

Radden (1995) discusses idioms related to the verbs *come* and *go* from a cognitive linguistic perspective. Feyaerts (1999) analyzes idioms of stupidity in German. Niemeier (2000) is an analysis of idioms related to the heart. Kövecses and Szabó (1996) outline the semantic aspects of the cognitive linguistic view of idioms, together with some implications for applied linguistics. Kövecses (n.d.) continues to outline the place of the cognitive linguistic view of idioms in applied linguistics. The notion of semantic transparency is discussed by Irujo (1993). Danesi (1993) describes what he calls "metaphorical competence." Moon (1998) examines the role of context, including verbal context, in the understanding of idioms. Several papers deal with applied and corpus-linguistic aspects of metaphor and metaphor-based idioms in Cameron and Low (1999a). Cameron and Low (1999b) survey the metaphor field in applied linguistics and provide an excellent summary of work by R. Alexander, F. Boers, L. Cameron, A. Deignan, P. Drew, G. Low, Z. Todd, and others. They also list a number of web resources for the study of metaphor and metonymy.

EXERCISES

1. Identify the specific metaphors or metonymies that underlie the following idiomatic slang or informal expressions:

   (a) *get all steamed up* "become angry/lustful"
   (b) *get cold feet* "be frightened"
   (c) *brew, chill* "beer"
   (d) *have a head like a sieve* "absent-minded"
   (e) *split up* "break up"

2. The following quote from *Macbeth* is the part where Macbeth has just stabbed King Duncan to death (2.2.59–62). Macbeth is *caught red-handed*. What is the motivation for this metaphorical idiom?

> Will all great Neptune's ocean wash this blood
> Clean from my hand? No, this my hand will rather
> The multitudinous seas incarnadine,
> Making the green one red.

3. Look at the following idioms related to the eyes. What cognitive mechanisms (metonymies, metaphors, conventional knowledge) are at work in these idiomatic expressions?

(a) catch someone's eye
(b) close one's eyes to something
(c) get stars in one's eyes
(d) give someone the eye
(e) have eyes in the back of one's head
(f) turn a blind eye to someone/something
(g) in one's mind's eye
(h) keep one's eyes peeled
(i) lay/set eyes on someone/something
(j) pull the wool over someone's eyes

4. In the following sentences, which come from a dictionary of idioms, identify (a) the special idiomatic meaning of the expressions; (b) the cognitive mechanisms (metaphors, metonymies, conventional knowledge) that motivate the meaning of the idiom.

(1) I am/my bank account is *in the red*.
(2) Criticizing the Liberal Party in front of him is *like a red rag to a bull*.
(3) When smoke was seen rising from the volcano, the area was put *on red alert*.
(4) He was a *red-blooded* male who could not be expected to live like a monk.
(5) The Prime Minister was given the *red-carpet treatment* when he visited the town.
(6) He is a *red-hot* socialist.
(7) The day I won a prize on the football pools was a real *red-letter day*.
(8) When he started criticizing my work, I really *saw red*.

Metaphor and
Metonymy in the
Study of Language

In the previous chapter we saw how the cognitive linguistic view of metaphor and metonymy can shed new light on one aspect of language studies: the study of idiomatic expressions—especially for applied linguistic purposes. In the present chapter, I will discuss some further implications of this view for the study of various additional aspects of language. Given our new perspective, I will deal with such well-known linguistic phenomena as *polysemy*, *historical semantics*, as well as *grammar* and *grammatical constructions*. Lastly, I will look briefly at metaphorical aspects of *linguistic theorizing*.

1. Polysemy

Polysemy involves words that have a number of *related senses* (as opposed to homonymy where the senses are completely unrelated). This is the traditional definition of polysemy that cognitive linguists also accept. A crucial question here is what is meant by two senses being related. It is by taking this question seriously that cognitive linguistics can greatly contribute to a fuller understanding of the phenomenon of polysemy. It can be suggested that polysemy is often based on metaphor and metonymy; that is, in many cases there are systematic metaphorical and metonymic relationships between two senses of a word.

The most obvious and most analyzed examples of how polysemy can be based on metaphor come from prepositions and adverbials, such as *over*, *up*, *down*, *on*, *in*, etc. The word *up*, for instance, can be said to have many senses. We can exemplify two of these with sentences such as the following:

(a) He went up the stairs, so that we can see him.
(b) He spoke up, so that we can hear him.

In (a), the sense of *up* is 'upward', while in (b) it is 'more intensity'. Now the problem is how these two senses of *up* are related. The explanation is that they are related by a conceptual metaphor: MORE IS UP, whereby, in this particular case, more intensity of sound is understood as being physically higher on some scale. Thus, the metaphor MORE IS UP provides a systematic link between two very different senses of the same word. In the traditional view, where there are no conceptual metaphors, this explanation would not be available because it could only be suggested that there is some kind of preexisting similarity between the two. But we saw that this notion is very vague to have any real explanatory value.

Now consider a content (or open class) word, such as *climb*. We can demonstrate three of its senses, or uses, with the following sentences:

(a) The monkey climbed up the pole.
(b) The prices are climbing up.
(c) She is climbing the corporate ladder.

It is obvious that in (a) *climb* means simultaneously "clambering" and "upward." The "clambering" component is canceled out in a sentence such as "The plane climbed to 30,000 feet." Planes do not have arms and legs, so they can't clamber, but they can "move upward." What about (b) and (c)? (b) is related to (a) by means of the same conceptual metaphor that we saw above for *up*: MORE IS UP. Prices cannot physically move up, but they can metaphorically do so by means of MORE IS UP: the increase in prices is understood as upward physical movement. (c) is also systematically related to (a), in that there is a productive conceptual metaphor, A CAREER IS AN UPWARD JOURNEY, that links them; to acquire a socially higher position is comprehended as upward physical movement in the course of a journey.

What is common to the two cases above (*up* and *climb*) is that the two words have a physical sense ('upward'), and this physical sense is extended to metaphorical senses by means of conceptual metaphors (MORE IS UP and A CAREER IS AN UPWARD JOURNEY). In other words, a central, physical sense serves as a source domain to conceptualize certain target domains, such as quantity and career, that are less clearly physical.

Let us now briefly reconsider the case of fire as a source domain with which we dealt in the previous chapter. There it was pointed out that the domain of fire is used to conceptualize a wide variety of intense states and events, such as anger, love, enthusiasm, imagination, conflict, energy, etc. This means that *fire*, and the near-synonymous word *flame*, will predictably have the sense of an intense state or event because there exists the mapping in the FIRE metaphor: "the (heat of) fire corresponds to an intense state or event." That is, the word *fire* (and *flame*) will be as many ways polysemous as the number of target concepts the source domain of fire applies to: anger, love, conflict, etc. Most of these are given in dictionaries as conventionalized senses. However, some of them are not, but it is not even necessary to give them. The reason is as follows:

The scope of metaphor and the main meaning focus of a source domain (see chapter 9) can determine the polysemy of words (e.g., *fire* and *flame*) in that source domain (e.g., FIRE) by means of the mappings that characterize that meaning focus (e.g., "the (heat of) fire corresponds to an intense state or event").

In this way, we get a powerful mechanism to account for many cases of polysemy.

The cases we have examined so far were all based on metaphor. What role does metonymy play in polysemy? To see this, let us take the word *love*, as used in the sentences below:

(a) I was overwhelmed by *love*.
(b) The *love* between them is strong.
(c) Her *love* of music knows no boundaries.
(d) Come here, *love*.
(e) I *love* ice-cream.
(f) They are *lovers*.
(g) I gave her all my *love*.

Love is used in different senses in the examples above:

(a) intense emotion, passion
(b) relationship
(c) enthusiasm
(d) the object of love
(e) liking
(f) sexual partners
(g) affection

How can we account for the fact that the word *love* has precisely these senses? The answer relies crucially on two notions: metonymy and ICM (see chapter 11). I have claimed in this book that metonymy, unlike metaphor, can be found between elements of a single ICM. The ICM for romantic love involves several elements: the lovers (subject and object of love), an intense emotion felt by the lovers, a relationship between them, and a variety of attitudes and behaviors typically assumed by the love emotion, including (but not exhausted by) affection, liking, enthusiasm, and sex. (All this is not to claim that there is only one kind of romantic love.) We can account for the extension of the basic sense of love, the love emotion, by postulating the following set of conceptual metonymies:

(1) LOVE FOR THE RELATIONSHIP IT PRODUCES (ex. b)
(2) LOVE FOR THE OBJECT OF EMOTION (exs. d and f)
(3) LOVE FOR THE SUBJECT OF EMOTION (ex. f)
(4) LOVE FOR THE PROPERTIES (ATTITUDES AND BEHAVIORS) IT
    ASSUMES (exs. c, e, f, g)

More generally, we can have the following corresponding metonymies:

THE EMOTION FOR THE RELATIONSHIP IT PRODUCES
THE EMOTION FOR THE OBJECT OF EMOTION
THE EMOTION FOR THE AGENT OF THE EMOTION
THE EMOTION FOR AN ASSUMED PROPERTY OF THAT EMOTION

However, the metonymies that account for the several distinct senses of *love* are not limited to the emotion domain. At the most general level, we find the metonymies below in connection with love:

CAUSE FOR EFFECT (EMOTION FOR THE RELATIONSHIP)
EFFECT FOR CAUSE (EMOTION FOR THE OBJECT)
STATE FOR AGENT (EMOTION FOR THE AGENT)
WHOLE FOR PART (EMOTION FOR ASSUMED PROPERTY)

The metonymy WHOLE FOR PART will include as special cases LOVE FOR AFFECTION, LOVE FOR LIKING, LOVE FOR ENTHUSIASM, and LOVE FOR SEX.

To conclude this discussion of polysemy, it can be claimed that meaning extension often takes place on the basis of conceptual metaphor and metonymy. These take as their source domains the more central senses of the words concerned. The metaphors and metonymies serve as cognitive links between two or more distinct senses of a word. But the most significant point is that *the metaphors and metonymies that serve as cognitive links between two or more distinct senses exist independently in our conceptual system.* MORE IS UP, A CAREER IS A JOURNEY, AN INTENSE STATE IS FIRE, CAUSE FOR EFFECT, WHOLE FOR PART, etc. have separate and independent existence in our conceptual system; nevertheless, we call on them to extend the range of the senses of the words we use.

2. Historical Semantics

Historical semantics studies, among other things, the historical development of the senses of words. A major question is whether the changes are random and unpredictable or there are systematic changes in the development of the senses of related words. Cognitive linguists have made interesting discoveries in this field as well, in light of which it has become possible to explain phenomena that were unaccounted for or simply unrecognized before. In many such cases, the cognitive mechanisms that helped scholars in their work were again metaphor and metonymy.

2.1. Modal Verbs

Following Len Talmy's work on force dynamics, Eve Sweetser suggested that *modal verbs* in English (and in many other languages) develop their senses in a certain direction: from the so-called *root* sense to what is called the *epistemic* sense. The root sense has to do with sociophysical obligation, permission, and ability, whereas the epistemic sense involves logical necessity and probability. The two senses can be illustrated in the case of the modal *must* as follows:

(a) John must be home by ten; mother won't let him stay out any later.
(b) John must be home already; I can see his coat.

In (a), we make a statement about a social obligation, while in (b) we make a logical inference on the basis of some evidence. Thus, (a) exemplifies the root sense and (b) the epistemic sense of *must*. The root senses of *must, may, might, can, will,* etc. tend to appear historically before the epistemic senses of the same modals.

Why is it the case that the epistemic senses of modals derive historically from the root senses? Sweetser's idea is that the root senses reflect a reality external to the speaker, while the epistemic senses a reality internal to the speaker. Given this, it becomes possible to conceptualize the internal in terms of the external (i.e., INTERNAL IS EXTERNAL), the less physical in terms of the more physical; that is, to apply what Sweetser terms THE MIND AS BODY metaphor. But what is the structure of the external reality associated with root modality, such as social obligation, permission, and so on? Following Talmy's work, Sweetser argues that it is structured by *force-dynamic notions* such as *force* (that compels one to act in some way) and *barrier* (to action). Thus, it is based on the metaphor THE SOCIAL WORLD IS THE PHYSICAL WORLD. In the case of the root sense of *must*, a social force (understood as a physical force) compels an entity to do something. But what corresponds to this social force in the case of the epistemic sense? Consider the following pair of examples, illustrating the two senses of *must* (*a* corresponding to the root sense, *b* to the epistemic one):

(a) You must come home by ten.
(b) You must have been home last night.

To reveal the difference in meaning between the two senses, we can distinguish the two sentences as follows:

(a) "A social authority (mother) compels you to come home by ten."
(b) "Some evidence (I saw the light in your room) compels me to conclude that you were home last night."

The social force of the root modal in (a) corresponds to some evidence available to the speaker in (b). In other words, the epistemic sense (the internal world of the speaker) is comprehended via the social sense as structured by physical forces.

In another example, let us take the modal *may*. This can be illustrated with the sentence pair:

(a) John may go.
(b) John may be there.
   (a) "John is not barred by authority from going."
   (b) "The speaker is not barred from the conclusion that John is there."

Here as well, the *social world* is understood in terms of the *physical world*, and the social world so understood is used as a source domain for the comprehension of the internal world of epistemic modality.

It should be noticed that the historical development of the modal senses from root to epistemic is at the same time a case of polysemy: meaning differentiation through time. It is thus not surprising that the same mechanisms that apply to polysemy, such as metaphor, apply and produce historically new senses. But, of course, the new senses coexist today and constitute true cases of polysemy.

2.2. Words of Vision for Words of Wisdom

But the process of *historical meaning shift* affects open-class items as well. It has been widely noticed that words denoting various psychological phenomena, such as knowing, emotion, judgment, derive historically from words denoting bodily sensations, such as sight, touch, taste, etc. It was again Sweetser who brought the two sets of words into systematic correspondence and suggested that the correspondences are special cases of the more general metaphor THE MIND IS THE BODY. She proposed the following set of mappings:

THE MIND-AS-BODY SYSTEM

Target domain:		*Source domain:*
Mental manipulation, control	⇒	Physical manipulation
Sight	⇒	Physical manipulation
Knowledge, mental vision	⇒	Sight
Internal receptivity	⇒	Hearing
Emotion	⇒	Feel
Personal preference	⇒	Taste

Let us take the domain of vision as an example. In English (and again in many other languages), words denoting vision also denote various aspects of knowing. It is this KNOWING IS SEEING metaphor that seems to account for many present-day linguistic metaphors, such as "I *see*," "*transparent* idea," "*murky* argument," etc. This extension of the domain of vision to that of knowledge is pervasive and systematic. And many of the words that we consider literal today turn out to be based on the same metaphor. Here are some examples from György László:

   aspect: from Latin *aspectus*, meaning seeing, look, appearance, from *ad-* at + *specere* to look

fantasy: from Latin *phantasia*, from Greek *phantasia* appearance, image,
  perception
idea: from Latin *idea* idea, archetype, from Greek *idéa* look, semblance,
  form, kind, ideal prototype, from *idein* to see
intuition: from Latin *intueri* look at, consider, contemplate, from *in-* at,
  on + *tueri* to look, watch over
speculate: modeled on Latin *speculatus*, past participle of *speculari* to
  watch, examine, observe, from *specula* watchtower, from *specere* to
  look at
theory: from Greek *theorein* to consider, speculate, look at, from
  theorós spectator. Greek *theorós* from *théa* a view + *horós* seeing,
  related to *horán* to see

Again, the shifts are unidirectional through time: they go from vision to
knowledge. In other words, these cases provide further evidence for the view
that historical meaning change occurs along "well-trodden" paths; conceptual metaphors govern the direction of shifts of meaning through history.

3. Grammar

Lakoff and Johnson showed that conceptual metaphor plays a role in *grammar* as well. Other researchers have found that conceptual metonymy should
also be taken into account if we wish to understand some grammatical phenomena in natural language. One aspect of grammar involves *morphology*,
that is, the study of the smallest meaningful elements (morphemes) of language and their combinations. One question that arises in morphology is the
following: What is the cognitive basis of shifting the grammatical status of
words and expressions from one class to another? It is a well-known phenomenon that speakers of languages often shift the grammatical classes of
words. This is called *functional shift*, or *conversion*, and involves cases such
as shifting nouns to verbs, verbs to nouns, adjectives to verbs, nouns to adjectives, etc. We will look at the cognitive basis of the shift from nouns to
verbs.

3.1. Metonymy and Denominal Verbs

The approach we outlined in chapter 11 on metonymy can be fruitfully applied to this issue. I take Clark and Clark's work on the so-called *denominal
verbs*, involving noun-to-verb shifts, as an example to demonstrate the point
that *metonymy* may be involved in various aspects of grammar and conceptualization, and it is not only and simply a property of isolated words.

Clark and Clark pose the question: Why is it that people readily create
and understand denominal verbs, like *porch the newspaper* and *Houdini
one's way out of a closet*, that they may have never heard before? The
denominal verbs in the expressions are *porch* and *Houdini*, which represent noun-to-verb shifts. Clark and Clark's proposal is that in using such

verbs people follow a convention: "the speaker means to denote the kind of state, event, or process that, he has good reason to believe, the listener can readily and uniquely compute on this occasion, on the basis of their shared knowledge" (1979, p. 767). Although Clark and Clark do not mention metonymy in this process in their account, I suggest that at least part of the explanation for why such denominal verbs are readily made and understood involves productive metonymic relationships that were described in chapter 11.

Clark and Clark distinguish eight classes of denominal verbs: (1) LOCATUM VERBS: *blanket* the bed, *sheet* the furniture, *carpet* the floor, etc.; (2) LOCATION VERBS: *porch* the newspaper, *kennel* the dog, *bench* the players, *short-list* the candidates, etc.; (3) DURATION VERBS: *summer* in Paris, *winter* in California, *honeymoon* in Hawaii, etc.; (4) AGENT VERBS: *butcher* the cow, *jockey* the horse, *author* the book, etc.; (5) EXPERIENCER VERBS: *witness* the accident, *boycott* the store, *badger* the officials, etc.; (6) GOAL VERBS: *powder* the aspirin, *dupe* the voter, *line up* the class, etc.; (7) SOURCE VERBS: *piece* the quilt together, *word* the sentence, *letter* the sign, etc.; (8) INSTRU-MENT VERBS: *bicycle* to town, *ski*, *ship* something, *paddle* the canoe, etc. The suggestion is that it is possible to reanalyze all these cases as cases of metonymic relationships. Here are the metonymies that apply to the eight classes:

(1) Locatum verbs: OBJECT OF MOTION FOR THE MOTION
(2) Location verbs: DESTINATION OF THE MOTION FOR THE MOTION
(3) Duration verbs: TIME PERIOD FOR A CHARACTERISTIC ACTIVITY IN THAT TIME PERIOD
(4) Agent verbs: AGENT FOR A CHARACTERISTIC ACTIVITY OF THAT AGENT
(5) Experiencer verbs: EXPERIENCER OF AN EVENT FOR THE EVENT
(6) Goal verbs: RESULT FOR THE ACTION THAT BRINGS ABOUT THAT RESULT
(7) Source verbs: COMPONENT PARTS OF A WHOLE FOR THE ACTION THAT PRODUCES THE WHOLE
(8) Instrument verbs: INSTRUMENT FOR THE ACTION INVOLVING THAT INSTRUMENT

As can be seen, all these metonymies are instances of what I called the ACTION ICM. The particular significance of this is that the ACTION ICM and the metonymic relationships that it defines account for literally thousands of denominal verbs. The kinds of metonymies that are based on the ICM are deeply entrenched in the conceptual system of speakers of English: for instance, DESTINATION FOR MOTION, AGENT FOR ACTION, RESULT FOR ACTION, and INSTRUMENT FOR ACTION. These metonymies apply well beyond denominal verbs. Because they are deeply entrenched and pervasive, they provide speakers with natural *cognitive links* that enable them to move from one entity (the vehicle) to another (the target) unconsciously and without any effort. They are a part of the mutual knowledge that speakers share and rely on in creating and understanding denominal verbs with ease.

3.2. The Diminutive

Consider now another case, the *diminutive*, as discussed by John Taylor. What is the range of cases to which diminutive morphemes can apply? How can we systematically account for this range? The central sense of diminutive morphemes in languages that have such morphemes is the 'small size' of a physical entity. For example, in Italian one such diminutive suffix is *-etto*. Attached to a noun, the noun indicates the small size of a physical object, like *villa*, which becomes *villetta* ('small villa') when diminutivized. But the same suffix can also be attached to, say, nonphysical nouns, such as *sinfonia* and *cena* ('symphony' and 'supper'), yielding *sinfonietta* and *cenetta* ('small-scale symphony' and 'small supper'). What we have here is the process of metaphorization, in which nonphysical domains, like symphony and supper, are conceptualized as physical domains, like physical objects that have small size. Thus, the range of cases to which the diminutive applies includes cases that are extensions of the central sense based on metaphor.

But *metonymy* is also at work in the use of the diminutive suffix. Another, and maybe an even more obvious, sense of the diminutive is the expression of affection. The Italian diminutive *-ina*, as applied to a noun like *Mamma*, yields *Mammina* and has the sense of affection on the part of the speaker. This extension is based on metonymy, not on metaphor. The metonymy involves a correlation in human experience; namely, that physically small things, like small children and animals, are regarded as helpless and thus in need of care and affection. This correlation in experience gives a new meaning to the diminutive suffix and accounts for its particular sense development.

3.3. The Past Tense Suffix

The central meaning of the *past tense suffix* in English, *-ed*, is to locate an event or state at some point in time prior to the time of speaking. But it has other uses as well. One such use involves the expression of counterfactuality, in such sentences as *If I had time . . .* and *It would be nice if I knew the answer*. Why can the *-ed* suffix be used in meanings (such as counterfactuality) that seemingly have nothing to do with past time? Taylor suggests that this happens because there is a metonymic transfer at work here. The metonymy involves an inference that can be drawn from the use of the past tense. As an illustration, consider the sentence *I was ill last week*. Here it is possible to draw the inference from the form *was* (i.e., the third person singular past tense of *be*) that the person is no longer ill. More generally, the use of the past tense implies that the event or state denoted by the verb does not hold in the present. This inference rests on a metonymic relationship: Given that use of the past tense implies present counterfactuality, it can be suggested that the past tense has a meaning ('past time') that is only part of a larger meaning that includes the inference that the state no longer holds in the present (i.e., it has a counter-factual sense as well). Now this PART FOR WHOLE metonymic relationship explains the counterfactual sense of -ed.

Another use of the past tense involves -ed as a pragmatic softener. Let us take the following pairs of sentences:

> Excuse me, I want to ask you something.
> Excuse me, I wanted to ask you something.
> Can you help me?
> Could you help me?

In both pairs, the second sentence is more polite or tactful than the first—that is, it is pragmatically softened. Why can the past tense -ed suffix express tactfulness? The reason is, Taylor suggests, that the basic sense of the past tense is extended by means of a metaphor: INVOLVEMENT IS CLOSENESS and LACK OF INVOLVEMENT IS DISTANCE. To be tactful and polite implies lack of involvement. If I say *I wanted to ask you something*, this suggests less of an intrusion on someone's privacy than using *I want*. The use of the past tense distances the person from the direct force of the utterance. This meaning has become conventionalized in English as the previous example *Could you help me?* also indicates.

3.4. Grammatical Constructions

So far we have considered only morphemes and words in our discussion of metaphor in grammar. But metaphor can also be found in larger *syntactic constructions* because polysemy applies to *grammatical constructions* in the same way as it does to words. One example of this is the *ditransitive con-struction*, which involves a verb that is followed by two objects, and is de-scribed extensively by Adele Goldberg. Consider the following case that ex-emplifies the construction: "Bill gave me an apple." The construction can be described as consisting of a verb, an agent (subject), a goal (indirect object), and a theme (direct object). The semantics can be given as follows: X CAUSES Y TO RECEIVE Z. This is the basic sense of the construction.

One extension of the basic sense involves sentences such as: "Bill gave me a headache." I already mentioned this kind of metaphor in chapter 8, where it was pointed out that it is a manifestation of the CAUSATION IS PHYSICAL TRANSFER metaphor. What is new and remarkable about it in the present context is that it can be seen as an extension of the basic sense and that the extension is motivated by a metaphoric link, which is the metaphor CAUSA-TION IS PHYSICAL TRANSFER.

An even subtler case of a metaphoric link between the basic sense and another, extended sense of the same construction is discussed by George Lakoff and Mark Johnson. Consider the pair of sentences:

I taught Harry Greek.
I taught Greek to Harry.

The difference in meaning between the two sentences is that the first implies that Harry did learn some Greek, while the second does not imply this; Harry either learned some Greek or he did not. The basic sense of the construction involves successful transfer (of knowledge). There appears to be a conceptual metaphor that is responsible for the difference in meaning: STRENGTH OF EFFECT IS CLOSENESS. This metaphor involves the forms and meanings of language. Lakoff and Johnson explain this metaphor as follows:

> If the meaning of form A affects the meaning of form B, then, the CLOSER form A is to form B, the stronger will be the EFFECT of the meaning of A on the meaning of B.

That is, in this metaphor, linguistic form is understood in spatial terms (i.e., as being close or distant to each other) and the forms themselves are given meaning (i.e., the notion of strength of effect) by means of the spatialization metaphors. (This account of the interpretation of the sentences above does not rule out the possibility that other linguistic mechanisms of meaning production are also at work in such cases. One such linguistic mechanism that may also play a role is "theme-rheme" distribution in such sentence pairs.)

4. Linguistic Theorizing

All scientific theories employ metaphors, and linguistic theories are no exception. The people who construct *linguistic theories* commonly and inevitably use metaphors that characterize our conceptual structure in general. Above, we just saw one such metaphor, in which *syntactic distance* is characterized by the image schema of linear scale: STRENGTH OF EFFECT IS CLOSENESS. Lakoff observes several other cases in which we use image schemas to characterize syntactic structure. For example, what we call *constituent structure*, the hierarchical structure of sentences, is conceived of as a part-whole schema: the mother node is the whole and the daughters are the parts. In addition, and obviously, the talk about mother, daughter, and trees in connection with syntactic structure is another example of metaphorically understanding language, though it is not image schematic understanding. Of greater significance for the purposes of comprehending linguistic structure are **image-schema metaphors**. Other such metaphors that linguists rely on include the *center-periphery schema* that characterizes head-and-modifier structures (e.g., adjective and noun constructions). *Link schemas* are used to understand and represent grammatical and coreference relations. Finally, the *container schema* characterizes syntactic categories, such as noun and verb. This is not surprising because it is the container schema that we evoke to understand categories in general.

SUMMARY

A major notion in the cognitive linguistic view of language is *polysemy*. Not only *words* but also other linguistic elements are often regarded as structured by polysemy. Thus, *morphemes* and *grammatical constructions* can be seen as polysemous. Many cases of polysemy at these various levels of language are such that the elements in question are linked by conceptual metaphors and metonymies.

These metaphors and metonymies are productive and very much alive in our conceptual system. It should be stressed that they exist independently of the linguistic elements for whose different senses they provide important *cognitive links*.

Conceptual metaphors and metonymies also "guide" *historical meaning shifts*. Most of the well-known cases of meaning change follow the same source-to-target directions that manifest themselves in well-established metaphors.

Finally, *linguistic theorizing*, including cognitive linguistic theorizing, abounds in metaphor. No scientific discipline is imaginable without recourse to metaphor.

FURTHER READING

The first work in cognitive linguistics that emphasizes the role of metaphor in grammar is Lakoff and Johnson (1980). In several articles, Talmy draws our attention to metaphorical aspects of grammar (e.g., in Talmy 1988). Goldberg (1995) analyzes the English ditransitive construction and points out the crucial role of metaphor in understanding the various uses of the construction. Taylor (1989/1995) and Taylor 1996 do the same for a variety of morphological and syntactic constructions. The most comprehensive treatment of cognitive grammar is Langacker (1987, 1991), where he also discusses the role of metaphor in linguistic theory. Heine and his colleagues (e.g., Heine, Claudi, and Hünnemeyer, 1991; Heine, 1997) examine the role of metaphor in the emergence of many grammatical constructions in diverse languages of the world. Dirven and Radden (n.d.) is a cognitive linguistic introduction to English grammar for students of English. They deal with several issues that were mentioned in the chapter.

The most extensive treatment of the issue of polysemy and its relationship to metaphor is Lakoff (1987). Taylor (1989/1995) and Ungerer and Schmidt (1996) offer very accessible accounts of the same phenomenon. Anthropologists and psychologists influenced by the results of cognitive linguistics also pay considerable attention to polysemy and metaphor. These authors include Palmer (1996), Gibbs (1994), and Gibbs et al. (1994). Several studies by Fillmore (e.g., 1982) deal with polysemy within a frame-semantic (roughly ICM) framework, though not making use of the notion of conceptual metaphor as linking the different senses.

Traugott (1985), Sweetser (1990), and Geeraerts (1997) have done much to help us understand the role of metaphor in historical meaning change. More recently, Haser (2000) examines the role of metaphor in semantic change. In addition, László (1997) contains many examples of meaning shifts based on the mind-as-body metaphor. Ibarretxe-Antunano (1999) extends Sweetser's ideas concerning regular processes of sense development, and Pelyvás (2000) is a reanalysis of Sweetser's work on modals, especially *may* and *must*. Goossens (2000) offers an alternative to the analysis of modal verbs as typically done by cognitive linguists. Clark and Clark (1979) analyze "denominal" verbs, reanalyzed as metonimies by Kövecses and Radden (1998).

EXERCISES

1. It was illustrated in the chapter that the word *love* has many senses. Listen to the song entitled "I Give Her All My Love" by the Beatles. Try to find synonyms for the many senses of *love* used in the song. Consider the role of metonymy in the extension of the basic sense of LOVE and give the corresponding metonymies in each case. (To do the exercise, first, you should distinguish between the basic and the nonbasic senses. Then analyze the nonbasic senses only.)
2. Take philosopher John Austin's example: the adjective *healthy*. *Healthy* is used in the sense of (1) healthy body; (2) healthy complexion; (3) healthy exercise. What metonymic relationships do you recognize concerning the three senses of *healthy*?
3. Look up the meanings of one of the following words in a dictionary: *ruin, field, flag, leg, flood, flower*. How can you account for the different senses of these words with the help of metonymy?
4. Consider the following words and their meanings, taken from György László's examples. Which conceptual metaphor motivates the meanings of these words?

analysis	from ML/Greek *analysis* a breaking up, from *analyein* unloose
detail	from F *détail*, from OF *detail* small piece or quantity
distinguish	from MF *distinguiss-*, stem of *distinguer*, also from OF *distinguer*, from Latin *distinguere* to separate between
inform	from OF *enformer, enfourmer*, from Latin *informare* to shape, form, train, instruct, educate
metaphor	from MF *metaphore*, from Latin or Greek and directly from Latin *metphora* or from Greek *metaphora* a transfer, from *metapherein* transfer, carry over
suppose	from OF *supposer* to assume, from Latin *supponere* put or place under
syntax	from F *syntaxe*, and directly from LL *syntaxis*, from Greek *sýntaxis* a putting together or in order, arrangement, syntax
synthesis	from Latin *synthesis* collection, set, composition (of a medication), from Greek *synthesis* composition (logical, mathematical)

16

Metaphors
and Blends

In this book, I have characterized metonymy as a *stand-for relationship* between two elements within a single conceptual domain and metaphor as an *is-understood-as relationship* between two conceptually distant domains. With this *one-domain* (for metonymy) and *two-domain* (for metaphor) model, we have been able to account for several aspects of the human conceptual system and many cases of linguistic and nonlinguistic behavior. Nevertheless, there are also additional aspects of the conceptual system and many additional linguistic and nonlinguistic examples that require us to extend the model we have used so far. This chapter will discuss some specific suggestions to this effect.

1. The Network Model of Fauconnier and Turner

Fauconnier and Turner have proposed that the issue of conceptual metaphor is a special case of a much larger one; namely, that of how the conceptual system operates with domains in general: how it projects elements from one to another, how it fuses two domains into one, how it builds up new domains from existing ones, etc. To a large extent, imaginative or figurative human thought is constituted by this manipulation of structured domains of experience or ICMs. Fauconnier and Turner make use of the notion of *mental*, or *conceptual space* to describe this process. A mental space is a conceptual "packet" that is built up "on-line," that is, in the moment of understanding. A mental space is always much smaller than a conceptual domain, and it is also much more specific. Mental spaces are often structured by more than one conceptual domain. For example, "Yesterday, I saw Susan" prompts us to build a space for the speaker's present reality and another space (yesterday) in which the speaker is seeing Susan. These are mental spaces, but they are not conceptual domains like JOURNEY or FIRE. The "yesterday" mental space contains the specific speaker and the specific Susan, but conceptual domains are much more general than that. Now consider something like "Yesterday, I asked Susan for her telephone number." The "yesterday" mental space is structured by the domain of temporal relation (yesterday versus today), by the domain of request and conversation, and potentially also by the domain for dating. A mental space is not a domain but is often structured by domains.

Fauconnier and Turner's basic suggestion is that to account for the many complexities of human thought we need not just a one-domain or two-domain model but a *network* (or *many-space model*) of human imaginative thought. Let us now see what the network model consists of. For lack of space for a more detailed presentation, the following description will have to simplify the network model and offer only its bare outlines. The examples used to demonstrate the model will be taken from Fauconnier and Turner's work.

1.1. Blended Space

First, consider the case of counterfactuals, for instance, sentences such as "If I were you, I would have done it." Suppose this sentence was said by a man to a woman who declined earlier to become pregnant. To account for the meaning of the sentence, we need several domains. There is the domain of the man and there is the domain of the woman. In the "man domain," it is impossible to become pregnant, while in the "woman domain" it is possible. The sentence integrates the two domains into a third one: the space which has the man with the possibility of becoming pregnant. In other words, we get a mental space in which the man and the woman domains are integrated into a single domain: the "man-woman" domain. In this new mental space, the man can become pregnant. The man domain with its impossibility of becoming pregnant is blended with the woman domain with its possibility of becoming pregnant. In the *blended space* there is a man with the possibility of pregnancy. (It is also possible to get a different blended space when we understand this sentence; namely, the blended space of a woman when younger but with the judgment of this man. It is important to see that the same statement can be understood via different blends. But this is not the interpretation that I am considering here.) This blended space is, of course, an impossible domain; men cannot really become pregnant. The **blend** is a matter of our imagination. Thus, in order to explain the meaning of the counterfactual sentence, we needed two conceptual domains and a mental space: the real domain of the man, the real domain of the woman, and the impossible space of the "man-woman"; that is, the space where the man domain is blended counterfactually and imaginatively with the woman domain.

Notice that the man domain and the woman domain here do not correspond to the source and the target domain. It is not the case that the man-speaker maps properties of the woman domain onto his man-domain in order to understand the man-domain. Rather, he conceptually blends his man-domain with the woman-domain on the basis of two domains. We can say, then, that there are two *input domains* that yield a third one, a *blended space*. In the blend, the man can get pregnant and would intend to get pregnant.

But what does all this have to do with conceptual metaphor as I have discussed it in this book? Fauconnier and Turner's proposal is that blended spaces (or domains) derive from input spaces (or domains) and that these input spaces may be related to each other as source and target; that is, they may form a conceptual metaphor. Input spaces are often not related metaphorically. As we just saw in the previous example, the relationship between the two input spaces of man and woman was not a source-target relationship; one was not metaphorically understood in terms of the other. The next example, however, will involve a source-target relationship between the two input spaces (i.e., they can be seen as constituting a case of conceptual metaphor). The two inputs, then, yield a third domain: a blended space.

Consider the expression *The Grim Reaper*, as it is used to mean death. The Grim Reaper is typically visualized as a skeleton dressed in a robe and cowl that holds a scythe in his hands. This personification of death assumes two conceptual metaphors: PEOPLE ARE PLANTS and EVENTS ARE ACTIONS. We have already dealt with both metaphors. To recapitulate, the PEOPLE ARE PLANTS metaphor gives rise to examples, such as "She's *withering away*," "He is a *late bloomer*," and "He's a *young sprout*." The mappings include: the plants are the people; the life-cycle of the plants is the life-cycle of human beings; the growth of the plants is the development and progress that people make in their lives; etc. EVENTS ARE ACTIONS is a generic-level metaphor that is used to conceptualize events as actions. One example of this is when we refer to the event of somebody's death as departure (e.g., "He *passed away*"), where death is an event and passing is a deliberate action.

In the PEOPLE ARE PLANTS metaphor, plants correspond to people who can be cut down by a reaper with a scythe. Death is an event and this event can be conceptualized as an action via the EVENTS ARE ACTIONS metaphor. The particular action in terms of which The Grim Reaper is conceptualized is either cutting down people with a scythe or simply appearing before the people whom he wants to die. In other words, we have two input domains, death and (the harvesting of) plants, that are metaphorically related as target and source. Now The Grim Reaper does not belong to either the source or the target domain; it belongs to a blended space between the two. Why doesn't he arise from either of these input domains?

- The Grim Reaper cannot reside in the target domain because there are no plants and reapers in the domain of dying. Death is an event in the course of which people die of illnesses and injuries, not because of illnesses or injuries inflicted on them by reapers.
- The Grim Reaper does not reside in the source space of the reaping and harvesting of plants either because the features of The Grim Reaper are incompatible with our stereotype of reaping and harvesting.
- First, there are many actual reapers and they are interchangeable. But there is only one Grim Reaper who is definite. This explains the use of the definite article *the* in the expression *The Grim Reaper*.

- Second, actual reapers are mortal, but The Grim Reaper is immortal; it is the same Grim Reaper who cut our own ancestors down that will cut us down.
- Third, stereotypical reapers use their scythes to reap, while The Grim Reaper doesn't necessarily do so; he may bring death merely by appearing before us.
- Four, stereotypical reapers work for long intervals and wear clothes appropriate to their work. The Grim Reaper, on the other hand, acts only once (brings death) and is dressed suitable to repose.
- Five, reapers typically do their work by reaping the entire field indiscriminately, not paying any attention to the individual existence of plants of wheat. By contrast, The Grim Reaper comes for a specific person at a specific time.
- Finally, we do not normally think of reapers as grim, but we think of death and the cause of death as grim. Again, the source space has connotations that are incompatible with those of the target.

These are only some of incompatibilities between the conceptual space of reaping and features of The Grim Reaper, as discussed by Turner. However, for our purposes they suffice to demonstrate the point that blends do not arise from either sources or targets but from conceptual blending in the literal sense of "blend."

A further general point here is that blended spaces are not necessarily projections of source and target counterparts into a third blended space; blended spaces may involve new elements that are not simple combinations of elements in the source and the target. In the present example, The Grim Reaper as a "skeleton dressed in a robe and cowl that holds a scythe" only exists in the blended space. The reaper in the source corresponds to the cause of the event of death, and not to the skeleton in the target. The skeleton is related to the cause of death metonymically in the target, in that the cause of death produces skeletons (as EFFECT FOR CAUSE). In the blend, The Grim Reaper is a combination of the cause of death and the skeleton from the target, as well as the reaper from the source, but the reaper and the skeleton are not source and target counterparts. This is an example of the way in which blending often tightens metonymies: The long metonymic chain from the general cause of death to a specific cause of death to a specific event of death to the corpse to the decay to the skeleton is very much tightened in the blend, in this case to a prototypical part-whole relationship, in which the skeleton is the structural form of Death.

1.2. Generic Space

Fauconnier and Turner's network model involves more than input spaces (such as source and target) and a blended space. A further crucial part of their model is what they call a *generic space*. The generic space contains the abstract structure taken as applying to both input spaces. What is the relevance of the generic space to conceptual metaphor? It is relevant in two ways: Either generic spaces can make metaphoric mappings between source and target domains possible or two inputs will share abstract structure because a conventional metaphor has established that abstract structure. For example, the reaper in the source domain of plants has death as a counterpart in the target domain of people dying. The shared generic structure has been established by the metaphor PEOPLE ARE PLANTS and it involves entities such as "organic things" and such predicates as "living and stopping living." People dying and plants dying are both cases where things cease to live. This enables us to see counterparts, or correspondences, between the two domains: between people and plants and between death as cause and reaper.

Generic space is most easily seen in proverbs. Consider the proverb "Look before you leap." This proverb comes with a generic meaning or space: You should consider the consequences of your actions before you act. Now the acts of looking and leaping function as one input domain, and all the cases to which they can apply serve as additional input domains. The proverb "Look before you leap" applies to a wide variety of actions and gives a warning: think before you marry; think before you hand in your resignation; think before you buy a new house; think before you break up with your girlfriend; think before you sign the contract; and so on. What establishes the generic space between the look-leap domain and these other domains is the metaphors THINKING/CONSIDERING IS LOOKING (for the looking part) and the Event Structure metaphor (for the leaping part), where ACTION IS SELF-PROPELLED MOTION.

But shared abstract structure between input domains need not be established by metaphors only. To see one such nonmetaphorical case, let us take an example that Fauconnier and Turner often discuss in their work. In a magazine article, a journalist reports on the passage of a catamaran, *Great America II*, from San Francisco to Boston in 1993:

> As we went to press, Rich Wilson and Bill Biewenga were barely maintaining a 4.5 day lead over the ghost of the clipper *Northern Light*, whose record run from San Francisco to Boston they're trying to beat. In 1853, the clipper made the passage in 76 days, 8 hours. (Turner 1996, p. 67)

There are two input spaces here: the passage of *Northern Light* in 1853 and the passage of *Great America II* in 1993. The two input spaces are fused into a blended space, one in which the two passages by the two boats are conceived as a race. It is only in the blend that there can be a race between the two boats; both in 1853 and 1993 there was only one boat sailing from San Francisco to Boston. The race constitutes a (possible) blended space. But the two input spaces also share abstract structure, that is, generic space, which includes a boat, a path, a departure point, a destination, etc. The generic space provides counterpart relations (mappings) between the two inputs, but they are not *metaphorical* mappings. The two inputs of the 1853 and the 1993 passages are not related as source to target. The counterparts are obvious:

the *Northern Light* corresponds to *Great America II*, 1853 to 1993, San Francisco to San Francisco, Boston to Boston, etc. In other words, some of the counterparts are identical, and so generic structure becomes identity structure. In general, shared generic space (sometimes in the form of identity structure) allows us to establish the counterparts, or mappings, between the input domains.

The overall picture, then, is shown in Figure 16.1.

In Fauconnier and Turner's analysis, metaphor is a special case of the situation in Figure 16.1. See Figure 16.2.

This completes our presentation of Fauconnier and Turner's network model. In the remainder of the chapter, I will discuss the issue of what this model can "buy" us.

2. The Advantages of the Network Model

The many-space model offers several distinct advantages. These include: (1) we can make previous metaphor analyses more precise; (2) we can provide more refined analyses of literary texts; (3) we can handle better certain problems that arise in connection with the metaphor analysis as presented so far.

2.1. The HOT FLUID Metaphor for Anger

Lakoff and Kövecses described in detail the ANGER IS A HOT FLUID IN A CONTAINER metaphor. We hypothesized the existence of this metaphor on the basis of such expressions as "*Simmer down*," "Let him *stew* for a little while," "She was *boiling with* rage," "*Steam was coming out of* his ears," etc. To account for these and other expressions, a number of correspondences between the source (hot fluid in a container) and the target (anger) can be suggested, including

the heat of the fluid ⇒ anger
the container ⇒ the body of the angry person
the high intensity of the heat ⇒ the high intensity of anger
the physical signals of the potential danger of the hot fluid ⇒ the
    behavioral signals of the potential danger of anger
keeping the fluid inside the container ⇒ controlling anger, etc.

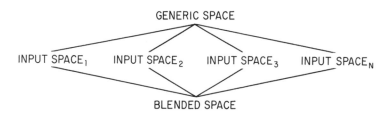

Figure 16.1. Blending.

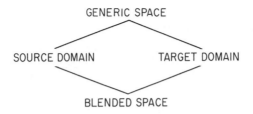

Figure 16.2. Blending and metaphor.

This analysis is adequate so far as it goes. However, it leaves out of consideration the fact that some blending also takes place here: The source and the target domains may both project elements into a blended space. One example of this blend is provided by the sentence "*Steam was coming out of his ears.*" In the source, there is a container with a hot fluid inside, like a pot, which produces steam when heated. In the target, there is a person who is getting more and more angry, showing signs of losing control over anger as a result of a continued cause. But there is also a blended space of an angry person with steam coming out of his ears. This blend is a result of projection from both the source and the target: The steam comes from the source, while the head of a person with ears comes from the target. There is no steam in the target and there is no head with ears in the source. But they are fused in a distinct conceptual space—the blend.

What the additional analysis of these examples shows is that there are complexities that have not been recognized in previous studies but which are clearly important for a fuller account of the cognitive work that goes into the creation of such expressions on the part of speakers.

2.2. King John

The cognitive mechanism of blending can also be found in literary works. As a matter of fact, literature produces a large number of blends, and many of these are of the impossible kind. Some authors use the device of creating fantastic blends with great skill and can thus convey subtle messages that can only be fully understood with the help of the kind of analysis that was presented above in this chapter.

As we saw in chapter 4, the notion of conceptual metaphor is extremely important in the study of literary texts. But this notion cannot, of course, be an "all-purpose" tool. There are texts where metaphor analysis, no matter how revealing, can only do so much, and large portions of the message of the literary work remain hidden. One good example where our analysis of a literary text should go beyond metaphor analysis is provided by the following quote from Shakespeare's *King John*. King John says to a messenger who just arrived with some bad news:

> So foul a sky clears not without a storm.
> Pour down thy weather.

Let us first see what the metaphor analysis of these two famous lines would involve. There are two domains here: the scene of an imminent storm as source and the scene of the king with a messenger who just came before him with some bad news. We could set up certain correspondences, or mappings, between the two domains. These include:

the appearance of the sky   ⇒   the appearance of the messenger's face
the imminent storm   ⇒   the bad message likely to be delivered
the rain   ⇒   the act of telling the bad news

This set of correspondences makes it clear for us that the lines are not about the weather; that what is really conveyed is another message, namely, that the king knows that the messenger is about to deliver some bad news to him. How do we know that this is what the lines are about?

The reason we know is that the mappings are the mappings of the conventional CONDUIT metaphor for communication, in which:

THE MIND IS A CONTAINER;

MEANINGS ARE OBJECTS;

LINGUISTIC EXPRESSIONS ARE CONTAINERS FOR MEANING OBJECTS;

COMMUNICATION IS SENDING MEANING OBJECTS FROM A MIND
   CONTAINER TO ANOTHER MIND CONTAINER ALONG A CONDUIT.

The correspondences above are special cases of these submetaphors of the CONDUIT metaphor complex: The sky-clouds as containers are the mind of the messenger, the rain falling "out of" the sky is the message, and the rain's movement from the sky down to the earth is the conduit along which the message travels. Thus, a large portion of the text's meaning can be captured by means of applying an ordinary, conventional conceptual metaphor to the two lines. But there is more to the text's meaning.

These lines are said in the play at a point where King John's rule as a king is increasingly questioned. He appears to be in command, but many things are happening that make his command less and less stable. His power as king is shrinking. This is an additional and subtler reading of the play's meaning at this point. But how does this reading arise? It can be proposed that it comes from the process of blending: Certain parts of the source are blended with certain parts of the target. The blended space derives from the counterpart relation, or correspondence, between the cloudy sky and the messenger. In the blend, a paradox arises: a messenger is completely under the king's command, but nature is something that is absolutely not under his command. The paradox is that, given the correspondence between nature and the messenger, the king commands nature (the messenger) to rain (to talk). This can only happen in the blend. Not even kings have control over nature and rain, but kings have control over their messengers. This comes from the target in the construction of the blend. On the other hand, they have absolutely no control over nature. This comes from the source. The blend combines these two conflicting aspects and provides a basic paradox: The king commands something that he does not command. The paradox is also signaled in linguistic structure: The king gives an order to nature in the form of an imperative sentence (*"Pour down"*), which is impossible, and uses the informal second-person pronoun (*"thy"*) to a subordinate, which is possible, given the king-messenger relationship. This subtler and fuller meaning of the lines can only be captured if we go beyond ordinary metaphor analysis and analyze the text as involving a case of conceptual blending.

2.3. The Generalization of Metaphorical Meaning along Mappings

Both the example of anger and the lines by King John represent blended spaces. As we have seen, with the help of this notion we were able to provide more accurate and revealing analyses of these cases. However, the notion of generic space also plays an important role in accounting for some other problematic cases. One such case involves some of the metaphors that we have dealt with in previous chapters.

A complex metaphor that was discussed in chapter 9 was the COMPLEX SYSTEMS ARE COMPLEX OBJECTS metaphor. We talk about *building* a country and an economic system or about *constructing* a theory, *laying the foundations* of a legal system, etc. These examples can be accounted for by the submappings of the COMPLEX SYSTEMS ARE BUILDINGS metaphor, including:

building a complex object $\Rightarrow$ creation of a complex system
(e.g., *build*)
foundation of a complex object $\Rightarrow$ basis of a complex system
(e.g., *lay the foundations*)

However, we find that in many instances of metaphoric usage the expressions that characterize this metaphor can be used in other cases as well. Consider some sample sentences from the *Cobuild Metaphor Dictionary* again:

During this time he *has built* a fine reputation for high standards in the field. (reputation)
The self-confidence that she *had built up* so painfully was still *paper-thin*; beneath it hid despair and cold anger. (self-confidence)
The *foundations are being laid* for a steady increase in oil prices. (increase)
At the same time the *foundations were laid* for more far-reaching changes in the future. (change)

Reputation, self-confidence, increase, and change are not abstract systems, and yet the metaphorical expressions of *build*, *build up*, *paper-thin*, and *lay the foundations* are used in connection with them. Reputation is an attribute, self-confidence is a property or trait, and increase and change are processes. To account for this usage, we can hypothesize the existence of some very general mappings. In the present examples, these are

building   ⇒   creation
foundation ⇒   basis

This means that the (sub)mappings of a metaphor can undergo a generalization process. In the present instance, this entails that they are no longer limited to complex systems as a target domain. The concept of the activity of building acquires the general meaning of 'creation' and the concept of foundation acquires the general meaning of 'basis.' Once this happens, the concepts of building and foundation can be extended beyond the domain of complex systems, such as country, economic system, law, theory, etc. to attributes, porperties, and processes. In other words, based on these mappings a generic space is created.

As another illustration, consider the sentence taken from the COMPLEX SYSTEMS ARE MACHINES metaphor: "He soon had the household *running like clockwork*." A household is a complex system, so the metaphorical expression *running like clockwork* is used here in a natural way. The meaning of the expression is based on the submapping:

regularity in the working of a machine   ⇒   regularity in the operation
                                              of complex systems

Now consider the following sentences that contain the same expression (*clockwork*) but not in connection with a complex system:

Each day a howling wind springs up from the south with almost
    clockwork regularity.
The journey there went like *clockwork*.

The wind is not a complex system, and neither is a journey. Both of these concepts are events. Here again, what makes this use possible is the generalization of the relevant mapping. The regularity in the operation of machines and (metaphorically) of complex systems becomes 'regularity' as such. In other words, a generic space for regularity is created which may then apply outside complex systems—for instance, to events.

In general, it seems that generic spaces related to conceptual metaphors arise from the generalization of mappings. The generic space will apply to cases beyond the original and most natural application. However, it cannot apply to anything indiscriminately: Only domains that do have or can be regarded as having the required abstract structure can take it.

SUMMARY

In this chapter, we saw that the cognitive linguistic theory of conceptual metaphor needs to be supplemented by an account of "on-line" processes of human understanding. Fauconnier and Turner replace the *two-domain* model of conceptual metaphor with a *network model*, which can account for several metaphorical and nonmetaphorical aspects of on-line understanding. The model consists of *input spaces*, a *blended space*, and a *generic space*. The model offers some distinct advantages, in that with its help we can account for certain metaphor-related phenomena more fully; we can provide subtler analyses of literary texts; and we can describe certain conceptual phenomena with greater systematicity than was available before.

FURTHER READING

In recent years, Fauconnier and Turner, and several others, have written extensively about many of the issues I have only touched on in the chapter. Much of this is available on the Internet. Some of the more "conventional" sources for the reader to get acquainted with their ideas include the following. The notion of "mental space" was introduced by Fauconnier (1985/1994). Fauconnier and Turner (1994) provide a detailed description of their ideas regarding "conceptual projection" and "middle spaces." Turner (1996) reviews the major ideas of blending and argues that at the heart of our cognitive capacity is the "literary mind," not the "logical mind." Fauconnier (1997) contains a comprehensive overview of the "network" model. Turner and Fauconnier (1995) discuss some of the implications of their theory for grammatical analysis. Grady, Oakley, and Coulson (1999) discuss the relationship between metaphor and blending.

EXERCISES

1. What generic abstract structure characterizes the following proverbs? Which metaphors, if any, establish the generic space in these cases? Find appropriate situations where these proverbs could be applied to describe the events at hand.

    (a) When the cat is away, the mice will play.
    (b) The early bird catches the worm.
    (c) It is no use crying over spilt milk.
    (d) A barking dog never bites.
    (e) Once burned, twice shy.

2. Some important aspects of the Puritan understanding of America can also be explained with conceptual blending. For instance, the Puritan writer Cotton Mather wrote a longish work about John Winthrop who was an important leader of the Puritans: He was elected governor of the Company of Massachusetts Bay in 1629. The colony was under his leadership for nearly twenty years. In this work, Mather talks about Winthrop's life and actions in terms of

Nehemiah's life and actions. Nehemiah was a high Jewish official in Persia, who led the Israelites back from Babylon to their promised land. Here, however, Winthrop in the target domain does not correspond to Nehemiah in the source domain. On the basis of the following quote from Mather, try to discover how blending applies to this case. What resides in the input, in the generic, and the blended spaces?

But whilst [John Winthrop] thus did, as our New English Nehemiah, the part of a ruler in managing the public affairs of our American Jerusalem, when there were Tobijahs and Sanballats enough to vex him, and give him the experiment of Luther's observation [A man in authority is a target at which Satan and the world launch all their darts], he made himself still an exacter parallel unto that governor of Israel, by doing the part of a neighbor among the distressed people of the new plantation. (Cotton Mather 1702, 231)

3. Blends of the human and the animal occur frequently in folk tales and literature. Consider the A. A. Milne's story, *Winnie The Pooh*. In this tale, there are a number of talking animals. What do you think is blended from the source space and the target space in the characters of Winnie The Pooh, Piglet, Eyore, Rabbit, Tigger, and Owl?

4. Take Turner's example of Arthur Koester's riddle about a Buddhist monk. How can you solve the riddle with the help of blending?

A Buddhist monk begins at dawn to walk up a mountain. He stops and starts and varies his pace as he pleases, and reaches the mountaintop at sunset. There he meditates overnight. At dawn, he begins to walk back down, again moving as he pleases. He reaches the foot of the mountain at sunset. Prove that there is a place on the path that he occupies at the same hour of the day on the two separate journeys.

5. In the chapter, "The Grim Reaper" was mentioned as a case of blending. Now read Ray Bradbury's short story "The Scythe."
   (a) In "The Scythe," the main character, Drew Erickson is at first just "the man with the scythe"; he is like an agricultural worker cutting the ripe wheat. What is the turning point, when does he become The Grim Reaper?
   (b) Read through "The Grim Reaper" analysis in the chapter, which describes a "prototypical" Grim Reaper. Name the main conceptual metaphors, lay out the mappings, and show what falls into the blended space. Pay special attention to elements that do not come from either the source or the target but exist only in the blended space.
   (c) Ray Bradbury takes the idea of The Grim Reaper one step further. What happens to The Grim Reaper? How does his situation become abnormal? Why does he become The Mad Reaper?

17

How Does All This
Hang Together?

G iven all the various strands of research on metaphor that has been surveyed in this book, it seems reasonable to distinguish three levels of metaphor: (1) the "supraindividual" level, (2) the individual level, and (3) the
"subindividual" level. Each conceptual metaphor can be analyzed on these
levels. Most of the research in cognitive linguistics takes place on and is directed at one or several of these levels. In this brief final chapter, I'll try to
bring together the many threads of research in cognitive linguistics on metaphor into a coherent picture, whose coherence seems to derive from the three
interrelated levels, or aspects, of metaphor.

In a nutshell, the supraindividual level is one at which linguists identify conceptual metaphors mainly on the basis of decontextualized linguistic examples.
The individual level is one at which metaphors exist in the heads of individual
speakers, as studied, for example, by psycholinguists in various experimental
situations. Finally, the subindividual level is one at which we find universal sensorimotor experiences that underlie and motivate conceptual metaphors.

Figure 17.1 on page 240 is a simple drawing that is intended to show the
three levels: the supraindividual level at the top (in the form of a cloud-like
formation), the individual level in the middle (with people communicating
with each other, surrounded by nature and man-made objects), and the subindividual level at the bottom of the drawing (representing people having all
kinds of preconceptual experiences throughout the duration of their lives).
This is no doubt an oversimplified picture of the three levels and their interaction, but it may serve us well in illustrating its main characteristics.

1. The Supraindividual Level

Let us begin with the supraindividual level. What "supraindividual" simply
means is that there is a level of metaphor that is based on the conventional-

Figure 17.1. Katalin Jobbágy, *Three Levels of Metaphor*, 2000. Property of the artist.

ized metaphors of a given language (such as English, Chinese, Zulu, Wolof, Hungarian, etc.). This is the level at which most of the cognitive linguistic research is taking place. Researchers typically collect conventionalized metaphorical expressions from dictionaries, thesauri, random other sources such as books, newspapers, magazines, and other news reports in the media, or from their own "mental lexcion" as native speakers of a language. They then analyze these collections of conventionalized metaphorical expressions by grouping them into conceptual metaphors that have a concrete source and an abstract target domain. For example, this is what Lakoff and Kovecses did in their study of anger-related metaphors in (American) English. We collected such examples as "*boil* with anger," "be *pissed off*," "*seethe* with anger," "make one's blood *boil*," and many others, from dictionaries and other sources. We concluded from these data that there exists a conceptual metaphor that we put as ANGER IS A HOT FLUID IN A CONTAINER.

The conceptual metaphors form larger systems. Source domains have a wide or narrow scope. There is a set of mappings that characterizes a source and the targets that belong to its scope. The mappings are conventionally fixed and they provide a certain structure for the abstract domains to which the source domain applies. Some of the mappings constitute simple, or primary, metaphors. The conceptual metaphors that we find in a language constitute large systems. Two large metaphor systems have been identified: the Great Chain metaphor that characterizes "things," and the Event Structure metaphor that characterizes "relations."

Source domains come with, or imply, a great deal of knowledge that metaphor researchers often explore. In other words, in addition to the basic, constituent elements that comprise source domains, the domains also give rise to metaphorical entailments. These entailments also structure target domains. However, only those entailments participate in this job that meet certain specific requirements. Three such requirements have been outlined in the book (but there are more). Each of these function independently in accounting for the question of what gets mapped from source to target. First is the requirement that only those conceptual materials are mapped from the source that are consistent with the image-schematic structure of the target. This is the invariance principle. Second is the view that what gets mapped depends on the primary metaphors that make up a complex one; the primary metaphors determine entailments. A third possible requirement suggests that each source is associated with a main meaning focus (or foci) and it is this that determines what gets mapped from the source; items outside the main meaning focus do not get mapped onto the target.

But many of the same metaphors that are identified on the basis of language can be found in all kinds of cultural institutions (as these are broadly conceived), such as art, science, politics, sports, and so forth. These are real-world enactments of metaphors identified initially in language. Thus, in addition to the linguistic dimension, this gives an important cultural dimension to the supraindividual level. Metaphors can be said to pervade and structure many aspects of language and culture. Do they also pervade and structure the thought, the conceptual system of people?

2. The Individual Level

The metaphors found on the supraindividual are mainly based on the analysis of linguistic expressions. But the question arises: Does this, or can this, analysis reveal anything about metaphors in the heads of individual speakers? In particular: Do people actually have the metaphors in their conceptual system that cognitive linguists discover on the basis of their linguistic analyses?

The breakthrough in answering these questions came with Ray Gibbs's psycholinguistic work on metaphor. In a variety of mental imagery tasks, he convincingly showed that conceptual metaphors actually exist in the heads of individual speakers. He asked subjects to form mental images of such anger-related idioms as *blow one's stack*, *flip one's lid*, and *hit the ceiling*. People's images were highly uniform and consistent about what they imagined: a container with heated fluid inside that explodes as a result of too much pressure inside the container. Why was this so? This is only possible if people's images are constrained by something in their conceptual system: something that can only be the conceptual metaphor ANGER IS A HOT FLUID IN A CONTAINER. That is, what Gibbs showed was that the metaphors discovered by cognitive linguists actually exist in the heads of speakers.

However, the same research also shows that the match between the supra-individual and the individual levels is not perfect or complete. The incompleteness of the fit can come from a variety of factors. The entire range of metaphors at the supraindividual level is not utilized by every single speaker of a language. The individual level is the level at which individual speakers of a given language use the metaphors that are available to them at the supraindividual level in actual communicative situations, but this level is also where they create new metaphors. This level is characterized by such issues as the selection of metaphors for particular communicative purposes; how people think on-line using metaphors; how the context of communication constrains the use of metaphors; and how metaphors can organize or otherwise structure actual texts or discourses. There are several other ways in which metaphor plays a role in communication between actual speakers of a language in real-world situations, but these are the issues that were briefly mentioned, or at least alluded to, in the references in various chapters of this book.

Not all the metaphors that have been, or could be, identified at the supra-individual level are available to all speakers of a language. Both individuals and social groups vary in the kinds of metaphors they use, and they also often invent new conceptual metaphors. This is what we called "within-culture" variation in metaphor in this book.

When people engage in on-line thinking in the course of communication, they commonly create blends—both in language and thought. This phenomenon incorporates blending properties of the source with properties of the target. However, this is part of a broader phenomenon than metaphor. We do not need metaphorical source and target domains to get blends; people often use blends on-line or in real time in the course of working conceptually with input domains of any kind. A nice example of a metaphorical blend is provided by Turner and Fauconnier. The example comes from the ANGER IS A HOT FLUID IN A CONTAINER metaphor we looked at in chapter 16. Take the sentence "God, he was so mad I could see *the smoke or steam coming out of his ears.*" In this novel elaboration of the metaphor, an element of the source is blended with an element of the target. There are no ears in the source and there is no smoke in the target, but in the blend both are present at the same time as *smoke or steam coming out of his ears*. A frame is created with smoke and ears in it that is novel with respect to both the source and the target.

The use of metaphors also depends on the context of communication as broadly conceived. The kinds of concerns speakers have, their life histories, and even the physical context (such as the particular season in which they communicate) can significantly contribute to arriving at the metaphors they use.

Individuals may also differ in whether or not they make use of all the mappings of a metaphor that are associated with it supraindividually when they use a particular metaphor in particular communicative situations. As a limiting case this can happen (and it can even happen in poetic texts), and all mappings may occasionally be utilized, but more often than not, only a selection of conventional mappings is utilized in actual speech situations, depending on one's communicative needs. Thus, it is not the case that all the mappings arrived at by cognitive linguists at the supraindividual level are activated by individual speakers in the course of on-line thinking and communication in the real world.

3. The Subindividual Level

What I call the "subindividual" level of metpahor is the level at which the conceptualization of a conceptual domain (the target) by means of another conceptual domain (the source) is made natural and motivated for speakers. Since the bringing together of the two domains into a conceptual metaphor is often motivated by sensorimotor experiences, and human beings (no matter which language they speak) share these experiences, this is a level that corresponds to the universal aspects of metaphor.

The most obvious cases in which two different kinds of experience are seen as being in correlation are those that involve the human physiology. Bodily experiences are often correlated with certain abstract or subjective experiences which give rise to conceptual metaphors that we find natural and well motivated. But it is not only direct bodily experience that can produce well motivated metaphors; perceptual, cultural, and category-based correlations in experience can also do so. But has anyone ever come up with any real evidence independent of linguistic claims about such correlations? The answer is yes. Ekman, Levenson, and their colleagues conducted several experiments which show that abstract domains such as emotions regularly correlate with physiological changes in the body. For example, anger has been shown to be correlated with an increase in skin temperature, blood pressure, and other autonomic nervous system activities. These changes make anger different from other emotions, which are characterized by a different ANS profile. These studies provide independent (i.e., nonlinguistic) motivation for the existence of the ANGER IS A HOT FLUID metaphor that was discussed as a test case for the three-level view of metaphor above. Similar to this one, many other metaphors could be characterized at each of the supraindividual, individual, and subindividual levels.

This is not to claim, however, that *each and every* conceptual metaphor is based on such correlations in experience. Many are not, and these may obtain their motivation from what we called "perceived structural similarity," or even real, objective, and preexisting similarity. The two types of motivation (correlations in experience and resemblance or similarity) should be seen as complementary rather than mutually exclusive. People in different cultures may take the same thing to be similar to different things, and different cultures can have unique concepts that may function as either source or target domains. Because of these possibilities, the subindividual level of metaphor is only partially universal—to the degree to which motivation is based on correlations in experience. The issue of how many conceptual metaphors can be accounted for by correlations in experience (as opposed to similarity of some kind) is one that requires a great deal more future research.

There are several distinct kinds of metaphor; metaphors can be classified according to their cognitive function (structural, ontological, etc.), their nature (knowledge-based or image-based), their conventionality (conventional or unconventional), their complexity (simple or complex), and so forth. Which of these distinct kinds of metaphors are based on correlations in experience? The kind of metaphor that is most studied by cognitive linguists is structural metaphor, but these are not all necessarily based on correlations in experience. Instead, it can be suggested that simple, or primary, metaphors are the ones that most obviously have a clear experiential basis. These simple metaphors function as mappings within larger, complex structural ones.

The notion of correlation brings with it an important implication in the study of the relationship between metaphor and metonymy. Correlation in experience brings together two (no matter how) distant domains of experience in a single one. If we characterize metaphor as involving two distant domains and metonymy as involving a single domain, then we should regard correlation as a metonymic relationship. In it, one domain correlates with, thus metonymically stands for, another domain. The implication is that correlation-based metaphors can all be seen as having a metonymic basis. Thus in this view, metonymy is a bridge between experiencing two domains simultaneously, on the one hand, and seeing them as metaphorically related (A-AS-B), on the other.

Where do metaphors "reside" in the human organism? The most natural location for metaphors, and especially for simple, or primary, metaphors, is in the brain. Given a source and a target domain, if one domain is activated, other, metaphorically connected domains are also activated. This shows that metaphors not only have linguistic and psychological reality but are also real in our neuroanatomy. But metaphors have further bodily motivation. As Lakoff and Johnson observe, we have three ways in which simple, or primary, metaphors are embodied: (1) as we just saw, the correlations are embodied in our neuroanatomy; (2) the source domains arise from the sensorimotor experiences of the human body; and (3) we repeatedly experience in the world situations in which source and target domains are connected.

Thus, the cognitive linguistic view of metaphor that has been discussed in this book works on three levels: the supraindividual level corresponding to how a given language and culture reflects metaphorical patterns, the individual level corresponding to the metaphorical cognitive system as used by individual speakers of a language, and the subindividual level corresponding to universal aspects of various kinds of embodiment. However, it is not claimed that the three levels are all equally well understood, researched, and described at the present time, and it is not claimed either that we know precisely how the three levels work together. But what is certain, as I hope this book has demonstrated, is that the cognitive view as presented here has produced significant results, perhaps the most important of which being the realization that language, culture, thought, and the body all come together and play an equally crucial role in the study of metaphor. We can safely predict that new results will continue to be produced and that the next two decades will be just as exciting as the twenty years we have left behind.

FURTHER READING

Lakoff and Johnson in their latest joint work (1999) put the issue of metaphor (together with many other things) in a philosophical perspective. Gibbs (1999) discusses the relationship between metaphor, cognition, and culture, and Gibbs (1994) is the best source for a survey of psychological research on metaphor in the head of actual speakers. The creative cognitive activity of individual speakers by using blends in relation to the ANGER IS A HOT FLUID metaphor is described by Turner and Fauconnier (2000). The idea that correlation in experience serves as a basis for many metaphors is elaborated by Grady (1999). A study on the physiological distinctiveness of emotions is Ekman et al. (1983), but see also references in chapter 12 on the universality of metaphors. Representative collections of recent research on metaphor as well as metonymy include Gibbs and Steen (1999), Panther and Radden (1999), and Barcelona (2000). Kövecses (2000) discusses the universal as well as the culture-specific aspects of the ANGER IS A HOT FLUID metaphor.

Glossary

Aspects of conceptual domains. Both source and target domains are characterized by a number of different dimensions of experience, such as purpose, function, control, manner, cause, shape, size, and many others. I call these "aspects of domains." Each such aspect consists of elements: entities and relations. Metaphorical mappings between a source and a target obtain between these elements. *See also* Conceptual domain.

Basis of metaphor. *See* Experiential basis (of metaphor).

Blend. These are cases where understanding of a sentence (or some non-linguistic message) involves the conceptual integration, or "fusion," of two domains into one—a new mental space. Thus, conceptual metaphor can be seen as a special case of blending. However, not all cases of blending are metaphors (e.g., counterfactual sentences like "If I were you . . ." are not). *See also* Mental space.

Bodily motivation (for metaphor). *See* Experiential basis (of metaphor).

Central mappings. Central mappings are mappings that are involved in projecting the main meaning focus (or foci) of the source onto the target. *See also* Main meaning focus (of conceptual metaphor); Entailments, metaphorical.

Combining. This is one way in which a conventional, ordinary metaphor can be reworked in literature. It works by combining several conventional conceptual metaphors in a few lines or even within a single line. Thus, the metaphorical linguistic expressions used within a small space can activate in the reader a number of distinct conceptual metaphors.

Complex metaphor. This is a metaphor that is composed of simple or primary metaphors. The latter function as mappings within the complex one. *See also* Mappings; Primary metaphor; Simple metaphor.

Complexity of conceptual metaphor. Conceptual metaphors can be placed along a scale of complexity, yielding simple metaphors at one end and complex metaphors at the other. *See also* Complex metaphor.

Concept. *See* Conceptual domain.

Conceptual domain. This is our conceptual representation, or knowledge, of any coherent segment of experience. We often call such representations concepts, such as the concepts of BUILDING or MOTION. This knowledge involves both the knowledge of basic elements that constitute a domain and knowledge that is rich in detail. This detailed rich knowledge about a domain is often made use of in metaphorical entailments. *See also* Entailments, metaphorical.

Conceptual metaphor. When one conceptual domain is understood in terms of another conceptual domain, we have a conceptual metaphor. This understanding is achieved by seeing a set of systematic correspondences, or mappings, between the two domains. Conceptual metaphors can be given by means of the formula A IS B or A AS B, where A and B indicate different conceptual domains. *See also* Mappings; Correspondences.

Conceptual metonymy. This is a cognitive process in which one conceptual entity, the vehicle, provides mental access to another conceptual entity, the target, within the same conceptual domain or ICM. It is important to note that in metonymy both the vehicle entity and the target entity are elements of one and the same conceptual domain.

Conceptual motivation for idioms. This is the idea that the meaning of many idioms seems natural, or "transparent," to us because either metaphor, metonymy, or conventional knowledge links the nonidiomatic meaning of the constituent words to the idiomatic meaning of these words taken together. *See also* Experiential basis (of metaphor); Multiple motivation for idioms.

Conventional knowledge. This is everyday, nonspecialist knowledge about a particular domain that is shared by speakers of a linguistic community.

Conventionality of metaphor. Conceptual metaphors may be more or less conventional; i.e., they can be placed along a continuum; that is, a scale of conventionality. Some conceptual metaphors are deeply entrenched and hence well known and widely used in a speech community (such as LOVE IS FIRE), whereas others are much less so (such as LOVE IS A COLLABORATIVE WORK OF ART). The less conventional ones can be called "novel (conceptual) metaphors." Metaphorical linguistic expression reflecting a particular conceptual metaphor can also be more or less conventional. These less conventional, or novel, metaphorical expressions are especially prevalent in poetry. Thus, although they both come from the conceptual metaphor LIFE IS A JOURNEY, the lines by Frost "Two roads diverged in a wood, and I / I took the one less traveled by" are more novel than the cliched expression "I'm at a crossroads in life."

Correlations in experience. *See* Experiential basis (of metaphor).

Correspondences. To understand a target domain in terms of a source domain means that we see certain conceptual correspondences between elements of the source domain and those of the target domain. *See also* Mappings.

Cultural variation (in metaphor). Conceptual metaphors may vary cross-culturally and within a single culture. The limiting case of within-culture variation is individual variation in the use of metaphor. In those cases where a conceptual metaphor is universal, its universality obtains at a generic level, while the same conceptual metaphor shows cultural variation at the specific level. *See also* Universality of metaphor.

Domain. *See* Conceptual domain.

Elaboration. This is one way in which a conventional, ordinary metaphor can be reworked in literature. It works by elaborating on an existing element of the source domain in an unusual way.

Elements (of aspects of domains). The aspects of domains are constituted by (conceptual) elements: entities and relations. Mappings between domains are based on these elements. *See also* Aspects of conceptual domains.

Entailment potential, metaphorical. Source domains have a large set of potential entailments that can lead to metaphorical entailments. These potential entailments constitute the metaphorical entailment potential of the source domains in structural metaphors.

Entailments, metaphorical. Metaphorical entailments arise from the rich knowledge people have about elements of source domains. For example, in the ANGER IS A HOT FLUID IN A CONTAINER metaphor we have rich knowledge about the behavior of hot fluids in a container. When such knowledge about the source domain is carried over to the target domain, we get metaphorical entailments.

Experiential basis (of metaphor). Conceptual metaphors are grounded in, or motivated by, human experience. The experiential basis of metaphor involves just this groundedness-in-experience. Specifically, we experience the interconnectedness of two domains of experience and this justifies for us conceptually linking the two domains. For example, if we often experience anger as being connected with body heat, we will feel justified in creating and using the conceptual metaphor ANGER IS A HOT FLUID IN A CONTAINER. The experiences on which the conceptual metaphors are based may be not only bodily but also perceptual, cognitive, biological, or cultural. The inter-connectedness between the two domains of experience may be of several types, including correlations in experience, perceiving structural similarities between two domains, etc. *See also* Conceptual motivation for idioms.

Extended metaphor. These occur mainly in literary texts. They are large-scale metaphors (megametaphors) "behind" a text that underlie other, more local metaphors (called "micrometaphors"). Their cognitive function is to organize the local metaphors into a coherent metaphorical structure in the text.

Extending. This is one way in which a conventional, ordinary metaphor can be reworked in literature. In it, a conventional conceptual metaphor that is associated with certain conventionalized linguistic expressions is expressed by new linguistic means. It is typically achieved by introducing a new conceptual element in the source domain.

Folk theory (of a conceptual domain). *See* Folk understanding (of a conceptual domain).

Folk understanding (of a conceptual domain). We have nonexpert, naive views about everything in our world. When this kind of naive, nonexpert knowledge comes in a more or less structured form, we call it "folk under-standing" or "folk theory." These folk understandings of the world include our knowledge about the behavior of hot fluids in a closed container, about how machines work, about what a journey is, about what wars are, and a huge number of other things. *See also* Conceptual domain.

Function of conceptual metaphors. Different types of metaphor serve different cognitive functions. Three major types have been distinguished: structural, ontological, and orientational (which see).

Generic-level metaphors. These metaphors occupy a high level on a scale of generality on which conceptual metaphors can be placed. They are composed of generic-level source and target domains. Generic-level metaphors are instantiated, or realized, by specific-level ones. Thus, the metaphor EMOTIONS ARE FORCES is instantiated, or realized, by the specific-level metaphor ANGER IS A HOT FLUID IN A CONTAINER. *See also* Specific-level metaphors.

Hiding. In hiding, of the several aspects of a target, only some will be focused on. The ones that are not in focus can be said to be hidden. *See also* Aspects of conceptual domains.

Highlighting. In highlighting, of the several aspects of a target domain, some will be focused on by the source domain. The source domain can be said to highlight these aspects of the target. *See also* Aspects of conceptual domains; Utilization.

ICM. *See* Idealized cognitive models.

Idealized cognitive models. These are structured conceptual representations of domains in terms of elements of these domains. *See also* Conceptual domain.

Image-schema metaphor. Image-schema metaphors are based on "skeletal" image-schemas, such as the path-schema, the force-schema, the contact-schema, etc. They are skeletal in the sense that these source domains do not map rich knowledge onto the target.

Intercultural variation (in metaphor). *See* Cultural variation (in metaphor).

Intracultural variation (in metaphor). *See* Cultural variation (in metaphor).

Invariance principle. This principle states: Map as much knowledge from the source domain onto the target domain as is coherent with the image-schematic properties of the target. *See also* Main meaning focus (of conceptual metaphor).

Kinds of conceptual metaphor. Conceptual metaphors can be classified in a variety of ways. We can classify them according to their conventionality, function, nature, level of generality, and complexity (*which see*).

Levels of generality of conceptual metaphor. Conceptual metaphors can be placed on a scale of generality: Some metaphors are at the specific level, while others are at the generic level. Thus, we have specific-level metaphors and generic-level metaphors (which see).

Literary metaphors. These are metaphors that can be found in literary works. They are especially prevalent in poetry. As conceptual metaphors, they are commonly conventional; as linguistic expressions, they are commonly unconventional.

Main meaning focus (of conceptual metaphor). Each source domain is associated with a particular meaning focus (or foci) that is (are) mapped onto the target. This meaning focus (or foci) is (are) conventionally fixed and agreed-upon within a speech community or subculture. For example, the main meaning focus of the source domain of fire is intensity. This is what is most commonly "imported" to target domains. *See also* Invariance principle.

Mappings. Conceptual metaphors are characterized by a set of conceptual correspondences between elements of the source and target domains. These correspondences are technically called "mappings."

Megametaphor. *See* Extended metaphor.

Mental space. This is a conceptual "packet" that gets built up "on-line" in the process of understanding sentences (or other nonlinguistic messages). Mental spaces are not the same as conceptual domains, although they make use of them in the process of understanding. Mental spaces are created in particular situations for the purpose of understanding and thus are smaller and more specific than conceptual domains. *See also* Blend.

Metaphor systems. We have metaphor systems when a number of different individual source domains jointly characterize various aspects of a single target domain. This can happen at a specific level (e.g., at the level of concepts such as ARGUMENT or ANGER characterized by their sources) or at a generic level (e.g., at the level of the superordinate concept of EVENT characterized by its several source domains).

Metaphor. *See* Conceptual metaphor.

Metaphorical entailments. *See* Entailments, metaphorical.

Metaphorical linguistic expressions. These are words or other linguistic expressions (e.g., idioms) that come from the terminology of the conceptual domain that is used to understand another conceptual domain. For example, when we use *to be at a crossroads* to talk about LIFE, this metaphorical expression comes from the domain of JOURNEY. Usually, there are many metaphorical linguistic expressions that reflect a particular conceptual metaphor, such as LIFE IS A JOURNEY.

Metonymy. *See* Conceptual metonymy.

Micrometaphors. These are local metaphors in a text that are organized into a coherent metaphorical structure by extended metaphors. *See also* Extended metaphor.

Motivation (of metaphor). *See* Experiential basis (of metaphor); Conceptual motivation for idioms; Prediction (of metaphor).

Multiple motivation for idioms. The meaning of an idiom is motivated in multiple ways when the idiomatic meaning can be linked to the non-idiomatic meaning of the constituent words by not only one but several cognitive mechanisms, such as metaphor, metonymy, and conventional knowledge. *See also* Conceptual motivation for idioms.

Nature of metaphor. Metaphors may be based on basic knowledge concerning conceptual domains (sometimes called "propositional knowledge") and knowledge concerning images. Image-based metaphors include image-schema metaphors and one-shot image metaphors. *See also* Image-schema metaphor; One-shot image metaphor.

One-shot image metaphor. These are metaphors that involve the superimposition of one rich image onto another rich image. For example, when we compare the rich image we have of a woman's body with the rich image of an hourglass, we get a one-shot image metaphor. These cases are called "one-shot" metaphors because, in them, we bring into correspondence two rich images for a temporary purpose on a particular occasion.

Ontological metaphors. These conceptual metaphors enable speakers to conceive of their experiences in terms of objects, substances, and containers in general, without specifying further the kind of object, substance, or container.

Orientational metaphors. These conceptual metaphors enable speakers to make a set of target concepts coherent by means of some basic human spatial orientations, such as up-down, in-out, center-periphery, etc.

Personification. This kind of conceptual metaphor involves understanding nonhuman entities, or things, in terms of human beings. It thus imputes human characteristics to things. Personification can be regarded as a type of ontological metaphor (which see).

Prediction (of metaphor). The cognitive view of metaphor does not claim that we can predict what metaphors there are either within a single culture or cross-culturally. Instead, it claims that the metaphors that do exist are motivated or have an experiential basis. *See also* Experiential basis (of metaphor); Conceptual motivation for idioms.

Primary metaphor. A primary metaphor is one that emerges directly from correlations in experience, e.g., MORE IS UP; PURPOSES ARE DESTINATIONS; (ABSTRACT) ORGANIZATION IS PHYSICAL STRUCTURE; PERSISTENCE IS BEING ERECT; etc. Several primary metaphors can be joined together to form complex metaphors, such as THEORIES ARE BUILDINGS, which is constituted by the last two primary metaphors. *See also* Complex metaphor; Simple metaphor.

Questioning. This is one way in which a conventional, ordinary metaphor can be reworked in literature. In it, the writer or the poet calls into question the appropriateness of a conventional conceptual metaphor.

Realizations of conceptual metaphors. Conceptual metaphors can become manifest in several ways. One major way is through language. However, they can also manifest themselves in nonlinguistic ways, such as in cartoons, social action, art, etc.

Scope of metaphor. This is the entire range of target domains to which a given source domain, such as journey, war, plant, human body, fire, etc., can apply.

Simple metaphor. A simple metaphor is one that emerges from what we find important in connection with basic physical entities and events that make up the human world, such as BUILDING, FIRE, PRESSURIZED CONTAINER, WAR, JOURNEY, BODY, PLANT, MACHINE, SPORTS, etc. All these entities and events have a main meaning focus (which see) for us within a culture. The mappings that constitute this meaning focus (or foci) are simple metaphors. For example, the central mapping (which see) (ABSTRACT) DEVELOPMENT IS PHYSICAL GROWTH derives from the PLANT source domain within the scope of the metaphor COMPLEX ABSTRACT SYSTEMS ARE PLANTS. *See also* Complex metaphor; Primary metaphor.

Source domain. This is a conceptual domain that we use to understand another conceptual domain (the target domain). Source domains are typically less abstract or less complex than target domains. For example, in the conceptual metaphor LIFE IS A JOURNEY, the conceptual domain of journey is typically viewed as being less abstract or less complex than that of life.

Specific-level metaphors. These metaphors occupy a low level on a scale of generality on which conceptual metaphors can be placed. They are composed of specific-level source and target domains. Specific-level metaphors are instantiations, or special cases, of generic-level ones. Thus, the metaphor ANGER IS A HOT FLUID IN A CONTAINER is an instantiation, or special case, of the generic-level metaphor EMOTIONS ARE FORCES. *See also* Generic-level metaphors.

Structural metaphors. These are conceptual metaphors that enable speakers to understand the target domain in terms of the structure of the source domain. This understanding is based on a set of conceptual correspondences between elements of the two domains. *See also* Mappings.

Target domain. This is a conceptual domain that we try to understand with the help of another conceptual domain (the source domain). Target domains are typically more abstract and subjective than source domains. For example, in the conceptual metaphor LIFE IS A JOURNEY, the conceptual domain of life is typically viewed as being more abstract (and more complex) than that of journey.

Unconventional metaphors. *See* Conventionality of metaphor.

Unidirectionality of conceptual metaphor. In conceptual metaphors, the understanding of abstract or complex domains is based on less abstract or less complex conceptual domains. With metaphors that serve the purpose of understanding, this is the natural direction; metaphorical understanding goes from the more concrete and less complex to the more abstract and more complex. The reverse direction can also sometimes occur, but then the metaphor has a special noneveryday function.

Universality of metaphor. Conceptual metaphors that can be found in all languages are universal. Obviously, because of the large number of languages spoken around the world, it would be impossible to obtain conclusive evidence for the universality of any single conceptual metaphor. Some candidates for universal metaphors have been suggested, such as the EVENT STRUCTURE metaphor. The (possible) universality of conceptual metaphors largely exists at the generic level. *See also* Cultural variation (in metaphor).

Utilization. In metaphorical utilization, only some aspects of the source are utilized in metaphorical mappings, while the others remain unutilized. *See also* Highlighting.

Solutions to

Exercises

Chapter 1

1. 1-d; 2-e; 3-a; 4-f; 5-c; 6-b
2. LIFE IS A GAMBLING GAME. (See Lakoff and Johnson 1980, 51.)
3. *waste/spend/gain/lose/buy/invest/budget/save/rob/give/steal time, run out of time, put aside some time, have some time left, cost some time, the thief of time*
4. *Source*: BUILDINGS   *Target*: THEORIES
   the foundation of a building   the basis of the theory
   support   evidence
   strength   plausibility
   construction   creation
   collapse of a building   fall of a theory

Chapter 2

1. (a) Source: JOURNEY; Target: POLITICS/HISTORY
   (b) Source: A SPORT RACE; Target: ECONOMIC DEVELOPMENT
2. (a) FATHER; (b) SHEPHERD; (c) KING/FATHER.
3. GOD IS A SEA CAPTAIN; (CHRISTIAN) LIFE IS A (SEA) JOURNEY
4. (a) MAGNETIC FORCE
   (b) (c) (d) NATURAL FORCE
   (a) LOVE IS A MAGNETIC FORCE
   (b) ANGER IS A NATURAL FORCE
   (c) LOVE IS A NATURAL FORCE
   (d) SADNESS IS A NATURAL FORCE
       ANGER IS A NATURAL FORCE

Chapter 3

1. (a) VIRTUE IS UP—DEPRAVITY IS DOWN
   (b) HIGH SOCIAL STATUS IS UP—LOW SOCIAL STATUS IS DOWN
   (c) HAPPY IS UP—SAD IS DOWN
   (d) HEALTH AND LIFE ARE UP—SICKNESS AND DEATH ARE DOWN
2. (a) HAPPINESS IS A CAPTIVE ANIMAL "C"
   (b) LOVE IS AN INCURABLE DISEASE "E"
   (c) LIFE IS A STORY "C"
   (d) HIGH SOCIAL STATUS IS UP "C"
   (e) LOVE IS A UNITY "C"
3. THE CITY IS A PERSON
4. See, for example, the following works: Richard Aldington: "New Love";
   Ezra Pound: "A Girl"; Emily Dickinson: "The distance that the dead . . .";
   Shakespeare's works; Sylvia Plath: *The Bell Jar*
5. Some examples of conventional metaphors: LOVE IS BLINDNESS, LOVE IS
   AN OBJECT, INTIMACY IS PHYSICAL CLOSENESS, THE OBJECT OF LIVE IS A
   CHILD, LOVE IS FIRE
   Some examples of unconventional metaphors: LOVE IS CLOCKWORKS,
   LOVE IS DEATH (DROWNING), NIGHT IS A BLANKET

Chapter 4

1. LOVE IS A NUTRIENT DRINK; LOVE IS THIRST; THE BODY IS A CONTAINER
   elaboration and combining ⇒ LOVE IS AN INTOXICATING DRINK
2. A PERSON IS A BUILDING (A PALACE)

roof	head
rampart	body
windows	eyes
throne	heart
pearl and ruby	teeth
palace door	mouth
banners	hair

3. PASSIONS ARE BEASTS INSIDE THE PERSON
4. A PERSON IS A BOUNDED ENTITY; PERSONAL SPACE IS PHYSICAL SPACE;
   SOCIAL CONSTRAINTS ARE PHYSICAL CONSTRAINTS
5. (a) check   the promise of equal human rights
       funds   guarantee of human rights
       to cash the check   to obtain the human rights
   (b) Source domain: FINANCIAL TRANSACTION OF VALUABLE COMMODITIES
       Target domain: ACQUIRING HUMAN RIGHTS
       Metaphor: ACQUIRING HUMAN RIGHTS IS A BUSINESS TRANSACTION/
          MONETARY EXCHANGE;
   (c) Mappings: HUMAN RIGHTS ARE VALUABLE COMMODITIES/CASH;
       GUARANTEEING HUMAN RIGHTS IS GRANTING FUNDS; THE PROMISE
       (OF PROVIDING EQUAL HUMAN RIGHTS) IS THE CHECK
   (d) elaboration ⇒ money

Chapter 5

1. e.g., the American flag—Union ⇒ THE UNION OF STATES IS THE PHYSICAL
   UNION OF STARS
   Uncle Sam—America ⇒ A STATE IS A PERSON
   Eagle—freedom ⇒ FREEDOM IS UNINHIBITED SELF-PROPELLED MOVEMENT
2. (i) (ii) & (iii) Harry
   (a) They express more content or meaning.
   (b) MORE OF CONTENT IS MORE OF FORM
3. (a) IMMIGRATION IS A FLOOD
   (b) negative (MOVEMENT IS A FLOW; LARGE QUANTITIES ARE MASSES)
   Immigration is seen as a threatening force from which the country
   should be protected.

Chapter 6

1. LOVE IS FIRE: Physical experience: felt increase in body temperature
   LOVE IS A JOURNEY: PURPOSES ARE DESTINATIONS conceptual metaphor
2. e.g., A CAREER/AN ARGUMENT/MARRIAGE IS A JOURNEY
3. sickness: passivity, lying (in bed)
   health: activity, walking/acting/standing erect
4. cultural root: dance evolved from sex

Chapter 7

1.

Metaphor	Example	Highlighted and Utilized Aspects
LOVE IS A JOURNEY	It's been a *long bumpy road.* Look *how far we've come.*	progress
LOVE IS A NUTRIENT	I am *starved for* love.	desire
LOVE IS FIRE	He is *burning with* love.	intensity
LOVE IS MAGIC	I am *under her spell.*	loss of control

2. (a)

Linguistic Examples	Conceptual Metaphors
1. Waves of depression came over him.	SADNESS IS A NATURAL FORCE
2. He brought me down with his remarks.	SAD IS DOWN
3. He is in a dark mood.	SAD IS DARK
4. I am filled with sorrow.	SADNESS IS A FLUID IN A CONTAINER
5. That was a terrible blow.	SADNESS IS A PHYSICAL FORCE
6. Time heals all sorrows.	SADNESS IS A DISEASE
7. He was insane with grief.	SADNESS IS INSANITY
8. He drowned his sorrow in drink.	SADNESS IS AN OPPONENT
9. His feelings of misery got out of hand.	SADNESS IS A CAPTIVE ANIMAL
10. She was ruled by sorrow.	SADNESS IS A SOCIAL SUPERIOR

(b)

Conceptual Metaphors	Highlighted Aspects	Hidden Aspects
1. SADNESS IS A NATURAL FORCE	Passivity Lack of control	Cause Attempt at control Behavioral responses
2. SAD IS DOWN	Negative character	Cause Attempt at control
3. SAD IS DARK	Negative character	Cause Attempt at control
4. SADNESS IS A FLUID IN A CONTAINER	Intensity Attempt at control Loss of control	Negative character
5. SADNESS IS A PHYSICAL FORCE	Passivity Sudden impact	Cause Attempt at control Behavioral responses
6. SADNESS IS A DISEASE	Negative character Passivity Behavioral responses	Attempt at control
7. SADNESS IS INSANITY	Lack of control	Attempt at control
8. SADNESS IS AN OPPONENT	Attempt at control	Passivity
9. SADNESS IS A CAPTIVE ANIMAL	Loss of control	Passivity
10. SADNESS IS A SOCIAL SUPERIOR	Lack of control	Attempt at control

(c) Some HAPPINESS metaphors are the opposites of SADNESS metaphors (e.g., HAPPINESS IS UP/LIGHT/VITALITY); others are the same because similar aspects are highlighted in the two target concepts.

3. Extension of the source concept SLEEP to DREAMING. Shakespeare questions the validity of the metaphor DEATH IS SLEEP.

Chapter 8

1. (a) LIFE IS A JOURNEY; LOVE IS A JOURNEY
   Entailments: circular movement—aimlessness of life
   (b) PEOPLE ARE PLANTS
   Entailments: flowers are easy to crush—women are easy to harm
2. Because a) both the cause and the effect must be durable entities (and in the second example the effect is not a durable entity) and b) the process of causation that takes place between the cause and the effect must be long-lasting (and in the second example it is a momentary action.)

Chapter 9

1. (a) ARGUMENT IS SPORT
   (b) LIFE IS SPORT
   (c) BUSINESS IS SPORT
   (d) POLITICS IS SPORT
   (e) LIFE IS SPORT
   (f) POLITICS/GOVERNMENT IS SPORT

    (g) A LOVE RELATIONSHIP IS SPORT
    (h) POLITICS IS SPORT (ELECTION IS A RACE)
2. COMPLEX SYSTEMS ARE MACHINES
    (a) LAW
    (b) POLITICS/DEMOCRACY
    (c) POLITICS/ELECTION
    (d) PROJECTS
    (e) ECONOMY
    (f) LAW
    (g) ECONOMY
    (h) MILITARY ORGANIZATIONS
    Overarching metaphor: COMPLEX ABSTRACT SYSTEMS ARE MACHINES
3. (a) UP/HIGH
    (b) GOOD QUALITY: (1) (6) (9)
        (SOCIAL) STATUS: (5) (7) (10) (12)
        HAPPINESS: (2) (4) (8)
        CAREER: (3)
        SUCCESS: (11) (13)
4. E.g., *fall short/sick/victim/prey to/in love/for somebody, his face fell*
    (a) HEALTH CONDITIONS, EMOTIONAL STATES, SOCIAL CONDITIONS, etc.
    (b) Scope: ANY ACCIDENTAL CHANGE OF STATE/CONDITION
    Falling is an accidental physical change. It is the accidental nature of
    falling that is mapped onto nonphysical changes of states.

Chapter 10

1. (a) ANIMALS—GREAT CHAIN
    (b) PLANTS—COMPLEX SYSTEMS
    (c) ANIMALS—GREAT CHAIN
    (d) COMPLEX OBJECTS—COMPLEX SYSTEMS
    (e) ANIMALS—GREAT CHAIN
    (f) PLANT—COMPLEX SYSTEMS
    (g) ANIMAL—GREAT CHAIN
2. Target domains:
    (a) AN ORGANIZATION
    (b) A STATE
    (c) POLITICS/FOREIGN POLICY
    (d) ECONOMY
    (e) POLITICS
    (f) THEORY/PLAN
    (g) SOCIETY
    Focus: THE STRUCTURE OF AN ABSTRACT COMPLEX SYSTEM IS THE
    PHYSICAL STRUCTURE OF THE HUMAN BODY
3. COMPLEX SYSTEMS metaphor (sub)system
    (a) FRIENDSHIP IS A BUILDING
    (b) FRIENDSHIP IS A MACHINE
    (c) FRIENDSHIP IS A PLANT
    (d) FRIENDSHIP IS A MACHINE
    (e) FRIENDSHIP IS A PLANT
    (f) FRIENDSHIP IS A PLANT

    (g) FRIENDSHIP IS A PLANT
    (h) FRIENDSHIP IS A MACHINE
    (i) FRIENDSHIP IS A PLANT
    (j) FRIENDSHIP IS A PLANT
    (k) FRIENDSHIP IS A PLANT

4. Jimmy is the bear and Alison is the squirrel. Jimmy is a big and strong man, but he is innocent, shy and somewhat lazy at the same time. He can become emotional, but he is ready to defend his beloved ones if necessary. Alison is an attractive woman with big eyes, though she doesn't seem to be too smart and experienced. We know that bears are big, heavy, strong and somewhat slow animals which become aggressive only when they have to defend their partners. Squirrels, on the other hand, are relatively small and nice animals, and they seem carefree but never careless.

5. Based on your own research.

Chapter 11

1. (a) PHYSIOLOGICAL/BEHAVIORAL EFFECT FOR EMOTION
    (b) PHYSIOLOGICAL/BEHAVIORAL EFFECT FOR EMOTION
    (c) PHYSIOLOGICAL/BEHAVIORAL EFFECT FOR EMOTION
    (d) PHYSIOLOGICAL/BEHAVIORAL EFFECT FOR EMOTION
    All of them are EFFECT FOR CAUSE metonymies.

2. (a) PRODUCER FOR PRODUCT (PRODUCTION ICM)
    (b) PRODUCER FOR PRODUCT (PRODUCTION ICM)
    (c) THE OBJECT FOR THE USER OF THE OBJECT (CONTROL ICM)
    (d) THE PLACE FOR THE INSTITUTION
    (e) THE PLACE FOR THE INSTITUTION
    (f) CONTROLLER FOR CONTROLLED (CONTROL ICM)

3. Metonymies: (a) (c) (f) (h)
    Metaphors: (b) (d) (e) (g)

4. In (a), the hitting is deliberate; in (b), it is accidental.

Chapter 12

1. (a) LOVE IS FIRE
    (b) LOVE IS AN ILLNESS

2. (a) & (i) SEXUAL DESIRE IS HUNGER, THE OBJECT OF SEXUAL DESIRE IS FOOD
    (b) & (ii) SEXUAL DESIRE IS FIRE, LACK OF SEXUAL DESIRE IS LACK OF FIRE

3. (a)

LANGUAGES

METAPHORS	English	Hungarian	Chinese	Japanese	Polish	Zulu
THE BODY IS A CONTAINER FOR THE EMOTIONS	+	+	+	+	+	+
ANGER IS FIRE	+	+	+	+	+	+
ANGER IS THE HEAT OF A FLUID IN A CONTAINER	+		+	+	+	+
ANGER IS INSANITY	+	+	+	+	+	
ANGER IS AN OPPONENT IN A STRUGGLE	+	+	+	+	+	
ANGER IS A DANGEROUS ANIMAL	+	+		+	+	+
THE CAUSE OF ANGER IS PHYSICAL ANNOYANCE	+	+				+
CAUSING ANGER IS TRESPASSING	+					
ANGER IS A BURDEN				+		
ANGER IS A NATURAL FORCE		+	+	+	+	+

(b) People have the same physiological experience concerning anger, that is, increase in body heat, pressure inside, etc.

(c) There are cultural differences, and the concepts may have culture-specific aspects to them.

Chapter 13

1. (1)–(5): THE LUSTFUL PERSON IS A WILD ANIMAL
   (6)–(10): THE LUSTFUL PERSON IS A DOMESTIC ANIMAL/AN ANIMAL THAT LIVES IN THEIR IMMEDIATE ENVIRONMENT
2. (a) (THE OBJECT OF) SEXUAL DESIRE IS A PHYSICAL FORCE
   (b) SEXUAL DESIRE IS INSANITY
   (c) SEXUAL DESIRE IS AN ELECTRIC FORCE
   (d) SEXUAL DESIRE IS A PHYSICAL (MAGNETIC) FORCE
   (e) SEXUAL DESIRE IS WAR
   (f) SEXUAL DESIRE IS INSANITY
3. (a)   (i) LUST IS FIRE
         (ii) LUST IS HUNGER
         (iii) LUST IS A HOT FLUID INSIDE A CONTAINER
         (iv) LUST IS AN OPPONENT IN A STRUGGLE
         (v) LUST IS INSANITY
         (vi) LUST IS PHYSICAL AGITATION
         (vii) LUST IS WAR
         (viii) LUST IS RAPTURE
         (ix) THE OBJECT OF LUST IS FOOD
         (x) LUST IS HUNGER/EATING
         (xi) A LUSTFUL PERSON IS A WILD ANIMAL
         (xii) LUST IS FIRE
         (xiii) LUST IS A HOT FLUID INSIDE A CONTAINER
         (xiv) LUST IS A MAGNETIC FORCE
         (xv) A LUSTFUL PERSON IS A FUNCTIONING MACHINE
   (b) In romance novels: LUST IS AN OPPONENT IN A STRUGGLE, LUST IS INSANITY, LUST IS PHYSICAL AGITATION, LUST IS WAR, LUST IS RAPTURE
   (c) In pornographic magazines: A LUSTFUL PERSON IS A WILD ANIMAL, LUST IS A MAGNETIC FORCE, A LUSTFUL PERSON IS A FUNCTIONING MACHINE
   (d) Romance novels use the LUST IS FIRE conceptual metaphor most frequently, the focus of which is the intensity of the desire. In pornographic magazines, the conceptual metaphors THE OBJECT OF LUST IS FOOD and LUST IS HUNGER/EATING are the most common, which focus on the satisfying of sexual desire.

Chapter 14

1. (a) ANGER IS A HOT FLUID IN A CONTAINER
   (b) DROP IN BODY TEMPERATURE STANDS FOR FEAR
   (c) THE MANNER OF PRODUCTION STANDS FOR THE PRODUCT
   (d) THE MIND IS A CONTAINER
   (e) LOVE IS A UNITY

2. Conventional knowledge: Stabbing someone causes the blood to flow out of the body, and your hands will probably be bloody. Blood is red, so if you are guilty, your hands are red.

3. (a) THE EYES ARE LIMBS = SEEING IS TOUCHING
   (b) (NOT) KNOWING IS (NOT) SEEING
   (c) LOVING VISUAL BEHAVIOR STANDS FOR LOVE
   (d) THE EYE STANDS FOR LOOKING
   (e) Conventional knowledge: If one has eyes at several places on the head, he/she will be able to see more.
   (f) (NOT) KNOWING IS (NOT) SEEING
   (g) THE MIND IS THE BODY
   (h) Conventional knowledge: The wider/more you open your eyes, the more you can see.
   (i) LOOKING AT SOMETHING STANDS FOR DESIRING IT
   (j) (NOT) KNOWING IS (NOT) SEEING or DECEIVING IS CAUSING NOT TO SEE

4. (a) (1) deficit
       (2) enraging experience
       (3) warning
       (4) lustful
       (5) respectful
       (6) extreme, committed
       (7) a day for celebration
       (8) be angry
   (b) (1) conventional knowledge, metonymy REDNESS FOR DANGER
       (2) conventional knowledge, metaphor THE CAUSE OF ANGER IS A PERCEPTUALLY SALIENT OBJECT
       (3) metonymy REDNESS FOR DANGER, metaphor INTENSITY IS SALIENCE
       (4) metonymy BLOOD FOR SEXUAL DESIRE
       (5) conventional knowledge
       (6) metaphor INTENSITY IS HEAT, metaphor INTENSITY IS SALIENCE
       (7) conventional knowledge, metaphor INTENSITY IS SALIENCE
       (8) metonymy INTERFERENCE WITH ACCURATE PERCEPTION STANDS FOR ANGER

Chapter 15

1. (1) affection—LOVE FOR THE PROPERTIES (ATTITUDES AND BEHAVIORS) IT ASSUMES
   (2) affection—LOVE FOR THE PROPERTIES (ATTITUDES AND BEHAVIORS) IT ASSUMES
   (3) darling/lover—LOVE FOR THE OBJECT OF EMOTION
   (4) admire/like—basic sense
   (5) admire/like—basic sense
   (6) admire/like—basic sense
   (7) love relationship—LOVE FOR THE RELATIONSHIP IT PRODUCES
   (8) intense emotion—basic sense
   (9) admire/like—basic sense

2. (1) *healthy* body: central/prototypical sense
   (2) *healthy* complexion: 'resulting from a healthy body'
   (3) *healthy* exercise: 'productive of healthy bodies'
   Healthy has senses (1), (2), and (3). (1) is the central member of this
   category of senses. (2) and (3) are extended senses, where metonymy is the
   principle of extension. Metonymical relationship between (1) and (2), and
   between (1) and (3) (see Lakoff 1987).

3. *Example:*

ruin	n	1. destruction, overthrow, serious damage	central sense
		2.a. state of being decayed, destroyed, collapsed	RESULT FOR ACTION
		2.b. something which has decayed, been destroyed, etc.	RESULT FOR ACTION
		3. cause of ruin	CAUSE FOR EFFECT
	v	1. to cause the ruin of	ACTION FOR RESULT

4. MENTAL ACTIVITY IS THE PHYSICAL MANIPULATION OF OBJECTS

Chapter 16

1. Proverbs often present a compact, implicit story, which can be interpreted
   through projection: we project the overt source story onto a covert target
   story. We can project a specific proverb onto an abstract story that might
   include a number of specific target stories.
   (a) Generic space: One agent or group of agents constrains another agent
       or group of agents in their behavior, and when those in control are
       inattentive, the otherwise constrained agent or agents behave more
       freely.
       Said at the office, it can be projected onto the story of boss and
       workers. PEOPLE ARE ANIMALS conceptual metaphor.
   (b) Generic space: Doing something before others ensures success in an
       undertaking.
       Said about business, it can be projected onto the story of business-
       men. PEOPLE ARE ANIMALS conceptual metaphor.
   (c) Generic space: One cannot change the thing(s) that he/she has done.
       Said about a divorce, it can be projected onto the story of the
       divorced partners.
   (d) Generic space: Threats rarely entail real aggression.
       Said about people who often shout, it can be projected onto their
       story. PEOPLE ARE ANIMALS conceptual metaphor.
   (e) Generic space: If we have been hurt, we take precautions not to get
       hurt again.
       Said about love relationships, it can be projected onto the story of
       the person involved in the (previous/future) relationship.
2. Generic space: strong leader/governor in a community
   Input I1: Old Testament story of Jewish leader, Nehemiah, in Jerusalem
   Input I2: Puritan governor, John Winthrop, in New England
   Blend: "New English/American Nehemiah," "American Jerusalem"
3. Talking animals are a conceptual blend: they reside in the blended space of
   animals with human characteristics. The blend includes specific informa-

tion from both source and target besides abstract information (event structure, etc.). Relation between two input spaces: ANIMALS ARE PEOPLE metaphor.

Generic space: Animate beings with characteristic features

Input I1: Human characteristics (e.g., talking)

Input I2: Animal characteristics (e.g., physical appearance, and psychological character ⇒ Winnie The Pooh: stupid, clumsy; Piglet: cowardly, stupid; Eyore: stupid; Rabbit: smart; Tigger: cunning, quick, strong; Owl: clever)

Blend: Animals with human characteristics

4. We can solve the riddle with the help of a blend: Imagine the Buddhist monk walking both up and down the path on the same day. Thus, there must be a place where he meets himself. This is the place that he would occupy at the same time of the day on the two separate journeys. The blend combines features of the journey upward and downward. We have only one mountain slope and one day of journey, but two moving individuals, which cannot be fused due to the preservation of input structure concerning the time of day and direction of motion. The generic space contains the moving individual, a path linking the foot and the summit of the mountain, and a day of travel.

5. (a) When Drew finds out that he kills people by reaping the wheat.

   (b) *Conceptual metaphors*:

   PEOPLE ARE PLANTS. Mappings: plants—people, life-cycle of plants—life-cycle of human beings, growth of plants—development and progress that people make in their lives, etc.

   EVENTS ARE ACTIONS. Mappings: actor . . . cause . . .

   Blending

   Generic space: Agent causing the end of an activity/process

   Input I1: Death (dying, grimness)

   Input I2: (The harvesting of) Plants (many mortal reapers, who use scythes to reap, and who work for long intervals, who wear appropriate clothes, who reap the entire field)

   Blend: The Grim Reaper (a skeleton dressed in a robe and cowl that holds a scythe; there is only one definite, immortal Grim Reaper, who doesn't necessarily use his scythe, who is dressed in black, who acts only once, who comes for one specific person at one time)

   (c) Bradbury's Reaper is mortal; he can go mad; he can lose his own family. Thus, the "supernatural" features (immortality, etc.) are taken away from this blend. Also, The Grim Reaper turns into The Mad Reaper, when he starts reaping/killing indiscriminately, without ever stopping, after his family becomes stuck between life and death.

References

Adamson, Tim, Greg Johnson, Tim Rohrer, and Howard Lam. 1996. Metaphors we ought not live by: Rush Limbaugh in the age of cognitive science. *Metaphor Center Online*. University of Oregon, Philosophy Department.

Alexander, R. J. 1987. Problems in understanding and teaching idiomaticity in English. *Anglistik und Englischunterricht* 32: 105–122.

Allbritton, David W. 1995. When metaphors function as schemas: Some cognitive effects of conceptual metaphors. *Metaphor and Symbolic Activity* 10(1): 33–46.

Balaban, Victor. 1999. Self and agency in religious discourse. Perceptual metaphors for knowledge at a Marian apparition site. In *Metaphor in Cognitive Linguistics*, ed. Raymond Gibbs and Gerard Steen, 125–144. Amsterdam: John Benjamins.

Barcelona, Antonio. 1986. On the concept of depression in American English: A cognitive approach. *Revista Canaria de Estudios Ingleses* 12: 7–33.

———. 1995. Metaphorical models of romantic love in *Romeo and Juliet*. *Journal of Pragmatics*, 24–6. Special issue: *Literary Pragmatics: Cognitive Metaphor and the Structure of the Poetic Text*, ed. Masako K. Hiraga and Joanna Radwanska Williams, 667–689. Amsterdam: North Holland.

———. 2000. On the plausibility of claiming a metonymic motivation for conceptual metaphor. In *Metaphor and Metonymy at the Crossroads*, ed. A. Barcelona, 31–58. Berlin: Mouton de Gruyter.

———, ed. 2000. *Metaphor and Metonymy at the Crossroads: A Cognitive Perspective*. Berlin: Gruyter.

Baugh, A. C. and T. Cable. 1983. *A History of the English Language*. 3d ed. London: Routledge and Kegan Paul.

Bellah, R. N., R. Madsen, W. M. Sullivan, A. Swidler, and S. M. Tipton. 1985. *Habits of the Heart: Individualism and Commitment in American Life*. Berkeley: University of California Press.

———, eds. 1988. *Individualism and Commitment in American Life*. New York: Harper and Row.

Boers, Frank. 1999. When a bodily source domain becomes prominent. In *Metaphor in Cognitive Linguistics*, ed. Raymond Gibbs and Gerard Steen, 47–56. Amsterdam: John Benjamins.

Bokor, Zsuzsanna. 1997. Body-based constructionism in the conceptualization of anger. *C.L.E.A.R. series*, no. 17. Department of English, Hamburg University and the Department of American Studies, ELTE, Budapest.

Brugman, Claudia. 1990. What is the invariance hypothesis? *Cognitive Linguistics* 1: 257–266.

Cameron, Lynne and Graham Low, eds., 1999a. *Researching and Applying Metaphor*. Cambridge: Cambridge University Press.

———. 1999b. Metaphor. *Language Teaching* 32: 77–96.

Carter, R. and M. McCarthy. 1988. *Vocabulary and Language Teaching*. London: Longman.

Cienki, Alan. 1998. Metaphoric gestures and some of their relations to verbal metaphoric expressions. In *Discourse and Cognition: Bridging the Gap*, ed. Jean-Pierre Konig, 189–204. Stanford, Calif.: CSLI Publications.

Chilton, Paul and George Lakoff. 1995. Foreign policy by metaphor. In *Language and Peace*, ed. Christina Schaffner and Anita L. Wenden, 37–59. Brookfield, Vt.: Dartmouth Publishing Company.

Croft, William. 1993. The role of domains in the interpretation of metaphors and metonymies. *Cognitive Linguistics* 4: 335–370.

Csábi, Szilvia. 1997. The concept of America in the puritan mind. *C.L.E.A.R. series*, no. 18. Department of English, Hamburg University and the Department of American Studies, ELTE, Budapest.

———. 1999. The conceptualization of lust in English, *Semiotische Berichte* 23(1): 29–49.

Clark, Eve V. and Herbert H. Clark. 1979. When nouns surface as verbs. *Language* 55: 767–811.

Danesi, M. 1993. Metaphorical competence in second language acquisition and second language teaching. In *Georgetown University Round Table on Language and Linguistics*, ed. J. E. Alatis, 489–500. Washington, D.C.: Georgetown University Press.

Dirven, René. 1993. Metonymy and metaphor: Different mental strategies of conceptualisation. *Leuvense Bijdragen* 82: 1–28.

———. 1994. *Metaphor and Nation: Metaphors Afrikaners Live By*. Frankfurt am Main: Peter Lang.

Dirven, René and Günter Radden. n.d. *Cognitive English Grammar*. Amsterdam: John Benjamins.

Ekman, P., R. W. Levenson, and W. V. Friesen. 1983. Autonomic nervous system activity distinguishes among emotions. *Science* 221: 1208–1210.

Emanatian, Michele. 1995. Metaphor and the expression of emotion: The value of cross-cultural perspectives. *Metaphor and Symbolic Activity* 10: 163–182.

Fauconnier, Gilles. 1985. *Mental Spaces*. Cambridge, Mass.: MIT Press. Rev. ed. 1994. New York: Cambridge University Press.

———. 1997. *Mappings in Language and Thought*. Cambridge: Cambridge University Press.

Fauconnier, Gilles and Mark Turner. 1994. Conceptual projection and middle spaces. (Department of Cognitive Science Tech. Rep. 9401). San Diego: University of California Press.

Feyaerts, Kurt. 1999. Metonymic hierarchies: The conceptualization of stupidity in German idiomatic expressions. In *Metonymy in Language and Thought*, ed. Klaus-Uwe Panther and Gunter Radden, 309–332. Amsterdam: John Benjamins.

———. 2000. Refining the inheritance hypothesis: Interaction between metaphoric and metonymic hierarchies. In *Metaphor and Metonymy at the Crossroads*, ed. Antonio Barcelona, 59–78. Berlin: Gruyter.

Fillmore, Charles. 1982. Frame semantics. In *Linguistics in the Morning Calm*, ed. Linguistic Society of Korea, 111–138. Seoul: Hanshin.

Forceville, Charles. 1996. *Pictorial Metaphor in Advertising*. London: Routledge.

Freeman, Donald C. 1993. According to my bond: *King Lear* and re-cognition. *Language and Literature* 2(1): 1–18.

———. 1995. Catch[ing] the nearest way: *Macbeth* and cognitive metaphor. *Journal of Pragmatics* 24: 689–708.

Freeman, Margaret H. 1995. Metaphor making meaning: Dickinson's conceptual universe. *Journal of Pragmatics* 24: 643–666.

———. 2000. Poetry and the scope of metaphor: Toward a cognitive theory of metaphor. In *Metaphor and Metonymy at the Crossroads*, ed. Antonio Barcelona, 253–281. Berlin: Gruyter.

Fuller, Margaret. 1843. The great lawsuit. MAN versus MEN. WOMAN versus WOMEN. *Dial*, 4 (July): 1–47.

Gairns, R. and S. Redman. 1986. *Working with Words*. Cambridge: Cambridge University Press.

Geeraerts, Dirk. 1997. *Diachronic Prototype Semantics*. Oxford: Oxford University Press.

Geeraerts, Dirk and Stefan Grondelaers. 1995. Looking back at anger: Cultural traditions and metaphorical patterns. In *Language and the Cognitive Construal of the World*, ed. John R. Taylor and Robert E. MacLaury, 153–179. Berlin: Gruyter.

Gentner, D. 1983. Structure-mapping: A theoretical framework for analogy. *Cognitive Science* 7: 155–170.

Gibbs, Raymond W. 1990. Psycholinguistic studies on the conceptual basis of idiomaticity. *Cognitive Linguistics* 1: 417–451.

———. 1994. *The Poetics of Mind: Figurative Thought, Language, and Understanding*. Cambridge: Cambridge University Press.

———. 1999. Taking metaphor out of our heads and putting it into the cultural world. In *Metaphor in Cognitive Linguistics*, ed. Raymond Gibbs and Gerard Steen, 146–166. Amsterdam: John Benjamins.

Gibbs, Raymond W. and J. O'Brien. 1990. Idioms and mental imagery: The metaphorical motivation for idiomatic meaning. *Cognition* 36: 35–68.

Gibbs, Raymond W., Dinara A. Beitel, Michael Harrington, and Paul Sanders. 1994. Taking a stand on the meanings of *stand*: Bodily experience as motivation for polysemy. *Journal of Semantics* 11: 231–251.

Gibbs, Raymond W. and Gerard Steen, eds. 1999. *Metaphor in Cognitive Linguistics*. Amsterdam: John Benjamins.

Giora, Rachel. 1997. Understanding figurative and literal language: The graded salience hypothesis. *Cognitive Linguistics* 7(1): 183–206.

Goatley, Andrew. 1997. *The Language of Metaphors*. London: Routledge.

Goldberg. Adele E. 1995. *Constructions: A Construction Grammar Approach to Argument Structure*. Chicago: University of Chicago Press.

Goossens, Louis. 1990. Metaphtonymy: The interaction of metaphor and metonymy in expressions of linguistic action. *Cognitive Linguistics* 1: 323–340.

———. 2000. Patterns of meaning extension, "parallel chaining," subjectification, and modal shifts. In *Metaphor and Metonymy at the Crossroads*, ed. Antonio Barcelona, 149–169. Berlin: Gruyter.

Goossens, Louis, Paul Pauwels, Brygida Rudzka-Ostyn, Anne-Marie Simon-Vanderbergen, and Johan Vanparys. 1995. *By Word of Mouth: Metaphor, Metonmy and Linguistic Action in a Cognitive Perspective*. Amsterdam: John Benjamins.

Grady, Joseph E. 1997. THEORIES ARE BUILDINGS revisited. *Cognitive Linguistics* 8: 267–290.

———. 1999. A typology of motivation for conceptual metaphor. In *Metaphor in Cognitive Linguistics*, ed. Raymond Gibbs and Gerard Steen, 79–100. Amsterdam: John Benjamins.

Grady, Joseph E., Sarah Taub, and Pamela Morgan. 1996. Primitive and compound metaphors. In *Conceptual Structure, Discourse, and Language*, ed. Adele E. Goldberg, 177–87. Stanford, Calif.: CSLI Publications.

Grady, Joseph E., Todd Oakley, and Seana Coulson. 1999. Blending and metaphor. In *Metaphor in Cognitive Linguistics*, ed. Raymond Gibbs and Gerard Steen, 101–124. Amsterdam: John Benjamins.

Hale, D. G. 1971. *The Body Politic. A Political Metaphor in Renaissance English Literature*. The Hague: Mouton.

Haser, Verena. 2000. Metaphor in semantic change. In *Metaphor and Metonymy at the Crossroads*, ed. Antonio Barcelona, 171–194. Berlin: Gruyter.

Heine, Bernd. 1995. Conceptual grammaticalization and prediction. In *Language and the Cognitive Construal of the World*, ed. John R. Taylor and Robert E. MacLaury, 119–135. Berlin: Gruyter.

———. 1997. *Cognitive Foundations of Grammar*. Oxford and New York: Oxford University Press.

Heine, Bernd, Ulrike Claudi, and Friederike Hünnemeyer. 1991. *Grammaticalization: A Conceptual Framework*. Chicago: University of Chicago Press.

Holland, Dorothy 1982. All is metaphor: Conventional metaphors in human thought and language. *Reviews in Anthropology* 9(3): 287–297.

Holland, Dorothy and Naomi Quinn, eds. 1987. *Cultural Models in Language and Thought*. Cambridge: Cambridge University Press.

Ibarretxe-Antunano, Iraide. 1999. Metaphorical mappings in the sense of smell. In *Metaphor in Cognitive Linguistics*, ed. Raymond Gibbs and Gerard Steen, 29–45. Amsterdam: John Benjamins.

Irujo, S. 1993. Steering clear: Avoidance in the production of idioms. *IRAL* 30(3): 205–219.

Jackendoff, Ray. 1988. *Semantics and Cognition*. Cambridge, Mass.: MIT Press.

———. 1991. *Semantics Structures*. Cambridge, Mass.: MIT Press.

Jackendoff, Ray and David Aaron. 1991. Review Article: More than cool reason: A field guide to poetic metaphor by George Lakoff and Mark Johnson. *Language* 67(2): 320–328.

Jäkel, Olaf. 1993. Is metaphor really a one-way street? One of the basic tenets of the cognitive theory of metaphor put to the test. In *C.L.E.A.R. Series*.

Department of English, Hamburg University and the Department of American Studies, ELTE, Budapest.

———. 1995. The metaphorical conception of mind: "Mental activity is manipulation." In *Language and the Cognitive Construal of the World*, ed. John R. Taylor and Robert E. MacLaury, 197–229. Berlin: Gruyter.

———. 1999. Kant, Blumenberg, Weinrich. Some forgotten contributions to the cognitive theory of metaphor. In *Metaphor in Cognitive Linguistics*, ed. Raymond Gibbs and Gerard Steen, 9–27. Amsterdam: John Benjamins.

Johnson, Christopher. 1997. Metaphor vs. conflation in the acquisition of polysemy: The case of SEE. In *Cultural, Typological and Psychological Issues in Cognitive Linguistics*, ed. M. K. Hiraga, C. Sinha, and S. Wilcox. Amsterdam: John Benjamins.

Johnson, Mark. 1987. *The Body in the Mind: The Bodily Basis of Meaning, Imagination, and Reason*. Chicago: University of Chicago Press.

———. 1992. *Moral Imagination*. Chicago: University of Chicago Press.

Johnson, Mark, ed. 1981. *Philosophical Perspectives on Metaphor*. Minneapolis: University of Minnesota Press.

King, Brian. 1989. The conceptual structure of emotional experience in Chinese. Ph.D. diss., Ohio State University.

Kövecses, Zoltán. 1986. *Metaphors of Anger, Pride, and Love: A Lexical Approach to the Study of Concepts*. Amsterdam: John Benjamins.

———. 1988. *The Language of Love: The Semantics of Passion in Conversational English*. Lewisburg, Pa.: Bucknell University Press.

———. 1990. *Emotion Concepts*. New York: Springer Verlag.

———. 1991a. A linguist's quest for love. *Journal of Social and Personal Relationships* 8: 77–97.

———. 1991b. Happiness: A definitional effort. *Metaphor and Symbolic Activity* 6: 29–46.

———. 1994. Tocqueville's passionate "beast": A linguistic analysis of American democracy. *Metaphor and Symbolic Activity* 9(2): 113–133.

———. 1995a. Understanding the Statue of Liberty. In *New Approaches to American English*, ed. Z. Kövecses, 129–138. Budapest: Eötvös Loránd University.

———. 1995b. Metaphor and the folk understanding of anger. In *Everyday Conceptions of Emotion*, James A. Russell et al., eds. 49–71. Dordrecht: Kluwer.

———. 1995c. American friendship and the scope of metaphor. *Cognitive Linguistics* 6: 315–346.

———. 1995d. Anger: Its language, conceptualization, and physiology in the light of cross-cultural evidence. In *Language and the Cognitive Construal of the World*, eds. John R. Taylor and Robert MacLaury, 181–196. Berlin: Mouton.

———. 1999. Metaphor: Does it constitute or reflect cultural models? In *Metaphor in Cognitive Linguistics*, ed. Raymond W. Gibbs and Gerard Steen, 167–188. Amsterdam: John Benjamins.

———. 2000a. *Metaphor and Emotion: Language, Culture, and Body in Human Feeling*. Cambridge and New York: Cambridge University Press.

———. 2000b. The scope of metaphor. In *Metaphor and Metonymy at the Crossroads*, ed. Antonio Barcelona, 79–92. Berlin: Mouton.

———. n.d. A cognitive linguistic view of learning idioms in an FLT context.

In *Applied Cognitive Linguistics: Theory, Acquistion and Language Pedagogy*, ed. Martin Putz and Susanne Niemeier, forthcoming.

Kövecses, Zoltán and Günter Radden. 1998. Metonymy: Developing a cognitive linguistic view. *Cognitive Linguistics* 9: 37–77.

Kövecses, Zoltán and Peter Szabó. 1996. Idioms: A view from cognitive linguistics. *Applied Linguistics* 17(3): 326–355.

Krzeszowski, Tomasz P. 1993. The axiological parameter in preconceptional image schemata. In *Conceptualizations and Mental Processing in Language*, eds. Richard A. Geiger and Brygida Rudzka-Ostyn, 307–329. Berlin: Gruyter.

Kusumi, Takashi. 1996. Image schema of emotion in drawing task. (manuscript), Department of Human System Science, Tokyo Institute of Technology.

Lakoff, George. 1987. *Women, Fire, and Dangerous Things: What Categories Reveal about the Mind*. Chicago: University of Chicago Press.

———. 1990. The invariance hypothesis: Is abstract reason based on image-schemas? *Cognitive Linguistics* 1: 39–74.

———. 1992. Metaphors and war: The metaphor system used to justify war in the Gulf. In *Thirty Years of Linquistic Evolution*, ed. Martin Putz, 463–481. Amsterdam: John Benjamins.

———. 1993. The contemporary theory of metaphor. In *Metaphor and Thought*, ed. Andrew Ortony, 202–251. Cambridge: Cambridge University Press.

———. 1994. What is a conceptual system? In *The Nature and Ontogenesis of Meaning*, eds. Willis F. Overton and David S. Palermo, 41–90. Hillsdale, N.J.: Lawrence Erlbaum.

———. 1996. *Moral Politics: What Conservatives Know that Liberals don't*. Chicago: University of Chicago Press.

Lakoff, George and Mark Johnson. 1980. *Metaphors We Live By*. Chicago: University of Chicago Press.

———. 1999. *Philosophy in the Flesh*. New York: Basic Books.

Lakoff, George and Zoltán Kövecses. 1987. The cognitive model of anger inherent in American English. In *Cultural Models in Language and Thought*, ed. Dorothy Holland and Naomi Quinn, 195–221. Cambridge: Cambridge University Press.

Lakoff, George and Mark Turner. 1989. *More Than Cool Reason: A Field Guide to Poetic Metaphor*. Chicago: University of Chicago Press.

Lakoff, George, Jane Espenson, and Adele Goldberg. 1989. *Master Metaphor List*. Berkeley: University of California Press, Cognitive Linguistics Group.

Langacker, Ronald W. 1987. *Foundations of Cognitive Grammar*. Vol. 1, *Theoretical Prerequisites*. Stanford: Stanford University Press.

———. 1991. *Foundations of Cognitive Grammar*. Vol. 2, *Descriptive Applications*. Stanford: Stanford University Press.

———. 1993. Reference-point constructions. *Cognitive Linguistics* 4: 1–38.

László, György. 1997. Metaphors of theories of mind. Master's thesis. Department of American Studies, ELTE, Budapest.

Lattey, E. 1986. Pragmatic classification of idioms as an aid for the language learner. *IRAL* 24(3): 217–233.

Levenson, R. W., L. L. Carstensen, W. V. Friesen, and P. Ekman. 1991. Emotion, physiology, and expression in old age, *Psychology and Aging* 6: 28–35.

Levenson, R. W., P. Ekman, and W. V. Friesen. 1990. Voluntary facial action generates emotion-specific autonomic nervous system activity, *Psychophysiology* 27: 363–384.

Levenson, R. W., P. Ekman, K. Heider, and W. V. Friesen. 1992. Emotion and autonomic nervous system activity in the Minangkabau of West Sumatra. *Journal of Personality and Social Psychology* 62: 972–988.

Levy, R. I. 1973. *Tahitians: Mind and Experience in Society Islands*. Chicago: University of Chicago Press.

Lutz, Catherine A. 1987. Goals, events, and understanding in Ifaluk emotion theory. In *Cultural Models in Language and Thought*, ed. Dorothy Holland and Naomi Quinn, 290–312. Cambridge: Cambridge University Press.

———. 1988. *Unnatural Emotions: Everyday Sentiments on a Micronesian Atoll and Their Challenge to Western Theory*. Chicago: University of Chicago Press.

Matsuki, Keiko. 1995. Metaphors of anger in Japanese. In *Language and the Cognitive Construal of the World*, ed. John R. Taylor and Robert E. MacLaury, 137–151. Berlin: Mouton.

McArthur, Tom. 1992. *The Oxford Companion to the English Language*. Oxford: Oxford University Press.

McNeill, David. 1992. *Hand and Mind: What Gestures Reveal about Thought*. Chicago: University of Chicago Press.

Mikolajczuk, Agnieszka. 1998. The metonymic and metaphoric conceptualisation of *anger* in Polish. In *Speaking of Emotions: Conceptualisation and Expression*, ed. Angeliki Athanasiadou and Elzbieta Tabakowska, 153–191. Berlin: Mouton.

Moon, Rosamund. 1998. *Fixed Expressions and Idioms in English. A Corpus-Based Approach*. Oxford: Clarendon Press.

Munro, Pamela. 1991. ANGER IS HEAT: Some data for a cross-linguistic survey. (manuscript), Department of Linguistics, UCLA.

Murphy, Gregory. 1996. On metaphoric representations. *Cognition* 60: 173–204.

Niemeier, Susanne. 2000. Straight from the heart—metonymyic and metaphorical explorations. In *Metaphor and Metonymy at the Crossroads*, ed. Antonio Barcelona, 195–213. Berlin: Gruyter.

Norrick, Neal R. 1981. *Semiotic Principles in Semantic Theory*. Amsterdam and Philadelphia: John Benjamins.

Ortony, Andrew. 1988. Are emotion metaphors conceptual or lexical? *Cognition and Emotion* 2: 95–103.

———. 1993. *Metaphor and Thought*. 2d ed. Cambridge: Cambridge University Press.

Palmer, Gary B. 1996. *Toward a Theory of Cultural Linguistics*. Austin: Texas University Press.

Panther, Klaus-Uwe and Linda Thornburg. 2000. The EFFECT FOR CAUSE metonymy in English grammar. In *Metaphor and Metonymy at the Crossroads*, ed. A. Barcelona, 215–231. Berlin: Gruyter.

Panther, Klaus-Uwe and Günter Radden, eds. 1999. *Metonymy in Language and Thought*. Amsterdam: John Benjamins.

Pelyvás, Péter. 2000. Metaphorical extension of *may* and *must* into the epistemic domain. In *Metaphor and Metonymy at the Crossroads*, ed. Antonio Barcelona. Berlin: Gruyter.

Ponterotto, Diane. 2000. The cohesive role of cognitive metaphor in discourse and conversation. In *Metaphor and Metonymy at the Crossroads*, ed. Antonio Barcelona, 283–298. Berlin: Gruyter.

Quinn, Naomi. 1987. Convergent evidence for a cultural model of American marriage. In *Cultural Models in Language and Thought*, ed. Dorothy Holland and Naomi Quinn, 173–192. Cambridge: Cambridge University Press.

———. 1991. The cultural basis of metaphor. In *Beyond Metaphor: The Theory of Tropes in Anthropology*, ed. James W. Fernandez, 57–93. Stanford, Calif.: Stanford University Press.

Radden, Günter. 1995. Motion metaphorized: The case of *coming* and *going*. In *Cognitive Linguistics in the Redwoods*, ed. E. H. Casad, 423–458. Berlin: Mouton de Gruyter.

———. 1997. Time is space. In *Human Contact through Language and Linguistics*, ed. Birgit Smieja and Meike Tasch, 147–166. Peter Lang.

———. 2000. How metonymic are metaphors? In *Metaphor and Metonymy at the Crossroads*, ed. Antonio Barcelona, 93–108. Berlin: Mouton.

Radden, Günter and Zoltán Kövecses. 1999. Towards a theory of metonymy. In *The Conceptual Basis of Metonymy*, ed. Günter Radden and Klaus Panther. Amsterdam: John Benjamins.

Reddy, Michael. 1979. The conduit metaphor. In *Metaphor and Thought*. 1st ed., ed. Andrew Ortony, 284–324. Cambridge: Cambridge University Press.

Rohrer, Tim. 1995. The Metaphorical Logic of (Political) Rape: The New Wor(l)d Order. *Metaphor and Symbolic Activity* 10(2), 115–137.

Rudzka-Ostyn, Brygida. 1995. Metaphor, Schema, Invariance: The case of verbs of answering. In *By Word of Mouth: Metaphor, Metonmy and Linguistic Action in a Cognitive Perspective*, ed. Louis Goossens et al., 205–243. Amsterdam: John Benjamins.

Ruiz de Mendoza, Francisco Jose. 2000. The role of mappings and domains in understanding metonymy. In *Metaphor and Metonymy at the Crossroads*, ed. Antonio Barcelona, 109–132. Berlin: Mouton.

Schön, Donald. 1979. Generative metaphor: A perspective on problem-setting in social policy. In *Metaphor and Thought*, ed. A. Ortony. New York: Cambridge University Press.

Semino, Elena. 1997. *Language and World Creation in Poems and Other Texts*. London and New York: Longman.

Shore, Bradd. 1996. *Culture in Mind: Cognition, Culture, and the Problem of Meaning*. Oxford: Oxford University Press.

Stearns, Peter. 1994. *American Cool*. New York: New York University Press.

Steen, Gerard. 1994. *Understanding Metaphor in Literature*. Harlow: Longman.

———. 1999. From linguistic to conceptual metaphor in five steps. In *Metaphor in Cognitive Linguistics*, ed. Raymond Gibbs and Gerard Steen, 57–77. Amsterdam: John Benjamins.

Stern, Gustaf. 1931. *Meaning and Change of Meaning*. Bloomington: Indiana University Press.

Sweetser, Eve. 1990. *From Etymology to Pragmatics: Metaphorical and Cultural Aspects of Semantic Structure*. Cambridge: Cambridge University Press.

Talmy, Leonard. 1988. Force dynamics in language and cognition. *Cognitive Science* 12: 49–100.

Taylor, John R. 1989. *Linguistic Categorization: Prototypes in Linguistic Theory*. 2d ed. 1995. Oxford: Clarendon Press.

———. 1996. *Possessives in English*. Oxford: Clarendon Press.

Taylor, John R. and Robert E. MacLaury, eds. 1995. *Language and the Cognitive Construal of the World*. Berlin: Gruyter.

Taylor, John R. and Thandi G. Mbense. 1998. Red dogs and rotten mealies: How Zulus talk about anger. In *Speaking of Emotions: Conceptualisation and Expression*, ed. Angeliki Athanasiadou and Elzbieta Tabakowska, 191–226. Berlin: Mouton de Gruyter.

Thornburg, Linda and Klaus Panther. 1997. Speech act metonymies. In *Discourse and Perspective in Cognitive Linguistics*, ed. Wolf-Andreas Liebert, Gisela Redeker, and Linda Waugh, 205–219. Amsterdam: John Benjamins.

Traugott, Elizabeth C. 1985. On regularity in semantic change. *Journal of Literary Semantics* 14: 155–173.

Turner, Mark. 1987. *Death Is the Mother of Beauty*. Chicago: University of Chicago Press.

———. 1990. Aspects of the invariance hypothesis. *Cognitive Linguistics* 1: 247–255.

———. 1991. *Reading Minds*. Princeton, N.J.: Princeton University Press.

———. 1993. An image-schematic constraint on metaphor. In *Conceptualizations and Mental Processing in Language*, ed. Richard A. Geiger and Brygida Rudzka-Ostyn, 291–306. Berlin: Mouton de Gruyter.

———. 1996. *The Literary Mind*. New York: Oxford University Press.

Turner, Mark and Gilles Fauconnier. 1995. Conceptual integration and formal expression. *Metaphor and Symbolic Activity* 10(3): 183–204.

———. 2000. Metaphor, metonymy, and binding. In *Metaphor and Metonymy at the Crossroads*, ed. Antonio Barcelona, 133–145. Berlin: Gruyter.

Ullmann, Stephen. 1962. *Semantics: An Introduction to the Science of Meaning*. Oxford: Blackwell.

Ungerer, Friedrich. 2000. Muted metaphors and the activation of metonymies in advertising. In *Metaphor and Metonymy at the Crossroads*, ed. Antonio Barcelona, 321–340. Berlin: Gruyter.

Ungerer, Friedrich and Hans Jorg Schmid. 1996. *An Introduction to Cognitive Linguistics*. London: Longman.

Waldron, R. A. 1967. *Sense and Sense Development*. London: Deutsch.

Werth, Paul. 1994. Extended metaphor—a text-world account. *Language and Literature* 3(2): 79–103.

Wierzbicka, Anna. 1986. Metaphors linguists live by: Lakoff and Johnson contra Aristotle. *Papers in Linguistics* 19(2): 287–313.

Wilcox, P. 2000. *Metaphor in American Sign Language*. Washington, D.C.: Gallaudet University Press.

Winter, Steven L. 1995. A clearing in the forest. *Metaphor and Symbolic Activity* 10: 223–245.

Yu, Ning. 1995. Metaphorical expressions of anger and happiness in English and Chinese. *Metaphor and Symbolic Activity* 10: 59–92.

———. 1998. *The Contemporary Theory of Metaphor: A Perspective from Chinese*. Amsterdam: John Benjamins.

General Index

Anger, 191–192
Aspects of the source domain, 94

Basis for metaphor
  experiential, 243–244
  metonymic, 244
  See also Motivation
Blends, 228, 242–243

Causes of cross-cultural variation, 186–
  189. *See also* Variation (in
  metaphor and metonymy), cultural
Clark, E., 219–221
Clark, H., 219–221
Combining (of metaphors), 49
Concern (in metaphor variation),
  human, 193–194
Constructions (and metaphor),
  grammatical, 222–223
Context, broader cultural, 186–187,
  191–193
Contiguity, 146. *See also* Metonymy
Conventionality of metaphor, 29–32
Correlations
  in experience, 159, 243, 244
  as metonymies, 244
Correspondences, metaphorical, 6, 7.
  See also Mappings
Csábi, Sz., 61

Diminutive, 221
Directionality of metaphor. *See*
  Unidirectionality, of metaphor

Dirven, R., 188
Domain, conceptual, 4. *See also* ICM
Domains, metonymic, 149–156

Ekman, P., 173, 190, 243
Elaboration, 47–48
  of conceptual metaphors, 184–185
  of metonymies, 185–186
Elements of aspects (of concepts), 94
Embodiment, 16, 174. *See also* Basis
  for metaphor; Motivation
Entailments, metaphorical, 93–104
Entities, conceptual, 123–124
Environment (in metaphor variation),
  natural and physical, 187–188
Evaluation (of metaphor), positive-
  negative, 36
Experience, sensorimotor, 243, 244.
  See also Motivation
Expressions, metaphorical linguistic, 1
Extending (of metaphor), 47

Fauconnier, G., 227–228, 230, 231,
  242
Fire metaphors, 113–118
Freeman, D., 52
Freeman, M., 48
Friendship, 190, 192–193
Fuller, M., 61, 191
Function (of metaphor)
  cognitive, 32–36
  understanding vs. directing
    attention, 147–148

Metaphor and Metonymy Index